# CEN® Exam Blueprint

| Current CEN® Blueprint | | January 2022 CEN® Blueprint | |
|---|---|---|---|
| • Cardiovascular | 20 | • Cardiovascular | 19 |
| • Respiratory | 16 | • Respiratory | 18 |
| • Neurology | 16 | • Neurology | 18 |
| • GI GU GYN OB | 21 | • GI GU GYN OB | 18 |
| • Psych/Medical | 25 | • Mental Health | 11 |
| • Maxillo/Ortho | 21 | • Medical | 14 |
| • Environ/Tox | 15 | • Musculoskeletal | 13 |
| • Professional | 16 | • Maxillo/Ocular | 11 |
| | | • Environ/Tox | 14 |
| | | • Professional | 14 |

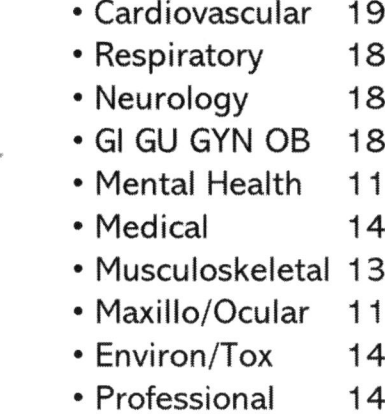

Reference: www.BCEN.org

## Quotes from CEN customers:

- "Huge thank you to Pam Bartley for providing an awesome CEN study guide. The information is concise and easy to follow, no extra fluff wasting my precious time. I only used your material and studied a section a day." Heather Oxford Finch, RN, CEN

- "The questions may as well be your key points, you hit the test on the nose." Samantha Schwartz-Phillips, RN, CEN, TCRN, CPEN, CFRN, CTRN

- "Thank you so much for all you do! I passed the CEN with 136/150, your material was spot on. Looking forward to more certifications with your help." Carly Ahern, RN, CEN

- "The CEN study guide is phenomenal, 100% on point, and low-cost. I passed the CEN exam today with 130/150, my only regret is that I didn't find Pam's material earlier." Lea Averill, RN, CEN

- "Thanks for helping me pass the TCRN and CEN exam. Your key points are on point, and thanks for the suggestion to take one exam after the other, that was a big help." Cris Valconcha, RN, CEN, TCRN

- "I passed the CEN on my first try! I would not have done it without your study material, thank you so much." Meagan White, RN, CEN

- "Thanks to Pam Bartley for helping me pass the CEN exam today! The study materials and key points are spot on. Hands down the best CEN prep material out there!" Abby Dunn, RN, CEN

- "I only studied Pam's CEN study guide and passed the first time. Her content is organized, condensed, and to the point." Ashley Davis, RN, CEN, TCRN

- "Pam's study materials are the best; I passed the CEN exam today! It was my second attempt at the exam, but the first time I used a different set of materials, not Pam's." Candy Churchwell, RN, CEN

ISBN: 978-1-7374277-4-2

# CEN Pretest by PDB Nurse Education, LLC

1. Pulse pressure is the difference between systolic blood pressure and diastolic blood pressure, and is widened in which of the following disorders?
    a. Early hypovolemic shock.
    b. Increased intracranial pressure.
    c. Cardiac tamponade.
    d. Neurogenic shock.
2. Parents bring in their 4-week-old infant with non-bilious projectile vomiting and persistent hunger. Which of the following conditions is suspected?
    a. Pyloric Stenosis
    b. Intussusception
    c. Appendicitis
    d. Volvulus
3. Systemic vascular resistance (SVR) is decreased in which type of shock?
    a. Hypovolemic
    b. Cardiogenic
    c. Obstructive
    d. Distributive
4. A 64-year-old female fell and transported to the ED via EMS for severe hip pain and inability to move. What classification of medications may mask the early signs of hypovolemic shock?
    a. Beta-blockers
    b. ACE inhibitors
    c. Angiotensin receptor blockers
    d. Calcium channel blockers
5. A patient is transported to the ED via EMS for headache, vomiting, and progressive confusion after a fall three days ago. Which of the following head injuries is the most likely cause of these symptoms?
    a. Concussion
    b. Epidural hematoma
    c. Subdural hematoma
    d. Basilar skull fracture
6. Which of the following is the hallmark symptom of Prinzmetal's angina?
    a. Chest pain with physical exertion
    b. Chest pain at rest due to coronary vasospasm
    c. Chest pain relieved by nitroglycerin and rest
    d. Atypical symptoms such as epigastric pain
7. A patient with a stab wound to the left flank area is unable to move his left side and unable to feel the right side of his body. These symptoms are associated with which of the following incomplete spinal cord injuries?
    a. Anterior cord syndrome
    b. Posterior cord syndrome
    c. Central cord syndrome
    d. Brown-Sequard syndrome
8. ST segment elevation in ECG leads II, III, and aVF indicates injury to which area of the heart?
    a. Inferior wall
    b. Anterior wall
    c. Posterior wall
    d. Lateral wall
9. Sutures placed in the eyebrows should be removed within:
    a. 4 to 5 days
    b. 5 to 7 days
    c. 7 to 10 days
    d. 10 to 14 days

10. A patient complains of ripping chest pain radiating to the back, has unequal bilateral blood pressures, and numbness in the lower extremities. The nurse suspects which emergent condition?
    a. Cardiac tamponade
    b. Tension pneumothorax
    c. Aortic dissection
    d. Posterior MI
11. A 40-year-old female who is 36-weeks pregnant patient presents to the ED with painless bright red vaginal bleeding. The nurse knows a pelvic exam is contraindicated since the most likely cause of the bleeding is:
    a. Abruptio placenta
    b. Placenta previa
    c. Uterine rupture
    d. Eclampsia
12. A 14-year-old complains of lightheadedness and palpitations. Which cardiac disorder is characterized by a short PR interval and a Delta wave?
    a. Torsades de Pointes
    b. R or T phenomenon
    c. AV Nodal Reentry Tachycardia (AVNRT)
    d. Wolff-Parkinson-White Syndrome (WPW)
13. A 22-year-old female complains of a thick, white, "cottage-cheese" like vaginal discharge, pruritis, vulvar burning, and dyspareunia. The nurse suspects a diagnosis of:
    a. Gonorrhea
    b. Chlamydia
    c. Candidiasis
    d. Trichomoniasis
14. Which atrioventricular block is characterized by a consistent but prolonged PR interval, and a consistent R to R interval?
    a. First degree AV block
    b. Second degree AV block, type 1
    c. Second degree AV block, type 2
    d. Third degree AV block
15. Fever, bloating, and pain at the right costal margin upon palpation is associated with which disorder?
    a. Pancreatitis
    b. Cholecystitis
    c. Appendicitis
    d. Diverticulitis
16. Jugular vein distention (JVD), and increased central venous pressure (CVP), hepatomegaly, and peripheral edema is seen in which disorder?
    a. Endocarditis
    b. Pericarditis
    c. Right heart failure.
    d. Left heart failure.
17. Which of the following signs/symptoms is typically seen in patients with Guillain-Barre syndrome?
    a. Prickly sensation in extremities and ascending symmetrical paralysis.
    b. Right-sided paralysis with left homonymous hemianopsia.
    c. Ptosis and descending symmetrical paralysis.
    d. Right-sided hemiplegia with left pupil dilation.
18. The following are signs of pericardial tamponade, **EXCEPT**?
    a. Kussmaul sign
    b. Pulsus paradoxus
    c. Electrical alternans
    d. Tracheal deviation
19. Which of the following is an early sign/symptom of left ventricular heart failure?
    a. Jugular vein distention (JVD)
    b. Paroxysmal nocturnal dyspnea

    c. Abdominal ascites
    d. Peripheral edema
20. Morphine is contraindicated in a right ventricular myocardial infarction (RV MI) because of what drug action?
    a. Morphine increases oxygen demand.
    b. Narcotics may lead to opioid dependence.
    c. Morphine decreases preload. ✓
    d. Morphine increases afterload.
21. A multi-trauma patient rapidly decompensates on arrival to the emergency department. ABG results are as follows: pH 7.25, CO₂ 50, HCO₃ 18. The patient is in which acid-base imbalance?
    a. Uncompensated respiratory acidosis.
    b. Uncompensated metabolic acidosis.
    c. Uncompensated respiratory and metabolic acidosis. ✓
    d. Partially compensated metabolic acidosis.
22. A 20-year-old male was discharged home yesterday after a femur fracture from a fall. He returns to the ED today with dyspnea, tachypnea, and tachycardia. You notice a petechial rash on the chest, so you suspect which disorder?
    a. Systemic inflammatory response syndrome.
    b. Disseminated intravascular coagulation.
    c. Rhabdomyolysis.
    d. Fat emboli syndrome. ✓
23. Which of the following signs/symptoms is **NOT** characteristic of Wernicke's encephalopathy?
    a. Confabulation
    b. Chronic memory loss ✓
    c. Ataxia
    d. Nystagmus
24. A patient complains of an excruciating unilateral headache with nasal congestion and excessive lacrimation on the affected side. The nurse suspects:
    a. Migraine
    b. Temporal arteritis
    c. Sinus headache
    d. Cluster headache ✓
25. A patient complains of crampy left lower quadrant abdominal pain with alternating episodes of explosive diarrhea and severe constipation. The nurse knows rehydration is critical since she/he suspects which disorder?
    a. Diverticulitis ✓
    b. Bowel obstruction
    c. Crohn's disease
    d. Volvulus
26. Which highly communicable infection is characterized by swollen salivary and parotid glands?
    a. Mumps ✓
    b. Measles
    c. Pertussis
    d. Diphtheria
27. A 68-year-old female with a history of atrial fibrillation complains of a sudden onset of painless unilateral vision loss and denies any trauma. Which ocular emergency does the nurse suspect?
    a. Acute angle closure glaucoma
    b. Central retinal artery occlusion ✓
    c. Retinal detachment
    d. Hyphema
28. Which of the following signs/symptoms should raise an index of suspicion that a patient is experiencing retinal detachment?
    a. "Tunnel vision" and seeing halos around lights.
    b. Reddish hue to vision after getting punched in the face.
    c. Crusty eyelids with yellow discharge from the eye.
    d. Photopsia and "floaters" in the visual field. ✓

29. A hazardous vulnerability assessment is completed in which phase of disaster management?
    a. Mitigation
    b. Preparedness
    c. Response
    d. Recovery
30. A patient complains of sharp chest pain that worsens with inspiration and lying down. Which sound is commonly heard in pericarditis?
    a. Systolic murmur
    b. Wheezing on exhalation
    c. Stridor on inspiration
    d. Friction rub
31. Pertussis is a highly communicable infection characterized by gagging, vomiting, and what hallmark sign?
    a. Inspiratory stridor
    b. Expiratory wheeze
    c. Paroxysmal cough
    d. Drooling
32. A patient complaining of chest pain exhibits restlessness, tachycardia, hypertension, dilated pupils, and paranoia so the nurse suspects which illicit drug use?
    a. Cocaine
    b. Heroin
    c. Phencyclidine
    d. Marijuana
33. A patient with a history of alcoholism has steady dull epigastric pain radiating to the back and elevated amylase and lipase levels. A common complication of pancreatitis is:
    a. Pneumonia
    b. Pleural effusion
    c. Pneumothorax
    d. Pulmonary embolus
34. The following are common signs/symptoms of Digoxin toxicity, EXCEPT:
    a. Ventricular dysrhythmias
    b. Yellow or green halos in vision
    c. Miosis
    d. Nausea and vomiting
35. Which of the following is not a cause of priapism?
    a. Sickle cell crisis
    b. Testicular torsion
    c. Spinal cord injury
    d. Antidepressants such as Trazadone
36. Which laboratory value will be decreased in thyrotoxic crisis (thyroid storm)?
    a. Calcium
    b. T3 and T4
    c. Alkaline phosphatase
    d. Thyroid stimulating hormone (TSH)
37. Which foreign body will more likely cause an infection?
    a. Bullet
    b. Glass
    c. Thorn
    d. Metal
38. Which is the priority for a patient with suicidal ideations?
    a. Inquiring if the patient has a history of depression.
    b. Providing a safe environment for the patient.
    c. Determining if the patient has a support person.
    d. Inquiring if the patient has a chronic illness.

39. Which of the earliest indicator of shock in pediatric patients?
    a. Hypotension
    b. Tachypnea
    c. Decreased capillary refill.
    d. Tachycardia ✓
40. Your patient has burning chest pain that awakens him at night. The following are recommendations for the treatment of esophagitis, EXCEPT:
    a. Avoid spicy foods and alcohol.
    b. Only eat three meals per day. ✓
    c. Eliminate smoking.
    d. Elevate head of bed.
41. Your patient has a history of Addison's disease. Which vital sign change would indicate adrenal crisis?
    a. Hypotension ✓   ALDOSTERONE
    b. Bradypnea
    c. Bradycardia
    d. Hypothermia
42. To assess the radial nerve the nurse asks the patient to:
    a. Make a tight fist.
    b. Abduct fingers.
    c. Oppose thumb to fingers.
    d. Give the "thumbs up" sign. ✓
43. A thin 16-year-old female complains of fatigue, dizziness, and feeling cold. You notice brittle nails and she states she has not had a period in 6 months. The nurse suspects:
    a. Bulimia
    b. Cushing's syndrome
    c. Anorexia ✓
    d. Hypothyroidism
44. Immerse the hand injured by a stingray in hot water until:
    a. Bleeding is controlled.
    b. Swelling decreases.
    c. Relief of pain. ✓
    d. The stinger is extracted.
45. Assessment of a patient who received metoclopramide (Reglan) reveals facial spasms and blepharospasms as well as tongue protrusion and lip-smacking. The patient is most likely experiencing:
    a. Myasthenia gravis
    b. A dystonic reaction ✓
    c. Seizure activity
    d. Bell's palsy
46. Parents bring in their 2-year-old child for a respiratory distress and a "barking" cough after a viral illness the last few days. Which of the following respiratory emergencies is this patient most likely experiencing?
    a. Epiglottitis
    b. Laryngotracheobronchitis (LTB) ✓
    c. Bronchiolitis
    d. Pertussis
47. Which consent allows healthcare providers to treat an unresponsive patient who is unable to give consent?
    a. Express consent
    b. Implied consent ✓
    c. Involuntary consent
    d. Informed consent
48. A 20-year-old male is transported to the ED via EMS after a high-speed MVC complaining of shortness of breath. Assessment reveals pain upon palpation, bony crepitus, and paradoxical chest wall movement. The nurse suspects:
    a. Flail chest ✓
    b. Pericardial tamponade
    c. Tension pneumothorax

d. Ruptured diaphragm
49. A patient with severe head trauma is diagnosed with syndrome of inappropriate antidiuretic syndrome (SIADH). The patient is most at risk for which of the following complications?
    a. Meningitis
    b. Seizures ✓
    c. Shock
    d. Torsades de Pointes
50. A 16-year-old female complains of fever, nausea, and right lower quadrant abdominal pain. Assessment reveals pain upon palpation at McBurney's point and rebound tenderness, so the nurse suspects:
    a. Cholecystitis
    b. Ruptured ovarian cyst.
    c. Appendicitis ✓
    d. Gastroenteritis
51. A victim of violence was unresponsive at the scene, awake on arrival to the ED, but had a second loss of consciousness in CT. Which of the following vessels is typically involved in an epidural bleed?
    a. Internal carotid artery
    b. Vertebral artery
    c. Middle meningeal artery ✓
    d. Vertebral vein
52. Which injury will least likely occur in a 6-year-old front-seat passenger secured only with a lap restraint?
    a. Duodenal rupture
    b. Pancreatic injury
    c. Chance fracture
    d. Pelvic fracture ✓
53. Which hemodynamic changes are typically seen in neurogenic shock?
    a. Bradycardia and hypotension. ✓
    b. Tachycardia and hypotension.
    c. Bradycardia and increased pulse pressure.
    d. Bradycardia and narrowed pulse pressure.
54. A patient with gestational hypertension is receiving magnesium sulfate IV. The most important parameter to monitor is:
    a. Blood pressure
    b. Heart rate
    c. Respiratory rate ✓
    d. Temperature
55. Laboratory results for a patient in disseminated intravascular coagulation (DIC) include:
    a. Decreased PT and PTT.
    b. Increased fibrin split products. ✓
    c. Increased platelets.
    d. Increased fibrinogen.
56. A 68-year-old male complains of severe pain in his "big toe". The joint is red and swollen and the uric acid level is elevated, so the nurse suspects:
    a. Gouty arthritis ✓
    b. Rhabdomyolysis
    c. Bursitis
    d. Bunion
57. Which medication is the priority treatment in anaphylaxis?
    a. Epinephrine ✓
    b. Diphenhydramine (Benadryl)
    c. Cimetidine (Tagamet)
    d. Solu-Medrol

58. A patient with a lower leg injury returns to the ED 24 hours later with severe throbbing pain not relieved by analgesia. The initial care includes:
    a. Elevating the injured leg above the level of the heart.
    b. Keeping the injured leg in neutral position.
    c. Applying compression to reduce swelling.
    d. Applying ice to reduce swelling.
59. A patient with a crush injury to his lower leg has an increased potassium, CK, myoglobin, and BUN. What is the hallmark sign of rhabdomyolysis?
    a. Loss of distal pulses.
    b. Increased intracompartmental pressure.
    c. Reddish-brown urine.
    d. Abdominal pain.
60. A 20-year-old male strikes a wall with a closed fist fracturing his fifth metacarpal. This is referred to as a:
    a. Colles fracture
    b. Scaphoid fracture
    c. Navicular fracture
    d. Boxer's fracture

## CEN Pretest Answers

1. **B** – Pulse pressure (SBP-DBP) is widened in increased ICP. Pulse pressure is narrow in early shock, cardiac tamponade, and aortic valve stenosis. (TNCC pg. 96)
2. **A** – Pyloric stenosis is characterized by non-bilious projectile vomiting and persistent hunger. Volvulus has bilious vomiting. (Sheehy pg. 570)
3. **D** - Afterload (pressure) is low in distributive shock (neurogenic, septic, and anaphylactic) due to vasodilation, and high in all other forms of shock due to vasoconstriction. (TNCC pg. 79)
4. **A** – Beta-blockers mask the early signs of shock and hypoglycemia. (TNCC pg. 272)
5. **C** – Subdural hematomas are slower bleeds since venous. Seen commonly in alcoholics, elderly, and from shaken impact syndrome. (TNCC pg. 108 and Sheehy pgs. 414-415)
6. **B** – The hallmark sign of Prinzmetal's angina is pain at rest. It is due to coronary vasospasm, so may be seen with stimulant use. (Sheehy pg. 236)
7. **D** – Brown-Sequard syndrome is the incomplete cord syndrome with ipsilateral motor loss and contralateral loss of sensation. It has a high rehab prognosis. (TNCC pg. 175)
8. **A** – Leads II, III, and aVF look at the inferior wall of the heart. V1-V4 look at the anterior wall, I, aVL, V5, and V6 look at the lateral wall of the left ventricle. (Sheehy pg. 24)
9. **A** – Eyebrow sutures should be removed in 4-5 days, lip 3-5, scalp 7-10, extremities 10-14, > 14 over joints. (Sheehy pg. 105)
10. **C** – Signs and symptoms of aortic dissection include ripping or tearing chest pain, with decreased circulation to kidneys and lower extremities. Obtain bilateral blood pressures. (Sheehy pg. 247)
11. **B** – Placenta previa is characterized by painless bright-red vaginal bleeding. Abruption has severe abdominal to back pain. (Sheehy pg. 284)
12. **D** – WPW is characterized by a short PR interval, and a slurred QRS on the upstroke, yielding a widened QRS complex. This morphology is referred to as a "Delta wave".
13. **C** – Candidiasis is characterized by pruritis and a thick white "cottage-cheese" like vaginal discharge. (Sheehy pg. 291)
14. **A** – First degree AV block has prolonged PR interval. Second degree type 1 has progressive elongation of PR interval. Second degree type 2 has a consistent PR interval, but inconsistent R to R interval. Third degree heart block has a consistent R to R interval, but the P waves get lost. (Sheehy pg. 244)
15. **B** – Cholecystitis or gallbladder disease is characterized by pain at the right costal margin, referred to as "Murphy's Sign". (Sheehy pg. 266)
16. **C** – Signs and symptoms of right heart failure include jugular vein distension (JVD), increased right atrial pressure (CVP), peripheral edema, ascites, hepatomegaly, and splenomegaly. Left heart failure has pulmonary edema.
17. **A** – Signs and symptoms of Guillain-Barre syndrome include prickly sensation in the extremities and ascending symmetrical paralysis. (Sheehy pg. 257)

18. **D** – Signs and symptoms of pericardial tamponade include Beck's Triad of hypotension, JVD, and muffled (distant) heart sounds. The pressure on the heart also causes pulsus paradoxus (decreased BP and pulse strength upon inspiration), and electrical alternans (low EKG amplitude). Tracheal deviation may be seen in tension pneumothorax. (Sheehy pg. 459)
19. **B** – Paroxysmal nocturnal dyspnea (PND) is an early S/S of left heart failure, along with dyspnea, and crackles. JVD, ascites, hepatomegaly, and peripheral edema are S/S of right heart failure. (Sheehy pg. 246)
20. **C** – Preload-reducing agents like morphine, Lasix (venodilator), and nitroglycerin are contraindicated in a right ventricular MI because they decrease preload. (Sheehy pg. 243)
21. **C** – A pH of 7.25 is uncompensated acidosis. $CO_2$ is > 45 (acidosis) and HCO3 is < 22 (acidosis), so it is a respiratory and metabolic (mixed) acidosis.
22. **D** – Fat emboli syndrome most commonly occur 24-72 hours after a long bone (femur) fracture. S/S include dyspnea, tachypnea, tachycardia, fever, confusion, and a reddish-brown nonpalpable petechial rash over the upper body, particularly on the chest and axillae. (TNCC pg. 391)
23. **B** – Wernicke's encephalopathy is characterized by confusion and confabulation, gait ataxia, and nystagmus. Chronic/permanent memory loss is a symptom of Korsakoff's syndrome.
24. **D** – Excessive tearing/lacrimation, along with unilateral nasal congestion are signs of a cluster headache. Temporal (Giant cell) arteritis has a palpable cord-like temporal artery. (Sheehy pg. 252)
25. **A** – Diverticulitis is characterized by crampy LLQ pain with alternating episodes of explosive diarrhea and constipation. It is often caused by a low fiber diet. (Sheehy pg. 267)
26. **A** – Mumps is characterized by swollen salivary and parotid glands (puffy cheeks). Measles has Koplik spots, Pertussis is "whooping cough", Diphtheria is gray pseudomembranous coating in throat.
27. **B** – Painless unilateral vision loss, curtain coming down, and amaurosis fugax are seen in central retinal artery occlusion (CRAO). Acute angle glaucoma has "tunnel vision", and halos around lights. Hyphema is blood in the anterior chamber of eye. (Sheehy pg. 374)
28. **D** – Flashes of light (photopsia) and floaters (spots in vision) are characteristic of retinal detachment. (Sheehy pg. 374)
29. **A** – Hazardous vulnerability assessment (HVA) is part of disaster mitigation. Disaster preparedness is stockpiling supplies, training, and mutual aid agreements. (Sheehy pg. 167)
30. **D** – One of the signs of pericarditis is a pericardial friction rub, heard best when the patient leans forward. Murmurs are audible in valve disorders. (Sheehy pg. 246)
31. **C** – The hallmark sign of Pertussis is a paroxysmal cough. Inspiratory stridor is heard in upper airway obstruction like croup. Expiratory wheeze is heard early in lower airway obstruction like asthma. Drooling with respiratory distress is the hallmark sign of epiglottitis. (Sheehy pg. 563)
32. **A** – Cocaine is a stimulant, so the patient is tachycardic, hypertensive, and hyperthermic. Pupils are dilated (mydriasis). Treatment includes benzodiazepines and manual cooling. (Sheehy pg. 636)
33. **B** – Pleural effusion is a complication of pancreatitis, which may lead to ARDS. Prepare for a thoracentesis. (Sheehy pg. 246)
34. **C** – Miosis is not a sign of Digoxin toxicity, but visual changes such as yellow vision or halos may be a symptom. (Sheehy pg. 351)
35. **B** – Testicular torsion is not a cause of priapism. Sickle cell, spinal cord injury, antidepressants, and leukemia are causes of priapism. (Sheehy pgs 277-78)
36. **D** – Thyroid stimulating hormone (TSH) is decreased in hyperthyroidism, while T3 and T4 are elevated. (Sheehy pg. 305)
37. **C** – Thorns, wooden splinters (vegetative materials) are most likely to cause infection, especially fungal infections. Remove vegetative materials quickly.
38. **B** – Providing a safe environment is the priority for suicidal patients. (Sheehy pg. 590)
39. **D** – Tachycardia is the best indication of shock in the pediatric patient. Tachypnea is seen in respiratory distress and shock. Capillary refill would be delayed, not decreased. Hypotension is a late sign of shock in children. Fluid boluses for pediatric patients are at 20 ml/kg. (TNCC pg. 237)
40. **B** – Eating three meals a day is not recommended in esophagitis. Treatment plans for esophagitis include eating small, frequent meals; avoiding spicy foods and alcohol; eliminating smoking; and raising the head of the bed. (Sheehy pg. 264)
41. **A** – Hypotension is seen in adrenal crisis due to hypovolemic shock from a lack of aldosterone. (Sheehy pgs. 307-08)

42. **D** – Asking the patient to make the "hitchhike" or "thumbs up" sign evaluates the radial nerve. Opposing the thumb to the fingers evaluates the medial nerve. Abducting the fingers assesses the ulnar nerve. (Sh pg. 483)
43. **C** – Anorexia is suspected when the patient is extremely thin, with brittle hair and nails. They have a distorted view of their weight, and an intense fear of gaining weight. Patients with bulimia are typically normal or larger weight, and commonly binge-purge. (Sheehy pgs. 584-85)
44. **C** – Immerse the part in hot water until the pain subsides, which may take 2 hours.
45. **B** – Dystonic reactions are involuntary repetitive movements such as facial grimacing, tongue protrusion, and lip smacking seen in the use of neuroleptics like Thorazine, Reglan, or Phenergan.
46. **B** - Croup (LTB) is characterized by low-grade fever and a "barking" cough after an URI. A-P chest film shows the "steeple sign". Nebulized epinephrine is the mainstay of treatment. (Sheehy pg. 562)
47. **B** - Implied consent allows appropriate treatment in an emergency. Express consent is an agreement to treatment. Informed consent means the patient understands the risks and benefits of the proposed treatment, is not under the influence, and has legal capacity. Involuntary consent ensures needed treatment when a patient refuses it as in suicidal or delusional patients. (Sheehy pg. 15)
48. **A** – Significant blunt chest trauma may cause a flail chest or free-floating segment of the thorax which results in paradoxical chest wall movement. Pulmonary contusion is usually associated with flail chest so decrease IV fluid rate. (Sheehy pg. 449)
49. **B** – SIADH is excessive secretion of antidiuretic hormone (ADH) seen in head trauma, meningitis, and oat cell carcinoma. The water retention leads to dilutional hyponatremia, which may cause seizures. (Sheehy pgs. 304-05)
50. **C** – Appendicitis is suspected with fever, nausea/vomiting, periumbilical to RLQ abdominal pain (McBurney's Point), and rebound tenderness (Rovsing's sign). (Sheehy pg. 265)
51. **C** – The middle meningeal artery is typically injured with a temporal lobe hit, resulting in an epidural bleed. The classic sign of an EDH is unresponsiveness, a lucid period, then a second loss of consciousness. (TNCC pg. 107)
52. **D** – A pelvic fracture is least likely to occur in a lap restraint injury. Common injuries include hollow organ like duodenal rupture, pancreatic injury, and lumbar "chance" fracture. (TNCC pg. 145)
53. **A** – Neurogenic shock is seen in spinal cord injury from a blocked sympathetic nervous system, resulting in the maldistribution of blood flow. Hemodynamically the vasodilation leads to hypotension and parasympathetic stimulation leads to bradycardia. (TNCC pg. 172)
54. **C** – Magnesium may cause a decrease in respiratory effort so monitor the respiratory rate and oxygen saturation closely. If it decreases, stop the Magnesium consider administering Calcium gluconate. (Sheehy pg. 284)
55. **B** – Lab values seen in DIC include prolonged bleeding times, elevated PT and PTT, positive d-dimer, and increased fibrin split products. (Sheehy pgs. 317-18)
56. **A** – Gouty arthritis causes intense pain, especially in the "big toe". Treat with colchicine and prednisone and reduce intake of alcohol and purine rich foods like red meats.
57. **A** – Maintaining airway and administering epinephrine IM are the priorities in treating anaphylaxis; then administer diphenhydramine, cimetidine, and solu-medrol. (Sheehy pgs. 567-68)
58. **B** – The hallmark symptom of compartment syndrome is pain out of proportion to the injury, unrelieved by analgesia. The initial nursing action is to keep the injured leg in a neutral position. Monitor the compartment pressure and prepare for a fasciotomy as needed. (TNCC pg. 196)
59. **C** – Signs and symptoms of rhabdomyolysis include myalgias and reddish-brown urine. Lab values include increased potassium, CK, myoglobin, and BUN. Treat aggressively with IVF's, sodium bicarbonate, and dialysis to prevent acute kidney injury. (TNCC pg. 396)
60. **D** – The 5th metacarpal fracture is known as the amateur "Boxer's fracture" and is treated with an ulnar gutter splint. (Sheehy pg. 488)

# PDB Nurse Education, LLC     CEN Study Tips (12 Step-by-Step Guide)

1. Thank you for allowing me to be your certification mentor! This is a commitment, but we WILL DO IT. Email me at **pbartleysc@gmail.com** if you have and questions about the study material.
2. If you are using other CEN study material, please email me to make sure it is reputable material. I have not found an app that I can confirm a nurse developing the content.
3. **Register for the CEN exam soon**, it makes it "REAL" and you will actively study. Do not tell anyone when your test date is, that just adds more pressure. You have **90 days to take the exam once you register**, but please do not schedule the exam on day 90, because something may go wrong. Check **www.BCEN.org** for exam information. With a medical statement of a learning disability, you can request a private testing space and additional time for testing.
4. **Schedule your exam at the best time of day for you, morning, or afternoon.** Night-shifters do not work all night, then taking the exam at 8:00am. The testing center is warm, and several have fallen asleep during the exam. When are you most alert – am or pm? Schedule your test for that time of day.
5. The CEN exam is **175 questions, and you have 180 minutes** to complete. All questions are multiple-choice, no "all of the above" or "select all that apply".
6. Yes, the 2020 pass rate was 55%, but if you follow my advice, you have a much higher chance of passing the exam. No, my pass rate is not 100%. Not everyone commits to following my advice.
7. **Twenty-five questions on the exam do not count**. The 25 questions can be anywhere on exam, but tend to be earlier, so if you see something not in my material, just make the **best educated choice**.
8. My CEN pretest is 60 questions so you can assess your timing. The goal is to make 75%, so did you get 45 correct? Why did you miss the questions? Was it a knowledge-deficit, or test-taking error? The pretest questions are a little easier than the actual exam, just to assess basic knowledge.
9. The CEN exam blueprint has **8 sections**, study one section per week.
10. Prepare a **dedicated study space**, just like students in virtual school. Have flashcards to write content you need to study more, and colorful pens to stimulate creative side.
11. **Study during your peak brain time** and consider playing instrumental music while you study to stimulate brain. Study in **30-45-minute intervals**, then get up and exercise before continuing.
12. What **study strategy** works best for you?
    a. Talk to a nurse who **recently passed** the CEN exam and ask for suggestions. This exam has evolved over the last 5 years, focusing more on prioritization and critical thinking, not memorization. Review ESI and TNCC to help with prioritization questions.
    b. Study buddy or group – I strongly suggest you have a study group or buddy.
    c. Develop **flash cards** of red bolded Key Concepts or concepts you do not fully understand, not everything. Take the flashcards to work and ask everyone to tell you everything they know about that concept. You learn while creating the flashcards.
    d. **Develop memory aids**, mnemonics, and acronyms for ECG concurrent leads, ABG interpretation, antidotes, etc.
    e. Practicing sample questions with BCEN's 150 questions, order at **www.BCEN.org** only if you feel you need more.
    f. **Record** yourself explaining "Key Points" in your own words and listen while driving or exercising, or before going to bed. You learn while recording the concepts and reinforce with listening.
    g. **Explain difficult material** to a co-worker and encourage questions.

# Cardiovascular Emergencies (19 items)

A. **Cardiac Assessment**
   1. Cardiac output = heart rate x stroke volume (amount of blood ejected per contraction)
      a. **Tachycardia** is the primary compensatory mechanism for low cardiac output in **pediatric** patients since they are unable to increase stroke volume. **Hypotension is a late** sign, and **bradycardia is an ominous sign in pediatrics**.
   2. **Stroke volume** influenced by **contractility, preload, and afterload**.
   3. **Preload** (volume) is evaluated by central venous pressure (CVP) on right.
      a. **Decreased when hypovolemic** and from vasodilators, increased by volume and vasoconstrictors. TX: **increase preload with fluids/blood, decrease with diuretics like venodilator Lasix (furosemide)**.
   4. **Afterload** (resistance to ventricular emptying) is evaluated by systemic vascular resistance.
      a. **Decreased in distributive shocks** (neurogenic, septic, and anaphylactic), and by vasodilators. TX: **Vasopressors** like Norepinephrine. Increased in hypertension, aortic stenosis, and through other **shock compensation.** TX: Vasodilators like NTG.
   5. **Sympathetic nervous system** (SNS) stimulation causes release of catecholamines epinephrine and norepinephrine, which **increases** heart rate in response to shock. Adrenal gland releases catecholamines increasing blood sugar.
   6. Parasympathetic nervous system **decreases heart rate**, like vagal response; and as seen in **neurogenic shock** (blocked sympathetic response, unopposed parasympathetic)
   7. Mean arterial pressure (**MAP**) = ((2 x DBP) + SBP) divided by 3. **EX: 120/80 = 280/3=93.3**.
   8. **Pulse pressure** (PP) = difference between the SBP and DBP. **Narrowed** PP seen in early shock; **Widened** PP seen in increased **ICP**.
   9. **Cushing triad** is indicative of **increased ICP** - widened pulse pressure or increased SBP, bradycardia, irregular breathing pattern.
   10. Cardiac Pharmacology
       a. Chronotropes affect the heart **rate** at the SA node – Cardizem (-) chronotrope.
       b. **Inotropes** affect **contractility** (force of contraction) – **Dopamine and Dobutamine are (+) inotropes.**
       c. Dromotropes affect **automaticity** (electrical impulse) of the heart at the AV node.
       d. **Beta-blockers** (olols) - Beta 1 medications affect the heart; beta 2 medications affect the heart and lungs. EX: Labetalol, Esmolol, Metoprolol, Propranolol. **Beta-blockers may mask signs of shock and hypoglycemia.**
       e. Angiotensin-converting enzyme **(ACE) inhibitors** - Affect the renin-angiotensin-aldosterone system (RAAS), **blocks conversion of angiotensin 1 to angiotensin 2** – reducing BP. EX: Lisinopril, Lotensin, Vasotec.
          - Adverse effects: most common - **dry nonproductive cough** (leads to noncompliance), most severe – **angioedema**.
       f. Angiotensin receptor blockers (ARBs) "sartans" Avapro, Cozaar, Diovan
          - Inhibits angiotensin 2 receptors, resulting in vasodilation to reduce BP.
       g. Calcium channel blockers "dipine" – EX: Diltiazem (Cardizem) to control ventricular rate in atrial fibrillation and hypertension, Norvasc, Nifedipine.
       h. Vasodilators
          - **Nitroglycerin** – coronary artery **vasodilator** that **reduces preload and afterload, BP, and oxygen consumption**. It is contraindicated within 24 hours of phosphodiesterase inhibitor use - Viagra (sildenafil), Cialis, Levitra (tadalafil).
          - **Nitroprusside** – strong **preload and afterload reduction** used in hypertensive crisis.

i. **Vasopressors** - Epinephrine, Norepinephrine (Levophed), and Phenylephrine. Vasopressin augments primary vasopressors.
- Watch for infiltration and **extravasation** – tissue necrosis. **Phentolamine (Regitine) is antidote for extravasation** (vasodilator). May use NTG ointment.

B. **Acute Coronary Syndromes**
1. Types
    a. **Stable** angina pectoris – chest pain that occurs with physical exertion, short duration, **relieved by rest or NTG**. (-) troponin. Unstable angina – chest pain with little physical exertion, longer, unrelieved; (-) troponin.
    b. NSTEMI – Plaque rupture, **(+) troponin**, absent ST elevation. **STEMI** – ST elevation, obstruction of vessel(s) with thrombosis, **(+) troponin.**
    c. **Prinzmetal's** or Variant Angina– Ischemia due to **coronary vasospasm** (stimulants), cyclical **pain at rest.** Vasospasm is precipitated by stress; ST elevation resolves and pain relief when vasospasm resolves. Beta-blockers **may** exacerbate vasospasm due to unopposed alpha stimulation.
2. S/S: Chest tightness, jaw, neck, left arm, epigastric (indigestion-like) pain, scapular discomfort; N/V; signs of shock; dysrhythmias; diaphoresis; dizziness. **Women complain of increased fatigue "atypical", diabetics more likely to have a silent MI.**
3. Labs: **Troponin** is best indicator of tissue damage due to acute MI, elevation in 3-12 hours, peaks at 10-24 hours. Myoglobin rises earlier, but not as specific.
4. HX: Use of phosphodiesterase inhibitors (sildenafil – Viagra) within last 24 hours, and cocaine (leaves unopposed alpha stimulation if given beta-blockers).
5. **12-lead ECG**
    a. **Lead Placement**
        - Limb leads – I, II, III (bipolar Einthoven's Triangle), aVR, aVL, aVF (unipolar)
        - Precordial leads- V1-V6 (unipolar over chest)
        - **V4R - 5th intercostal space (ICS) right mid-clavicular line (MCL)**
        - V7-V9 – posterior (get ECG when see **ST depression in V1 & V2**)
    b. **Contiguous Leads** (changes in 2 or more contiguous leads is significant)
        - **Inferior – II, III, aVF**
        - **Anterior** – V1-V4 (Septal V1 & V2)
        - **Lateral** – I, aVL (High Lateral) V5, V6

## Contiguous Leads

- Leads II, III, aVF    Inferior (RCA)
- Leads $V_1$-$V_4$    Anterior (LAD)
- Leads I, aVL, $V_5$, $V_6$    Lateral
- $V_4R$    Right Ventricle
- $V_7$-$V_9$    Posterior

c. Reciprocal Leads – leads that oppose (opposite view) contiguous leads.
- I and aVL in Inferior. II, III, and aVF in High Lateral (I and aVL)
d. Patterns
- Ischemia = **ST segment depression** and/or inverted or tall T waves.

- **Injury** = ST segment elevation (**STEMI**), T wave may invert.
- Infarction (old) = Abnormal (deep and wide) Q wave.
  e. STEMI/Vessel Occluded – ST segment elevation in at least 2 contiguous leads.
    - **Inferior** (II, III, aVF)
      - Most commonly **Right Coronary Artery** (RCA) – supplies SA and AV nodes also (pacemakers), so see **bradycardias** and heart blocks.
      - S/S: Epigastric pain, **bradycardias resulting in hypotension**, Second degree heart block type 1, N/V, risk of mitral regurgitation and papillary muscle rupture (new onset heart murmur).
    - **Anterior** (V1-V4)
      - Most **Left Anterior Descending** (LAD) "widow maker".
      - S/S: Crushing chest pain, ventricular dysrhythmias (VF), tachycardia, feeling of impending doom, BBB, SOB, **crackles in lungs and S3. from left ventricular failure (cardiogenic shock)**, second degree type 2 (Mobitz 2) is ominous sign. New onset heart murmur = ventricular septal defect – emergency.
    - **Right Ventricle** (30-50% of inferior MI's – **get right-sided ECG with inferior MI**) - Proximal RCA.
      - S/S: JVD, hypotension, shock, ST elevation at **V4R** at 5th ICS, right MCL).
      - TX: **Caution with preload-reducing agents, such as NTG and morphine**. Prepare to infuse a **NS bolus**, and **Dobutamine** infusion to increase contractility.
    - **Lateral MI** (LAD/Circumflex)
      - I and aVL high lateral, V5 and V6
      - See reciprocal changes (ST depression in II, III, aVF for high)
    - **Posterior MI** (ST segment elevation in V7-V9 or **depression in V1 & V2**).
  6. STEMI Treatment:
    a. **Oxygen** at 4 L via NC only if SpO$_2$ **< 94%** or respiratory distress.
    b. **Nitroglycerin** SL tablet 0.3-.04 or spray initially **1 tablet every 5 minutes, up to 3**, IV infusion as needed, contraindicated if SBP < 90, HR < 50, recent phosphodiesterase inhibitor (sildenafil).
    c. **Aspirin** 162-325 mg in chewable form to prevent platelet aggregation.
    d. Percutaneous catheterization intervention (PCI) goal is < 90 minutes; fibrinolytic therapy if PCI unavailable within 90-120 minutes; **expect reperfusion dysrhythmias like Accelerated IVR (AIVR) or Ventricular Tachycardia (VT) - good sign of reperfusion.**
    e. Beta-blockers early for hypertensive STEMI patients.
    f. ACE inhibitors/ARBs to reduce infarct size and improve ventricular remodeling.
    g. Antiplatelets – aspirin, clopidogrel (Plavix), Prasugrel (Effient), Ticagrelor (Brilinta) to prevent blood clots from forming.
    h. Anticoagulants – heparin, enoxaparin (Lovenox), warfarin (coumadin), apixaban (Eliquis), rivaroxaban (Xarelto), dabigatran (Pradaxa).

C. **Aortic dissection**
  1. Tear in intimal layer of aorta because of HTN, age > 60, cocaine use, trauma (**1st and 2nd rib fractures**), heart disease, connective tissue diseases like **Marfan's** and **Ehlers Danlos.**
  2. S/S: Sudden onset of **tearing, ripping pain** to chest, shoulders, flank, or **back** not relieved by analgesics; **difference of 20 mm Hg in SBP between arms, pulsatile mass.**
    a. Ascending – stroke-like symptoms, Horner's Syndrome (**P**tosis, **A**nhidrosis, **M**iosis).
    b. Descending – loss of distal pulses, lower extremity weakness, decreased UO.
  3. DX: Transthoracic or transesophageal echocardiogram (TTE or TEE), chest CT or MRI. See **widened mediastinum** and **obscured aortic knob** on films.

4. TX: Support ABC's; anticipate **rapid deterioration** so start **2 large-bore IV's**; maintain **heart rate of 60-80 and SBP of 100-120 mm Hg** with **IV beta-blockers first** to avoid reflex tachycardia, nitroprusside, or nitroglycerin; analgesia; prepare for surgical repair.

D. **Cardiopulmonary arrest**
   1. BLS/**CPR** - 100-120 compressions per minute at 30:2 compressions/ventilations, continuous compressions with 1 breath q 6 seconds once advanced airway (do not delay BLS and defibrillation for advanced airway), allow for full chest recoil, minimize interruptions, switch compressors every 2 minutes. Keep **ETCO$_2$ > 10 mm Hg**. Encourage or switch compressors if < 10 Mm Hg.
   2. **CPR and Defibrillation** for shockable cardiac arrest (**VF and pulseless VT**) (Pre-charge defibrillator prior to pulse check to increase compression time)
      a. Adult biphasic 120-200 joules, monophasic 200-360 joules.
      b. Pediatric **2-4 joules/kg** initially, then 4 joules/kg, then 4-10 joules/kg.
      c. Immediately resume chest compressions after shock, **no pulse checks** after defibrillation unless organized rhythm is present.
   3. **Medications for cardiac arrest**
      a. Epinephrine (1 mg/10 ml) 1 mg IV/IO every 3-5 minutes.
      b. Antiarrhythmic - Amiodarone 300 mg IV/IO or Lidocaine 1-1.5 mg/kg for refractory VF.
      c. Sodium Bicarbonate **1 mEq/kg** for metabolic acidosis-induced cardiac arrest only.
   4. Find cause of cardiac arrest and treat (**H's and T's**), especially for **Asystole and PEA with POCUS (point-of-care US)**
      a. Hypovolemia, Hypoxemia, Hydrogen Ion, Hyper or Hypokalemia, Hypothermia.
      b. Toxins, Trauma, Tension pneumothorax, Tamponade, Thrombosis.
   5. **Family Presence**
      a. Family is more likely to understand seriousness of patient's condition, able to begin the grieving process, and able to **provide needed history.** Assign a staff member to family, explain procedures in simple terms, allow family to hold patient's hand and speak to family member.
   6. Traumatic Cardiac Arrest – prepare for emergency **thoracotomy** for penetrating cardiac tamponade, seen on FAST (focused assessment sonography for trauma) exam.
   7. **Maternal cardiac arrest** – DIC, embolism, eclampsia, **abruption**
      a. Provide chest compressions higher and **manually displace the uterus** to the left to prevent **vena cava syndrome, prepare for emergency Cesarean-section.**
   8. Post Arrest Resuscitation (**ROSC**- return of spontaneous circulation)
      a. Secure airway and optimize ventilation/oxygenation (**ET CO$_2$ 35-45** and O$_2$ sat 90%)
      b. Increase circulation with 1-2 L of NS and vasopressor by weight to get **SBP of > 90 mm Hg.**
      c. Targeted temperature management (TTM) at **32-36 degrees** Celsius for at least 24 hours. Control shivering, provide sedation, analgesia, and neuromuscular blockade.

E. **Dysrhythmias**
   1. Medications for **Stable Tachycardia** (alert, **normal BP**)
      a. **Vagal** maneuvers for narrow-complex tachycardia.
      b. **Adenosine 6 mg** rapid IV push with flush to slow SA and AV node conduction for narrow (SVT) or **monomorphic** wide-complex tachycardia (VT); repeat with **12 mg** only if effective.
      c. Calcium-channel blockers (Cardizem) or beta-blockers (Labetalol) for stable SVT.
      d. **Amiodarone 150 mg** slow for stable ventricular tachycardia, OR
      e. Lidocaine for PVC's and stable ventricular tachycardia (esp. if due to prolonged QTi), OR Procainamide 20-50 mg/minute up to 17 mg/kg, OR Sotalol for stable ventricular tachycardia – **monitor for hypotension and prolonged QT.**
   2. **Synchronized Cardioversion** for **Unstable Tachycardia** (SVT or VT – has pulse, conscious but crashing) - SYNC on "R" wave (ventricular contraction)

a. Consider sedative prior to procedure as appropriate, 50-200 joules biphasic. **0.5-1 joule/kg, up to 2 joule/kg for pediatric patients.**
3. **Implantable cardioverter defibrillator (AICD)**
   a. Inappropriately firing – medical management of rate or apply magnet over generator.
   b. Persistent VT/VF – **Defibrillate ASAP** keeping defib pads 10 cm away from generator of ICD.
4. Atrial fibrillation – quivering atria, rapid ventricular rate (RVR – ventricular rate > 100), **and risk is emboli (stroke).** Atrial flutter – saw-tooth waves, fixed (2:1, 3:1) or variable.
5. Wolff-Parkinson-White Syndrome (**WPW**)
   a. Accessory (extra conduction) pathway carrying impulses rapidly through heart, leading to tachycardia, presence of a **delta wave** (short PR interval, slurring on the upstroke of the QRS).

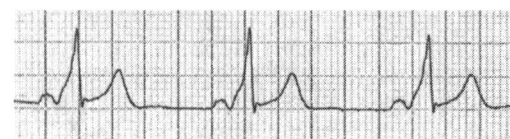

6. **Prolonged QT Interval** (> ½ the total R-R length)
   a. Medications that prolong QTi - Cardiac meds like Sotalol or Procainamide, antibiotics like **Erythromycin,** Levofloxacin, and Ciprofloxacin, psychiatric meds like **Haldol** and Lithium, **tricyclic antidepressants** (TCAs like Elavil and Tofranil), antihistamines, antifungals. Risk of causing **R on T phenomenon,** leading to **polymorphic VT** (Torsades de points).

ABCDE...
You are such a QT...prolong QTi

- A  AntiArrhythmics (Sotalol, Amiodarone, Procainamide)
- B  AntiBiotics (Flouroquinolones, Macrolides, Aminoglycosides)
- C  AntiCychotics (Haloperidol, Risperidone, Thorazine, Geodon)
- D  AntiDepressants (SSRI's, TCA's – Elavil, Tofranil)
- E  AntiEmetics (Ondansetron, Droperidol, Compazine)

7. **Torsades de pointes** (polymorphic VT due to prolonged QT)
   a. Cardioversion and **magnesium sulfate** slow infusion if pulse palpable.
   b. BLS, defibrillation, epinephrine, and magnesium **2 grams IV push if pulseless.**
8. **Bradycardias**
   a. Causes: **respiratory distress**, aging, coronary artery disease (CAD) and cardiac defects, or **medication induced.**
   b. S/S: Hypotension, altered mental status, signs of shock, cardiac ischemia, acute HF.
   c. Heart blocks
      - **First degree** – prolonged PR interval (> .20), consistent PR and R to R intervals (PR and RR consistent)
      - **Second degree, type 1** – progressive prolongation of the PR interval that eventually blocks an impulse, inconsistent PR and R to R (both inconsistent)
      - **Second degree, type 2** – consistent PR interval with blocked P waves yielding an inconsistent R to R interval (PR consistent, RR inconsistent)
      - **Third degree** – R to R intervals are consistent, hidden P waves (inconsistent)
   d. TX: Correct underlying cause (**respiratory - assist breathing with BVM**), **Atropine 1** mg IVP every 3-5 minutes for low degree blocks (up to 3 mg), Consider **transcutaneous pacing**,

Epinephrine infusion at 2-10 mcg/min or **Dopamine infusion** at 5-20 mcq/kg/min infusion, pacemakers for refractory bradycardia or heart blocks.
- **Atropine ineffective** for high degree HB and **heart transplants**. Administer **isoproterenol (Isuprel) for transplanted heart**.
  e. **Transcutaneous pacing (TCP)**
  - Anterior-posterior pad placement preferred, may place anterior-lateral.
  - Rate of 60-80 at 60 mA and increase until capture is obtained. Electrical capture – pacer spike precedes waves; Mechanical capture – palpable pulse that correlates to paced beat, **not judged by carotid pulse.**
  f. **Pacemaker** – failure to pace if no spikes, failure to capture if no QRS, failure to sense if pacemaker continuing to pace without regard to patients own pulse.

F. **Pericarditis**
  1. Inflammation of the pericardial sac from infection, MI (Dressler's), renal failure, etc.
  2. S/S: Sudden onset of **retrosternal** chest pain **exacerbated by inspiration, activity, and supine position**; and relieved by leaning forward or sitting up; pericardial **friction rub heard best while leaning forward**; tachycardia and tachypnea; low-grade fever.
  3. DX: Chest x-ray and echo; 12 lead ECG: **concave, global (widespread, diffuse) ST segment elevation in most leads** without reciprocal changes; tall, peaked T waves in all leads except aVR.
  4. TX: **NSAIDs (ibuprofen, Indocin, aspirin; and steroids)**, not NTG; **allow to lean forward**.

G. **Endocarditis**
  1. Inflammation of the endocardium from cardiac surgery, **IV drug use**, or **body piercing** affecting the cardiac valves.
  2. S/S of infection: **fever**, chills, night sweats, myalgia's, **new onset murmur** (vegetation on valves); pleuritic chest pain; splinter hemorrhages in nail beds; conjunctival petechiae; Osler's nodes (tender nodules on digits); Janeway lesions (macules on palms and soles); Roth spots (retinal hemorrhages).
  3. DX: increased WBC, blood cultures, **increased erythrocyte sedimentation rate** (ESR), **echocardiogram to assess valves.**
  4. TX: Administration of **IV antibiotics**, prepare for admission and possible valvular repair.

H. **Heart failure**
  1. Inadequate cardiac output, stroke volume, and oxygen delivery to tissues. Increased peripheral vasoconstriction, **brain natriuretic peptide (BNP)** over 100.
  2. Systolic HF – inability to pump effectively; diastolic – inability to adequately fill.
  3. **Left (lungs) HF** – **SOB**, paroxysmal nocturnal dyspnea (PND), dyspnea, crackles, **S3 heart sound**, Kerly B lines on x-ray, pulmonary edema; most from Anterior MI.
  4. **Right (rest of body) HF** – JVD, peripheral edema, ascites, hepatomegaly, increased CVP pressure; most from **Cor pulmonale** from COPD or pulmonary HTN, or RV MI.
  5. TX: Support ABC's, cardiac monitoring, titrate oxygenation to > 90%, **consider NIPPV (Bi-Pap or CPAP)**, caution with IVF's, **loop diuretics (Lasix is a venodilator) to decrease preload so watch K+**, vasodilators (NTG), ACE/ARB to interrupt RAAS (Renin-angiotensin, aldosterone system).

I. **Hypertensive Emergency/Crisis**
  1. SBP > 180 mm Hg or DBP > 120 mm Hg **PLUS** evidence of impending end-organ damage, i.e., AMI, aortic dissection, heart failure, pulmonary edema, intracranial hemorrhage; hypertensive encephalopathy; and eclampsia. Hypertensive urgency (no end-organ damage) can be treated over days.
  2. S/S: Altered LOC, chest pain, dizziness, epistaxis, headache, seizures, visual disturbances.
  3. DX: 12-lead ECG, chest x-ray, urinalysis, BUN, and creatinine.
  4. TX: $O_2$, IV, consider an arterial line (**Allen's Test prior to radial arterial line insertion**) with transducer leveled at **phlebostatic axis**.

a. Nitroglycerin or **nitroprusside (Nipride)** via infusion to slowly decrease MAP by a maximum of **25% in the first 2 hours of treatment, calculate MAP. Goal to get SBP to 140-160 mm Hg.** Labetalol slower onset; safe and effective during pregnancy.

J. **Pericardial (Cardiac) tamponade**
   1. Life-threatening condition in which the pericardial sac accumulates additional fluid (typically 20-50 ml of fluid) from pericarditis, trauma, MI leading to **obstructive shock.**
   2. S/S: **Beck's Triad** of JVD, hypotension, and **muffled (distant) heart sounds**; Kussmaul sign (increase in JVD on inspiration); **Pulsus paradoxus** (decrease in BP upon inspiration); small ECG amplitude; **Electrical alternans** (alternating amplitude of QRS); tachycardia, anxiousness, restlessness; risk of PEA.
   3. TX: Prepare **for needle pericardiocentesis** subxiphoid approach emergently or **resuscitative thoracotomy** (surgical pericardiectomy - window); support blood pressure with vasopressors.

K. **Peripheral vascular disease**
   1. **Peripheral artery disease** (PAD) signs are shiny skin, hair loss, constant excruciating burning pain, cold extremity, decreased pulses or pulseless.
      a. **DX: Ankle brachial index (ABI) – normal 0.9-1.3 (some manuals 0.8-1.2).**
      b. TX: **Do not elevate**, prepare for embolectomy for critical limb ischemia.
   2. Peripheral venous disease (**PVD**) is due to damaged venous valves. Signs are leg pain, delayed wound healing, cellulitis, and ulcers.
   3. **Deep vein thrombosis** (DVT) is a blood clot in a peripheral vein in the pelvis, thigh, or lower leg due to sluggish blood flow. Risk factors: **Virchow's Triad – venous stasis** (immobility, air travel), vein damage (fracture), hypercoagulability (estrogen therapy, pregnancy). S/S: Achy, throbbing pain more common **with walking** (dorsiflexion). **Major risk is pulmonary embolism.** TX: Elevate affected extremity, **compression**, anticoagulants.
   4. **Raynaud's disease** – episodic intense **vasospasm of the digits**, nose, or ears in response to stress or cold. Buerger's disease from smoking.

L. **Blunt Cardiac Injury (Cardiac contusion)**
   1. Blunt force to chest from MVC, acts of violence, or sports injuries that results in damage to the heart, especially the **right ventricle** due to positioning of heart.
   2. S/S: Chest pain unrelieved by NTG, **dysrhythmias (ST and PVC's most common**, VT, heart blocks), **ST segment elevation**, hypotension, cardiac failure.
   3. DX: ECG monitoring and **echocardiogram to assess heart damage.**
   4. TX: **oxygen**; prepare for admission for **continuous cardiac monitoring**; possible vasopressors and positive inotropes to increase BP.

M. **Cardiogenic Shock (left ventricular heat failure)**
   1. Inadequate tissue perfusion due to **pump failure**, most commonly from anterior wall MI.
   2. S/S: Tachypnea, **crackles**, pulmonary edema, **S3 heart sound**, Kerly B lines on chest x-ray, cool clammy skin, hypotension.
   3. TX: Oxygenation, **decrease preload** with NTG and diuretics, **decrease afterload** with NTG or Nitroprusside, **increase contractility** with positive inotropes like **Dobutamine** and intra-aortic balloon pump (IABP), and treat dysrhythmias.

N. **Ventricular assist device** (VAD) – audible **hum** with barely palpable pulses, **MAP 60-90 (one number) with Doppler over brachial or radial artery**. Contact **VAD coordinator** and defibrillate (AP pads) as needed, but **CPR** may damage device.

O. **Obstructive Shock**
   1. Resistance to ventricular filling from **pericardial tamponade, tension pneumothorax**, massive pulmonary embolism, **supine vena cava syndrome** in advanced pregnancy, abdominal compartment syndrome.

2. TX: **Correct underlying condition**
   a. Pericardiocentesis and surgical repair (pericardial window) for pericardial tamponade.
   b. **Needle decompression** and chest tube placement for tension pneumothorax.
   c. Thrombolytics for pulmonary embolism.
   d. Turn **pregnant patient on side** (left preferred) 15-30 degrees to relieve pressure on superior and inferior vena cava (aortocaval syndrome).

P. **Hypovolemic Shock**
   1. Non-hemorrhagic – infuse isotonic crystalloid solutions (NS or LR), repeat as needed. 20 ml/kg fluid boluses in children, repeat as needed.
   2. **Hemorrhagic** hypovolemic shock
      a. **Stop the bleeding process** with direct pressure, **tourniquets** tightened until bleeding stops, **pelvic binder** over greater trochanter.
      b. Transfuse **blood products** plasma, platelets, and pRBC's at **1:1:1 ratio**. Do not dilute with NS or increases risk of **lethal triad** – hypothermia, acidosis, and coagulopathy.
      c. **Hypocalcemia** common after massive transfusion protocol, so replace calcium. Administer blood products based on TEG lab values.
      d. Allow **permissive hypotension** in blunt abdominal trauma and pelvic fractures to reduce bleeding, do not pop the clot.

## Shock

- Insufficient oxygen to meet the metabolic demands of cells and organs, **inadequate tissue perfusion**.
- Degree of shock is dependent on cardiac output, hemoglobin, and the oxygen saturation of the hemoglobin.
  - Apply $O_2$, start IVs, transfuse blood.
- Shock can be associated with a hypotension, **but shock is NOT defined by hypotension**.
- Monitor serum lactate, pH, and base deficit.

## Classification of Shock

- **Hypovolemic (tank)** – loss of circulating volume, fill the pump and plug the leaks.
- **Obstructive** – obstructs blood flow, relieve the obstruction.
- **Cardiogenic (pump)** – the pump is pooped, increase contractility.
- **Distributive (pipe)** – maldistribution of blood.
  - Anaphylactic – bronchospasm and vasodilation.
  - **Septic** – hyperdynamic phase initially, flash capillary refill.
  - **Neurogenic** – bradycardia and hypotension.

**Respiratory Emergencies (18 items)**

A. **Respiratory Assessment**
1. Respiratory Patterns - Eupnea – normal, Tachypnea – rapid rate, Bradypnea – slow rate, Dyspnea – labored breathing, **Orthopnea** (pulmonary edema) – dyspnea when laying down, Apnea – absence of breathing, **Kussmaul** respirations (DKA) – rapid and deep breathing, Cheyne Stokes – rhythm pattern including periods of apnea.
2. **Respiratory distress** – dyspnea, **nasal flaring**, retractions, accessory muscle use and increased work of breathing, grunting, pallor. (Great chart in PALS).
3. **Respiratory failure** – decreased level of consciousness (lethargic), **bradypnea, bradycardia.**
4. **Abnormal breath sounds – stridor from upper** airway obstruction (croup LTB, epiglottitis, anaphylaxis), **wheezing from lower airway** bronchial obstruction (asthma and bronchiolitis), crackles from excess fluid, pleural friction rub from friction.
5. **Pertinent history** – recent travel, fever, hemoptysis (TB), smoker, HIV +, COPD, history of or risk for DVT.
6. **Noninvasive Positive Pressure Ventilation** (NIPPV – Bi-Pap, CPAP) – requires tight-fitting mask, must be **hemodynamically stable** since **decreases venous return to heart**, risk is **aspiration** and barotrauma.
    - Mostly used for **acute pulmonary edema, asthma, and obstructive sleep apnea.** Not used in head injury, decreased LOC.
    - **CPAP** – continuous airflow at single set pressure to keep airway open. **BiPAP** – higher pressure on inhalation, **lower pressure on exhalation.**
7. **Intubation/Mechanical Ventilation**
    - Insert an oropharyngeal (OPA) with BVM ventilation (measure from corner of mouth to ear for correct size).
    - Nasotracheal intubation used primarily for cervical spine injuries or angioedema in awake patient, not in facial injury. May be used in angioedema with conscious patient.
    - Preoxygenate with **high-flow cannula** and keep on patient during intubation. Increase head of bed 30 degrees. Drug-assisted intubation (DAI) to reduce risk of aspiration during intubation.
    - **Succinylcholine (Anectine)** (depolarizing neuromuscular blocker) **contraindicated** if history of **malignant hyperthermia,** conditions that **precipitate hyperkalemia** (burns, **crush injuries**, renal failure), neuromuscular disorders like Guillain Barre, multiple sclerosis, myasthenia gravis.
    - Fentanyl may cause chest wall rigidity. Etomidate has little effect on blood pressure, so good choice in trauma. Propofol lowers MAP. Ketamine may cause increases secretions.
    - Confirm tube placement by **auscultation** over epigastrium first, then four lung fields, pulse oximetry, continuous wave capnography $ETCO_2$ **(normal 35-45) capnography**, and chest x-ray.
    - If patient decompensates, **manually ventilate patient** and check **DOPE** – Tube is **D**isplaced, there is an **O**bstruction, **P**neumothorax, or **E**quipment failure.

# ABG: Who is the Baby Daddy?

- 1st Step   Look at pH (Baby first name)
  - If 7.35 to 7.45 either Compensated or Normal
  - If < 7.35 or > 7.45 – Uncompensated
- 2nd Step   Look at pH again (Baby last name)
  - If < 7.35 it is Acidosis, If > 7.45 it is Alkalosis
- 3rd Step   Look at $pCO_2$ (Respiratory Component)
  - If < 35 it is Alkalosis, If > 45 it is Acidosis
  - Does it go acid/alkalosis with pH? Baby Daddy
- 4th Step   Look at $HCO_3$ (Metabolic Component)
  - If < 22 it is Acidosis, If > 26 it is Alkalosis
  - Does it go acid/alkalosis with pH? Baby Daddy

|    | pH   | $CO_2$ | $HCO_3$ |
|----|------|--------|---------|
| 1. | 7.20 | 35     | 15      |
| 2. | 7.15 | 69     | 26      |
| 3. | 7.35 | 55     | 30      |
| 4. | 7.50 | 35     | 35      |
| 5. | 7.50 | 25     | 25      |

| |
|---|
| **#1 is uncompensated metabolic acidosis** – seen in **DKA**, alcoholic acidosis (high anion gap from ethylene glycol poisoning), **shock**, renal disease, diarrhea (from the ass), or salicylate poisoning. |
| **#2 is uncompensated respiratory acidosis** – respiratory depression from drugs, head injury, asthma, sedation. |
| **#3 is compensated respiratory acidosis** – seen in chronic COPD. |
| **#4 is uncompensated metabolic alkalosis** – prolonged **vomiting** (purging). |
| **#5 is uncompensated respiratory. alkalosis** – hyperventilation from anxiety, infection, or **pulmonary embolus.** |

B. **Aspiration** – highest risk in obese, **head injury**, intoxicated, advanced pregnancy.
   1. Keep **head of bed at 30-45 degrees** to reduce risk, thicken liquids, decrease use of straws. Place patient in the recovery position on side if unable to sit up.
C. **Asthma**
   1. **Chronic** reactive airway disease characterized by airway hyper reactivity, inflammation, and bronchial constriction; triggered by **environmental irritants** like exercise, allergies, and seasonal changes.
   2. S/S: Chest tightness, dyspnea, **tachypnea**, decreased oxygen saturation, increased work of breathing, **cough, prolonged expiratory time, respiratory alkalosis to acidosis, wheezing early to silent chest**. Pulsus paradoxus and silent chest are ominous signs.
   3. DX: **Peak expiratory flow rate** (PEFR) by **exhaling forcefully**. 70-90% of personal best- use inhalers; < 70% seek medical attention; < 40% severe. See **"shark-fin"** appearance on capnography with bronchospasm.
   4. **TX:** Short-acting beta-agonists (**SABA**) such as **albuterol** or levalbuterol (Xopenex) every 20 minutes times 3 to relax smooth muscles (side effect is tachycardia); Anticholinergics (Ipratropium bromide,

Atrovent) to limit secretions of mucus and inhibit bronchial muscle contraction; oral or inhaled corticosteroids to reduce inflammation; magnesium to inhibit bronchial muscle contraction. **Treatment effective if increase in PEAK flow.**

5. Ventilation: Consider NIPPV first. When intubating, ketamine is induction agent of choice since it is also a bronchodilator, **increase** inspiration: expiration ratio from 1:2 to 1:3-4, low PEEP in mechanical ventilation (causes barotrauma).
6. **Education**: **Prevention of attacks is best control of asthma**, use **spacer** with inhalers or use **nebulizers** to increase medication delivery, avoid allergens and NSAIDs, smoking cessation, pretreat with medication before exercise. (May see discharge education questions).

D. **Chronic obstructive pulmonary disease (COPD)** – decreased lung capacity.
   1. **Chronic bronchitis** – increased work of breathing, **pursed-lip breathing**, hacking cough with **sputum production** for at least 3 months during two consecutive years, "Blue bloater", stocky build, **polycythemia** (thicker blood and increased hemoglobin leads to **clots**), **Cor pulmonale** (pulmonary hypertension), enlarged heart on x-ray, rhonchi, and wheezes.
   2. **Emphysema** – destruction of alveoli from toxins or alpha-1 antitrypsin deficiency, "Pink puffer", thin, **barrel chest** (increased anterior: posterior diameter), pursed-lip breathing, lung over inflation and low diaphragm on x-ray.
   3. **TX: Keep SpO$_2$ 88-92%** via nasal cannula or venturi mask (**reduce oxygen if decreased RR** – hypoxia required for respiratory drive), **Bi-Pap**, bronchodilators, sit on edge of bed leaning forward with feet dangling.
   4. **Education**: Encourage **smoke cessation to prevent progression**, encourage pneumonia **immunizations**, avoid exposure to persons with respiratory infections, sleep upright.

E. **Pulmonary Hypertension**
   1. Causes **right heart failure** (Cor pulmonale). S/S include exertional dyspnea and fatigue, peripheral edema, and hepatomegaly. DX: Echocardiogram and shows right ventricular hypertrophy and right bundle branch block on ECG. TX: Oxygen, vasodilators like phosphodiesterase inhibitors **sildenafil** or tadalafil, diuretics, anticoagulants, and digoxin to increase contractility.

F. **Infections**
   1. **Acute bronchitis** - Viral inflammation due to Influenza A or B, RSV, etc.
      - S/S: Non-productive **dry cough for > 5 days** and worse at night, airway hyper reactivity, pleuritic chest pain, sore throat, stuffy nose, fatigue, low-grade fever.
      - DX: Chest x-ray to rule out pneumonia.
      - TX: Cough medication, bronchodilators, corticosteroids, **no antibiotics** needed.
   2. **Bronchiolitis** – Viral infection, usually **RSV** in premature infants, producing **copious nasal secretions** (rhinitis)
      - S/S: Respiratory distress, **wheezing, crackles**, grunting, poor feeding.
      - DX: Nasopharyngeal culture to rule out influenza and chest x-ray.
      - TX: **Suction nares**, bronchodilators, admission if RR > 70 breaths/min.
      - D/C education: Teach hand hygiene to reduce spread of RSV since most spread through direct contact.
   3. **Epiglottitis** – bacterial infection decreased since HIB vaccine.
      - S/S: Triad of **d**rooling, **d**ysphagia, and **d**istress; abrupt onset of high fever; **thumbprint sign on lateral neck x-ray**; **tripod position**; "turtle sign" (extend neck) to open airway.
      - TX: Keep **in caregiver's arms and keep child calm** (no IV or labs) and consult expert to secure airway STAT. "If they cry, they die."
   4. **Croup (Acute Laryngotracheobronchitis - LTB)** – viral infection 6 months – 3 years
      - S/S: Gradual onset of URI; **barky, seal-like cough**; low-grade fever; **steeple sign on chest x-ray**.

- TX: **Racemic nebulized epinephrine** (wears off leaving rebound effect, so consider hospital admission), and **dexamethasone**.

| Epiglottitis | Croup (Acute LTB) |
|---|---|
| • Bacterial Infection (HIB) | • Viral Infection (RSV) |
| • **D** Triad of **D**rooling, **D**ysphagia, **D**istress | • **Barky**, seal-like cough |
| • **Abrupt onset** of high fever | • **Gradual** onset URI |
| • "Hot potato" voice | • Low-grade fever |
| • "Turtle Sign" | • Inspiratory stridor |
| • "**Thumbprint**" Sign on neck film | • "**Steeple**" Sign on AP chest x-ray |

5. **Pneumonia** – Viral or bacterial (faster onset) infection; community or hospital-acquired
   - S/S: Fever, chills, malaise, pleuritic CP, **productive cough**, egophony, increased **fremitus** (vibration) over the affected area with decreased breath sounds.
   - DX: Increased WBC, chest x-ray, blood cultures.
   - TX: Antibiotics, bronchodilators, oxygen, and fluids as indicated, **pneumococcal vaccine recommended** for under age 2 and above age 65.
   - **Pleural effusion** – same S/S. **Thoracentesis** to remove purulent **empyema**.

G. **Inhalation injuries**
   1. **Immediate intubation** if oral burns, stridor, and/or carbonaceous sputum. **Perform escharotomy** if circumferential chest burn, and unable to ventilate.
   2. Combustible fumes from malfunctioning furnace, exhaust, etc. – **CO poisoning - shifts the oxyhemoglobin dissociation curve to the left**, impairing the ability of hemoglobin to release $O_2$, so **$SpO_2$ is 100% (unreliable)**; arterial $PaO_2$ reliable.
   3. S/S: headache, confusion, nausea/vomiting, **cherry-red skin, ST segment depression on ECG due to hypoxia.**
   4. DX: **Carboxyhemoglobin** (COHb) level and airway evaluation.
   5. TX**: 100% oxygen until carboxyhemoglobin < 10%,** Hyperbaric oxygenation (HBO) for pregnant female since **fetus most vulnerable.**

H. **Spontaneous Pneumothorax** – most common in **males 20-40**, COPD, pulmonary fibrosis, smokers, **Marfan's**.
   1. S/S: dyspnea, decreased or **absent breath sounds on affected side**, pleuritic chest pain, **hyperresonance on percussion**, subcutaneous emphysema if large pneumothorax.
   2. TX: High-fowler position, supplemental oxygen, potential **chest tube placement at 5-6th ICS, mid-axillary line** (> 15% pneumothorax typically).

I. **Non-cardiogenic Pulmonary Edema/Acute Respiratory Distress Syndrome (ARDS)**
   1. Causes: submersion injury, **rapid ascent while scuba diving**, HAPE (high altitude pulmonary edema), inhalation of toxic gases, heroin overdose.
   2. S/S: severe dyspnea, tachypnea, cough, crackles, wheezing, pink frothy sputum, skin cool pale and moist.
   3. TX: **judicious fluid administration**, NIPPV or intubation/ventilation with **low tidal volumes** (4-6 ml/kg due to sick lungs) and **high PEEP** to decrease chance of ARDS, IV NTG, **diuretics.**
   4. ARDS (acute respiratory distress syndrome) - **severe hypoxemia that is refractory to high concentrations of oxygen**, and loss of surfactant. TX: Mechanical ventilation and prone positioning.

J. **Pulmonary embolus**
   1. Blood clot from **DVT** (Risk factors - Virchow triad of immobility, damage, or hypercoagulopathy), air emboli from diving, or amniotic fluid emboli.
   2. S/S: **Sudden onset of SOB, tachypnea, tachycardia,** restlessness, **sense of impending doom,** chest pain, cough with hemoptysis, syncope, fever, accentuated $S_2$ heart sound.
   3. **Fat emboli** typically seen 12-48 hours post **long-bone fracture**, "hallmark sign" is chest and axilla **petechiae,** sudden onset of altered mental status, and hypoxia.
   4. DX: **elevated D-dimer**; new right bundle branch block and right axis deviation, peaked P waves and depressed T waves on ECG; V/Q scan, **pulmonary angiography definitive test, ABG - low $PaO_2$ and low $CO_2$ – respiratory alkalosis and hypoxemia.**
   5. TX: **Oxygen** is the priority, anticoagulants and/or fibrinolytics (r-TPA) as indicated, embolectomy.

K. **Chest Trauma (Leave impaled object like knife or ice pick in place!)**
   1. **Rib fractures**
      - **1ˢᵗ or 2ⁿᵈ rib fractures** associated with great vessel (**aortic dissection** – widened mediastinum and obscured aortic knob on chest x-ray) and/or pneumothorax.
      - **4ᵗʰ to 9ᵗʰ ribs** most often fractured – risk is **pulmonary contusion** and blunt chest injury, so decrease IVF rate.
      - **9ᵗʰ to 12th rib** fractures associated with **spleen (L) and liver (R) injury, renal injury if posterior.**
      - Rib fractures demonstrate **significant injury in pediatrics** (pliable ribs) so suspect maltreatment and in geriatrics due to lack of pulmonary reserves.
      - **Pain management with NSAIDs, lidocaine patches, intercostal nerve blocks.**
      - Aggressive pulmonary care cough and deep breath and **incentive spirometry** to prevent atelectasis.
   2. **Pulmonary contusion**
      - Lung injury and edema from chest trauma or barotrauma 24-48 hours after event.
      - S/S: Respiratory distress, **chest wall bruising,** increased work of breathing, restlessness, crackles, wheezes.
      - DX: Chest x-ray may not reveal infiltrates **until 12 hours or later.**
      - TX: **Oxygen is the priority**, patient in semi-fowlers position, NIPPV to intubation/mechanical ventilation, **judicious use of fluid administration** (euvolemia) to prevent ARDS (refractory hypoxemia).
   3. **Flail chest**
      - Typically seen in high-speed MVC, sternal fracture from airbag
      - Two or more adjacent ribs fractured in two or more places resulting in a **free-floating** unstable segment with **paradoxical chest wall** motion (asymmetry) during respiration, muscle spasm obscures flailing initially.
      - TX: Oxygen, intubation/ventilation with PEEP, prepare for **surgery for rib fixation**, judicious fluid administration since causes **pulmonary contusion**, monitor for associated pneumothorax or hemothorax (breath sounds, percussion).
   4. Simple **pneumothorax** (Air-leak syndrome)
      - S/S: Decreased or absent breath sounds on affected side, **hyperresonance** (tympanic) to percussion, tachypnea, tachycardia.
      - TX: High-fowlers position, oxygen, potential small-bore **chest tube or catheter placement** at 5-6ᵗʰ ICS, mid-axillary line (ML) for > 20% pneumothorax.
   5. **Open pneumothorax**
      - Sucking chest wound from penetrating trauma, visible open chest wound with sucking sound and **bubbling of blood** around wound, with **SQ emphysema.**
      - **If impaled object like an ice pick still in chest, stabilize it in place.**

- TX: Cover wound with **3-sided occlusive** (non-porous) dressing at **end-exhalation** and prepare for chest tube (ask patient to exhale fully).
- **Remove dressing if tension pneumothorax develops** (decreasing O$_2$ saturation, tracheal deviation).

6. **Tension pneumothorax**
   - **Life-threatening** pneumothorax with severe respiratory distress, absent or decreased breath sounds, jugular vein distention, hypotension due to impaired venous return to heart, and **trachea deviated to unaffected side** (late sign along with cyanosis). X-ray shows mediastinal shift.
   - TX: **Immediate needle decompression** with 14-16-gauge 7 cc needle at 2$^{nd}$ ICS over 3$^{rd}$ rib (**or 4-5$^{th}$ ICS**), and immediate chest tube insertion. Treatment is **effective if assisted ventilation become easier** after decompression.

7. **Hemothorax**
   - Accumulation of blood in pleural space from tear of internal mammary artery.
   - S/S: Severe SOB, dullness to percussion, S/S of **hemorrhagic shock** (tachycardic, delated capillary refill, cool and clammy skin, hypotension).
   - DX: **FAST bedside ultrasound**
   - TX: **Two large-bore IVs, transfuse blood products**, large-bore 32-36 Fr chest tube placement at 5-6$^{th}$ ICS, **emergent surgery if initial drainage > 1500 ml**, or 200 ml/hour over next 2-4 hours.
   - Consider **autotransfusion** for **blunt injury less than 4-6 hours ago.**
   - **Advantages**: Fresh, warm, whole blood without risk of transfusion reaction
   - Contraindicated if lower chest injury (risk of bowel injury) or ruptured diaphragm. Increased risk of contamination with penetrating injury.
   - Chest drainage system – tape all connections, keep upright below the level of the chest, no dependent loops, **tidaling is normal**.

8. **Ruptured diaphragm**
   - Abdominal contents herniate into chest and **compress the lungs**, heart, and vessels, most on the left side from lateral impact MVC, unable to breathe.
   - S/S: Dyspnea, "gurgling" **peristaltic sounds** in lower left chest with **progressive scaphoid abdomen**, abdominal pain radiating to left shoulder (**Kehr's sign**), elevated left diaphragm on chest x-ray.
   - TX: **ABC's**, prepare to intubate, emergent exploratory **laparotomy.**

9. **Tracheobronchial Injury**
   - Direct blow to neck (karate blows) or all-terrain vehicle (ATV) or snowmobile driver into suspended cable "clothesline injury".
   - S/S: Dyspnea, dysphagia (difficulty swallowing), odynophagia (painful swallowing), **SQ emphysema**, Hamman's crunch synchronized with heartbeat, anterior neck pain, hemoptysis, hematoma.
   - TX: Increase head of bed 30-45 degrees, fiberoptic bronchoscopy for intubation and prepare for surgery, **positive pressure ventilation may worsen subcutaneous air.**

10. **Fractured Larynx** – dysphonia (hoarse voice), seen with tracheobronchial injury.
11. **Esophageal injury** – food particles in chest tube, seen with tracheobronchial injury.

**Neurological Emergencies (18 items)**

A. **"Da Brain"** - Cerebral blood flow – MAP – ICP = CPP (cerebral perfusion pressure); **maintain > 60 mm Hg in head injury** (normal in absence of injury = 70-90 mm Hg).
   1. Normal ICP = <15 mm Hg, **abnormal if sustained > 20 mm Hg.**
   2. Monro-Kellie doctrine – an increase in one element must be accompanied by a corresponding decrease in one of the other elements, Brain 80%, CSF 10%, Blood 10%.

B. **Neurological Assessment**
   1. LOC assessment – AVPU – **A**lert, responds to **V**erbal stimulus, responds to **P**ain, or **U**nresponsive.
   2. **Glasgow Coma Scale** – best eye opening, verbal response, and motor response (3-15). 13-15 minor head injury, 9-12 moderate, **8 or < severe head injury** (secure airway).
   3. **FOUR** (full outline unresponsiveness score) score – useful for ventilated patients since includes reflexes and respiratory pattern.
   4. NIHSS (www.stroke.org) – predicts outcomes in stroke - LOC, best gaze, visual fields, facial palsy, motor, ataxia, sensory, language, inattention.
   5. Assess blood glucose and treat as needed, add **Thiamine (Vitamin B1)** 50-100 mg if malnourished to prevent **Wernicke's** encephalopathy (**C**onfusion/**C**onfabulation – unintentional fabrication of memory, **A**taxia – impaired balance, **N**ystagmus - repetitive uncontrolled eye movements).
   6. Pupils - Pinpoint – opioids (consider naloxone if apneic too), or exposure to OP pesticides or chemical warfare agent (CWA); Nystagmus – drugs, tumor.
   7. Posturing - Flexion – decorticate (cerebrum); Extension – decerebrate (brainstem)
   8. **CSF leakage** (otorrhea from ear, rhinorrhea from nose)
      a. **Clear drainage – check for glucose** (66% of serum glucose); **bloody – look for halo.**
      b. **Do NOT pack**, just let it drain, place **sterile nasal drip pad to prevent infection, not to prevent drainage.** Instruct patient to not blow nose. Do NOT insert an NG tube.
   9. Brain Reflexes
      a. Babinski – fanning of toes abnormal finding in adults.
      b. Oculocephalic reflex "Doll's eyes" – if brainstem intact eyes deviate to opposite side head moved to. No movement of eyes in brain death.
      c. Oculovestibular reflex "cold caloric" – eyes look toward ear irrigated, no response in brain death.
   10. **Cranial nerves** – 2 is responsible for vision; 3, 4, & 6 assess extraocular movements (EOMs); **3 (oculomotor) leads to limited upward gaze;** 5(V) – **Trigeminal neuralgia;** 7(VII) – **Bell's palsy.**

## Cranial Nerves    7 S's

- Smell — 1
- Sight /EOM — 2, 3, 4, 6
- Sensation — 5, 7
- Sound — 8
- Swallow/gag — 9, 10
- Shrug Shoulders — 11
- Stick out Tongue — 12

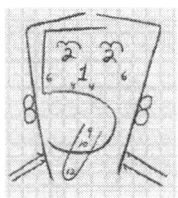

C. **Chronic neurological disorders – Assess for depression.**
   1. Multiple sclerosis - demyelination of axons leads to weakness, unsteady gait, and altered sensation in extremities and face; treated with steroids and immunosuppressants (interferon).
   2. **Myasthenia gravis** – autoimmune affecting women 20-30; affects acetylcholine binding sites leading to muscle fatigue, **ptosis** (drooping eyelids), dysphagia, and respiratory paralysis; DX with **Tensilon,** have Atropine at bedside in case of cholinergic crisis; TX with Neostigmine. Atropine if Neostigmine OD.
   3. Parkinson disease – chronic degenerative disease affecting the dopamine pathway; S/S: tremor at rest, facial "mask", **"cogwheel" rigidity**; bradykinesia. TX: Carbidopa (levodopa).
   4. Amyotrophic lateral sclerosis (ALS) "Lou Gehrig Disease" – genetic disorder that leads to progressive loss of voluntary muscle control (grip strength) but retains intelligence and personality.
D. **Guillain-Barre syndrome** – damage to myelin sheath leading to a **tingling prickling sensation in extremities**, loss of DTR and difficulty walking, urinary retention, and **ascending symmetrical weakness/paralysis; monitor respiratory effectiveness**; care is supportive.
E. **Headache**
   1. **Red flags** – sudden onset with peak intensity **"explosive" "worst of life"** within minutes (**SAH**), nuchal rigidity and fever (meningitis), trauma and decreased LOC (intracranial bleed), escalating (tumor).
   2. **Temporal arteritis** "giant cell arteritis" – inflamed temporal artery (**palpable cord-like**) in age > 50, resulting in a throbbing headache in temporal area and **jaw pain (with chewing)**, fever, and temporary unilateral vision loss; treated with **corticosteroids.**
   3. **Tension** – "band-like" pain across forehead. Teach relaxation techniques.
   4. **Migraine** –**unilateral pulsating pain**, photophobia and phonophobia, N/V, possible aura. Teach to journal to determine triggers.
   5. **Cluster** – excruciating, unilateral (periorbital/temporal), episodic (multiple per day, short-lived), **excessive tearing (lacrimation)** and nasal congestion on affected side. Treat with oxygen initially.
F. **Meningitis** – acute inflammation of the meninges from virus or bacteria (group B streptococcus or Neisseria meningitides – meningococcal)
   1. S/S: Altered LOC, fever, headache, nuchal rigidity, photophobia, **Kernig's and Brudzinski's** (legs pull up when head is bent) signs.
   2. **Infants - bulging fontanelles, opisthotonos (backward arch), and high-pitched cry.**
   3. **Meningococcemia - non-blanching petechial rash on torso/legs.** Don PPE and isolate patient immediately.
   4. TX: Assume bacterial and institute **isolation** immediately, antibiotics STAT, assist with lumbar puncture (LP) – side-lying position preferred. **Bacterial CSF** – high pressure, cloudy, **low glucose.**

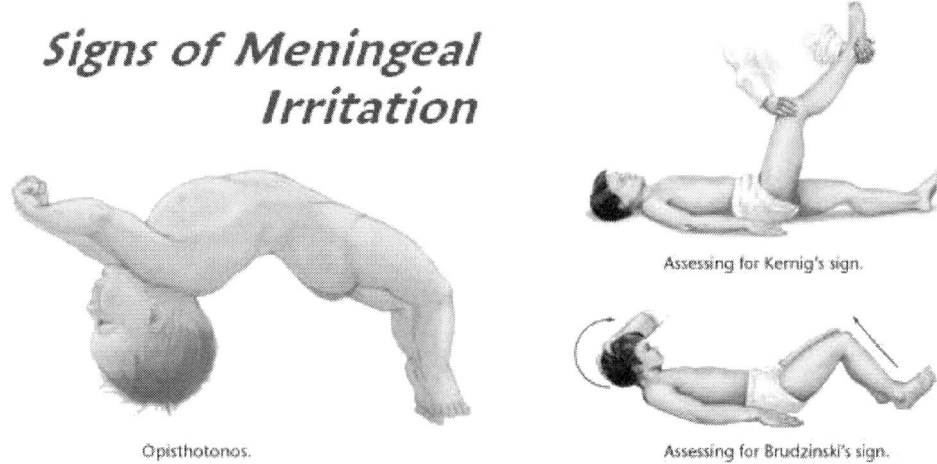

*Signs of Meningeal Irritation*

Opisthotonos.

Assessing for Kernig's sign.

Assessing for Brudzinski's sign.

G. **Seizure disorders**
   1. Causes: electrolyte disorders (**low sodium and glucose**), alcohol withdrawal, hypoxia, meningitis, illicit drugs, trauma, tumor, stroke, **febrile (rapid rise** in temperature, familial).
   2. Classifications: partial, complex, general, convulsive, non-convulsive, febrile. Infants demonstrate **repetitive movement "bicycling"**.
   3. Mainstay of treatment is **benzodiazepines (lorazepam).**
   4. **Status Epilepticus**: series of or continuous seizure lasting 5 minutes that is unresponsive to traditional therapy; sequelae of hypoxia, acidosis, and **hypoglycemia.**
   5. TX: Monitor **airway and safeguarding from injury**; identify and treat the cause (antipyretics); continue **lorazepam** (Ativan) and phenytoin (Dilantin) or fosphenytoin (Cerebryx); Thiamine and dextrose; consider paralytics. Mix **Dilantin in 0.9% NS only** and infuse **no faster than 50 mg/minute, monitor closely for infiltration.** Cardiac, BP, and RR monitoring **during infusion and 20 minutes post** infusion. Educate on seizure medication (Keppra) – causes **drowsiness**.

H. **Stroke** – Rule out hypoglycemia, atypical migraines, Bell palsy, Lyme disease facial paralysis.
   1. **Ischemic (92% from embolus or thrombus formation)**
      i. HX: of uncontrolled HTN, atrial fibrillation, diabetes, prostatic heart valves; focus on **last time normal** and symptom onset (Time Zero).
      ii. S/S: unilateral facial and extremity weakness/paralysis (**contralateral to clot**), **dysarthria** (slurred speech), dysphagia (difficulty swallowing, drooling), expressive (difficulty speaking) or receptive (difficulty understanding spoken word) **aphasia**, and visual disturbances (homonymous hemianopsia).
      iii. DX: Non-contrast head CT within 45 minutes to **r/o bleed** (does not show ischemia).
      iv. TX: peripheral rTPA (alteplase) within **3-4.5 hours** or intra-arterial reperfusion or mechanical thrombectomy to revascularize the ischemic penumbra.
         1. **rTPA 0.9 mg/kg** (maximum 90 mg), **bolus 10%** of dose over 1 minute, remainder as a drip over the next hour (**waste extra prior to administration**). Flush with NS at same rate.
         2. **Exclusion criteria**: evidence of intracranial bleed, tumor, or head trauma; AV malformation; current internal bleeding; **platelets < 100,000 mm²**.
         3. **Monitor for decreased LOC**, and bleeding during infusion.
      v. BP control for **SBP > 185 mm Hg or DBP > 110 mm Hg**.
   2. **Transient ischemic attack** (TIA – mini stroke) – warning sign - 10-15% experience a stroke within 3 months with 50% of those within next 48 hours.
      i. Symptoms typically **resolve within 10-20 minutes**, classified as **resolving within 24 hours.** Reversible ischemic neurologic deficit (RIND) is a cerebral infarct that lasts > 24 hours, but < 72 hours. Manage **BP**, blood sugar, and coagulation.
   3. **Hemorrhagic stroke**
      i. Intracerebral hemorrhage – rapid onset of headache and **focal deficits**; neurosurgical consult; manage ABC's and BP; administer vitamin K, FFP, and/or TXA to stop bleeding. Reverse anticoagulants with Kcentra and vitamin K for coumadin or Andexxa for Xarelto.
      ii. **Subarachnoid hemorrhage** – usually caused by aneurysm or AV malformation; explosive or **"worst HA of my life"** in 74%, altered LOC in 53%, N/V in 77%, photophobia, focal deficits, and nuchal rigidity in 35%. TX: Manage ABC's, raise head of bed, control SBP, and prepare for surgical intervention (clipping or coiling), **calcium-channel blockers (Nimodipine)**.

I. **Head Trauma**
   1. Primary injury from the event - MVC, fall, sports, assaults.
   2. Secondary brain injury from cerebral edema from **hypotension, hypoxia, hypercarbia.**
   3. Degrees of brain injury
      i. Mild – GCS 13-15 with loss of consciousness < 30 minutes and no deficits.
      ii. Moderate – GCS 9-12 with loss of consciousness and focal deficits.
      iii. **Severe – GCS of 8 or less** with significant loss of consciousness, abnormal pupils, and posturing.

## Increased ICP (Normal 0-15 mm Hg)

- Early signs
  - Restlessness, drowsiness, headache, vomiting, pupils sluggish to light, amnesia of event
  - Tachycardia, mild HTN
- Late signs
  - Responds to pain only or unresponsive on AVPU scale
  - Dilated nonreactive pupils(s)
  - Abnormal motor posturing – decorticate, decerebrate
  - Cushing's Triad
    - Profound **bradycardia**, abnormal respirations (Cheyne-Stokes), **increased SBP** with widened pulse pressure

## Herniation

- Uncal /Transtentorial
  - **Ipsilateral pupil dilation** early, bilateral fixed and dilated pupils
  - Contralateral hemiparesis to abnormal posturing
- Central Herniation
  - **Change in LOC** - restlessness progressing to coma (reticular activating system impairment)
  - Abnormal breathing rate/pattern (Cheyne-Stokes)
  - Dilated/nonreactive pupils
  - Bradycardia

   4. **Scalp lacerations** – Very vascular so apply **direct pressure**.
   5. **Concussion**
      i. Short period of impaired neurologic function that **resolves spontaneously**, GCS 13-15 with headache, dizziness, retrograde amnesia, vomiting, answers questions slowly.
      ii. **Head injury precautions** – acetaminophen only for pain, **no narcotics**; no caffeine to stimulate brain; **cognitive brain rest and graduated return to play.**
      iii. **Medical clearance** for return to play, too early return – **secondary impact** syndrome from minor injury may lead to death.
      iv. Complication is post concussive syndrome - cognitive impairment, slowed reaction time, memory difficulties.
   6. **Diffuse Axonal Injury** (severe diffuse TBI)
      i. Widespread microscopic hemorrhage (no focal lesion) leads to immediate and **prolonged coma** (reticular activating system affected), hypertension, hyperthermia, excessive sweating, and **abnormal posturing.**
   7. **Basilar Skull Fractures**
      i. Fracture of the bones at the skull leading to altered LOC, **combative behavior**, headache, and vomiting. Assessing **cerebral spinal fluid (CSF)** – "halo" test for bloody drainage, glucose test for clear drainage.
      ii. **Anterior fossa fracture** - "raccoon's eyes" – **periorbital ecchymosis** and rhinorrhea, anosmia. **Middle fossa fracture** - "battle's sign" – **mastoid ecchymosis** and otorrhea, ruptured tympanic membrane.
      iii. **Place sterile drip pad under nose** and over ears to prevent infection, **do not pack ears and nose, let it drain**, no NG tube.

8. **Epidural Hematoma**
    i. Rapidly forming hematoma between the skull and dura because of a **temporal** bone impact and laceration or tear of the **middle meningeal artery.**
    ii. Classic presentation in 75%: **Period of unconsciousness**, followed by **lucid period** with severe headache, then second loss of consciousness; **ipsilateral pupil dilation** with contralateral weakness or paralysis. Appears as lens-shape on CT scan.
9. **Subdural Hematoma** (Acute, subacute 48 hours to 2 weeks, chronic). Crescent-shape on CT scan.
    i. Collection of blood between the dura and subarachnoid layer due to **tearing of the bridging veins** seen most in **older patients** (anticoagulants) and in chronic **alcohol** abuse (fall often).
    ii. **Shaken impact syndrome** – triad of subdural hematoma, fractured (posterior) ribs, **retinal hemorrhage** seen more in infants and young children, and in interpersonal violence.

### Intracranial Bleeding "Typical Signs"

| Epidural Hematoma | Subdural Hematoma |
|---|---|
| • **Sudden loss of consciousness**, or<br>• Short period of unconsciousness followed by **lucid period**, and subsequent deterioration<br>• **Cushing's Triad**<br>   • Wide PP (Increased SBP)<br>   • Bradycardia<br>   • Altered respiratory pattern | • **Progressive** or decreasing loss of consciousness from **venous** bleed<br>• Headache<br>• Vomiting<br>• More common in older and alcoholics<br>• **Shaken Impact Syndrome** |

10. **Management of Increased Intracranial Pressure (ICP)**
    - Monitor intracranial pressure and **keep < 20 mm Hg.**
    - Elevate the **HOB to 30-45°**, neutral alignment (chin to umbilicus), avoid hip flexion (increases intra-abdominal pressure, which increases ICP).
    - Maintain **SBP 100 or above** (110 in older adult) with vasopressors to maintain cerebral perfusion pressure (CPP) 50-70 mm Hg.
    - Maintain $SpO_2$ above 94% and $CO_2$ at 35-37 mm Hg (low normal).
    - Administer the **osmotic diuretic Osmitrol (Mannitol)** 1 gram/kg IV bolus or **Hypertonic saline** 3%, 7.5%, or 10% IV, **effective if urine output increases**.
    - **Avoid hypotonic** solutions.
    - Monitor **sodium** and serum osmolality closely, especially if administering Mannitol.
    - Keep hemoglobin up since RBCs carry oxygen using 1:1:1 transfusion with plasma, platelets, and RBCs; reverse anticoagulants to reduce bleeding.
    - Avoid venous compression of neck (**remove rigid cervical collar**).
    - Maintain normothermia by treating fever aggressively.
    - Dark, low-stimulus environment, limit visitors, speak softly.
    - Control agitation with benzodiazepines and short-acting opioids so you can assess.

J. **Spinal cord injuries** – from hyperflexion "whiplash", hyperextension, axial loading/compression (diving or landing on feet), rotation, or penetrating injury.
   1. **NEXUS** Criteria (99.6% accurate) to guide need for radiography. Use NSAID mnemonic – **N**euro deficit, **S**pinal tenderness, **A**ltered mental status, **I**ntoxication, or **D**istracting injury.
   2. **SCIWORA** – spinal cord injury without radiographic injury seen in children under age 8, get **MRI** to assess edema.
   3. "**Chance**" fracture of T12-L2 seen in hyperflexion "**lap belt**" only injuries, with concurrent hollow organ bowel or stomach injury.
   4. **Cauda equina** syndrome – cord compression of L5-S1 "horse-tail" from fall onto coccyx, resulting in "**saddle anesthesia**", sciatica-type back pain, bowel, bladder, and sexual dysfunction.
   5. **Complete spinal cord injuries**
      i. Lose all motor/sensory function and reflexes below level of injury.
      ii. Loss of bowel and bladder function.
      iii. **P**riapism, **p**oikilothermia (difficulty to regulate body temperature), loss of **p**roprioception (sense of relative position of one's own body parts and strength of effort being employed).
      iv. Spinal or **neurogenic shock.**
      v. TX: Protect airway, **monitor breathing effectiveness** and assist breathing as needed, keep warm, remove from backboard early to **protect skin early**, insert gastric tube to prevent ileus, insert urinary catheter if not contraindicated.
      vi. Complications: Pressure ulcers, DVT to pulmonary embolus, pneumonia.

## Spinal Cord Injury

- **Cervical** - Tetraplegia or Quadriplegia when all four limbs are involved.
  - C1-C4 – Requires 24-hour-a-day care, may be able to use powered wheelchair.
  - C5-C8 – May be able to breath on their own and speak normally, needs assistance with ADL's. Little or no control of bowel or bladder.
- **Thoracic** – Paraplegia, can use a manual wheelchair, learn to drive a modified car, stand in standing frame.
- **Lumbar** – May walk with braces, no control of bowel and bladder.
- **Sacral** – Most able to walk, no control of bowel and bladder.

6. **Incomplete cord injuries** (voluntary anal sphincter tone - **sacral sparing**)

   - **A**nterior Cord
     - Loss of motor function, pain, crude touch, & temperature; retains proprioception.
   - Brown-Sequard Syndrome *(2 words – 2 sides)*
     - Transverse hemisection *(Stab or GSW)*
     - Loss of motor function on side of injury (ipsilateral)
     - Loss of pain & temperature on opposite side of injury (contralateral)
   - Central Cord
     - Loss of motor & sensory function, more pronounced in arms than legs *(walk to table, but can't eat)*
   - Posterior Cord
     - Loss of proprioception, vibration, fine touch, & fine pressure. Intact motor function

K. **Neurogenic shock**
   1. Injury at T6 or above with **loss of sympathetic nervous system (SNS) innervation** leaving **unopposed parasympathetic nervous stimulation**, prevents compensatory increase in heart rate in response to hypotension.
   2. S/S: **Warm, flushed skin with full pulses**, **hypotension**, and **bradycardia** (or lack of expected tachycardia), temperature instability (poikilothermia).
   3. TX: Spinal motion restriction; support airway and breathing; **augment vascular tone with IV fluids, vasopressors, and positive inotropes.**

### Neurogenic Shock

- Spinal cord injuries above T6 cause a disruption of sympathetic regulation leaving unopposed parasympathetic stimulation, which prevents a compensatory increase in the heart rate in response to hypotension.
- Neurogenic shock is **distributive shock**, maldistribution of blood.
- S/S: **Bradycardia** and hypotension, venous pooling in the periphery, warm skin with normal color, and temperature instability.
- TX: **Augment vascular tone** with IVFs, vasopressors (Norepinephrine), and positive inotropes (Dopamine).

L. **Spinal shock** – injury at any level, loss of motion/sensation below level of injury, transient episodes of hypotension, **flaccid paralysis,** and loss of reflexes.

M. **Autonomic Dysreflexia**
   1. Complication of SCI above T6.
   2. **Noxious stimulus** leads to massive sympathetic nervous system response, resulting in a sudden onset of **severe HTN**, pounding headache, nausea, nasal congestion, anxiety, flushed face, sweating with piloerection ("goose bumps").
   3. TX: **Identify and treat cause** – over-distended bladder, bowel impaction, skin pressure, infection, ingrown toenail; **lower blood pressure.**

# Gastrointestinal, Genitourinary, Gynecology, and Obstetrical Emergencies (18 items)

## Gastrointestinal

A. **Abdominal Assessment**
   1. Look for bruising, **pulsating masses** (AAA), and scars. Auscultate for bowel sounds, ask if "passing gas". Percuss – tympany (hyperresonance) over hollow organs, dullness over solid organs.
   2. Palpate for rigidity, pain, rebound tenderness (palpate painful quadrant last); Lying **rigidly still** is a classic peritonitis sign. Fever and pain prior to vomiting, and/or syncope are suggestive of surgical conditions.

B. **Gastric Tube Insertion**
   1. Patient in **high-fowler position if alert**, flex head forward, sips of water; **left side if altered mental status** to decrease risk of aspiration. Measure from tip of nose to earlobe to xyphoid process. Benzocaine, Tetracaine, or lidocaine may be sprayed x 2 in nose/mouth. Increased risk of rupture if esophageal varices.

C. **Acute abdomen**
   1. **Peritonitis** – inflammation of the peritoneum from ruptured appendix, pancreatitis, penetrating trauma, or **peritoneal dialysis** characterized by diffuse pain, **rebound tenderness, guarding**, and fever. TX: with gastric tube, IVF's, analgesics, antiemetics, and antibiotics.
   2. **Appendicitis** – obstruction of the appendix leads to peritonitis, most common in males 10-30. Extremes of age more likely to have atypical presentations.
      a. S/S: dull, steady **periumbilical pain** with anorexia and nausea early; **RLQ pain (McBurney's point)** later (12-48 hours) with **rebound tenderness** (Rovsing's sign), Markle sign (heel jar), Obturator sign (pain on right hip flexion), Psoas sign (pain on extension of hip).
      b. DX: CBC to detect **leukocytosis** (> 10,000 with > **10% bands**); initial CT or ultrasound; frequent reassessment with **ultrasound.**
      c. TX: IVF, analgesics, antiemetics, prepare for possible surgery (keep NPO).

D. **Bleeding**
   1. **Upper GI Bleed** - from **PUD**, Mallory-Weiss syndrome, and **frequent NSAID use.**
      a. S/S: Hematemesis (bloody vomit), signs of **shock** (dizziness, tachycardia).
      b. DX: Serial H & H, coagulation panel, TXM, **endoscopy** (**vasopressin** may cause cardiac ischemia, consider nitroglycerin), high BUN (dry).
      c. TX: **Suction and secure airway if actively bleeding, IV access for fluid and blood replacement** (hemoglobin < 7 g/dL), questionable gastric tube (OK for PUD, not for bleeding varices), **vasopressin, octreotide** (Sandostatin).
      d. **Mallory-Weiss syndrome** from violent retching with alcohol or **bulimia**, aspirin use, or heavy lifting.
   2. **Esophageal varices** – bleeding from dilated blood vessels **secondary to liver disease from portal hypertension.**
   3. **Lower GI Bleed** – from inflammatory bowel disease. S/S: Hematochezia (blood from anus), painless bleeding, signs of shock. DX: Colonoscopy, serial H & H. TX: IV access for fluid and **blood replacement**

E. **Cholecystitis** – inflammation of gallbladder.
   1. S/S: severe crampy **RUQ pain radiating to right shoulder** aggravated by deep breathing; pain often after **fatty foods** or large meal; fever; jaundice (sclera) and dark urine; **Murphy sign** (point tenderness under right costal margin); flatulence.
   2. DX: elevated WBC (**leukocytosis**), ALT, and bilirubin; abdominal ultrasound.
   3. TX: IV access, antiemetics, analgesics, NPO/possible gastric tube, antibiotics, possible surgery. If no surgery, D/C instructions focus on decreasing fat in diet.

F. **Pancreatitis** inflammation and autodigestion of the pancreas
   1. S/S: sudden onset of **sharp epigastric pain radiating to the back**, aggravated by eating, alcohol intake, or lying supine; pain relieved by leaning forward; fever; N/V/A; fever; signs of shock. Most common cause is **alcohol** abuse.
   2. DX: **elevated WBC, amylase (early), lipase (late, but more specific), glucose,** and **triglycerides**; CT or ultrasound of abdomen, **low calcium level.**
   3. TX: IV access for **fluid resuscitation**, antiemetics, analgesics (opioids), IV **calcium gluconate**, $H_2$ blockers and **glucagon** to suppress pancreatic enzymes.
   4. Complications: **hypocalcemia** (see Chvostek's, Trousseau's, and tetany), **pleural effusions (may need thoracentesis)**, ARDS, hemorrhagic (Grey-Turner and Cullen sign), sepsis.

G. **Hepatitis** – "Vowels (A & E) from the Bowels" (Fecal-Oral), B-Body fluids (sex), C-Circulation (blood)
   - **A** – fecal-oral (vaccination available) – teach and return demonstration of **handwashing.**
   - **B – body fluids** – sexual, human bites (vaccination available).
   - **C** – circulation – blood exposure.
   - **D** – requires HBV for HDV, so protected by Hep B vaccine.
   - **E** – enteric (contaminated food or water).
   1. S/S: malaise N/V/A (early); jaundice, clay-colored stool, steatorrhea, **dark-colored foamy urine** (later).
   2. TX: Fluid resuscitation for acute A & E. **Interferon** or Ribavirin for chronic hepatitis.
   3. DC instructions: A & E – do not prepare food for others; **B, C, D – do not donate blood, no sharing needles or razors, safe sex practices.**

H. **Cirrhosis/Liver Failure**
   1. Etiology: Most common cause is alcohol abuse.
   2. Labs: **Increased direct bilirubin (jaundice), LFTs, PT, PTT, and ammonia (hepatic encephalopathy)**; decreased urea, albumin, calcium.
   3. TX: **Lactulose or PEG (MiraLAX) to remove ammonia**, Neomycin to decrease production of ammonia, replacement of albumin, calcium, potassium, and vitamin K. Treat effective if **ammonia decreases** and LOC increases.
   4. Monitor for esophageal varices from **portal hypertension.**

I. **Diverticulitis** – inflammation of (sigmoid-large) colon
   1. S/S: abrupt onset of **crampy pain**, localizes to **LLQ**, anorexia, nausea, vomiting, alternating episodes of **explosive diarrhea and severe constipation.**
   2. TX: fluid resuscitation, **bowel rest**, antibiotic, surgery if ruptured.
   3. DC instructions: avoid straining, low-fat, low-fiber, **low-residue diet during acute phase**; then increase fiber in diet, take stool softeners, and **increase water** intake.

J. **Bowel Obstruction**
   1. **Esophageal Obstruction** – difficulty swallowing and drooling from "something stuck" or "food bolus"; TX: keep patient upright and consider a carbonated beverage, **glucagon** IV or **NTG** SL; esophagoscopy for removal.
   2. **Bowel Obstruction – high-pitched hyperactive bowel sounds early** to absent late.
      a. **Small Bowel Obstruction** – rapid onset, minimal distension, copious **fecal vomiting**, crampy pain.
      b. **Large Bowel Obstruction** – gradual onset, **marked distension**, rare vomiting, crampy pain.
      c. TX: **fluid and electrolyte replacement** for **hypovolemic shock**, bowel rest, prepare for surgery.
   3. **Bowel (mesenteric) infarction** – history of **atrial fibrillation**, severe abdominal pain with soft abdomen.
   4. **Bowel perforation** – peritoneal signs (rigidity and guarding) after colonoscopy. Prepare for surgery.

K. **Pediatric Disorders**
   1. **Gastroenteritis – 20 mL/kg of isotonic crystalloid solution boluses,** administer ondansetron (Zofran) and frequently 5 mL sips of pediatric rehydration solution.
   2. **Cyclic vomiting** – recurrent disabling vomiting. Treat with fluid boluses and antiemetics. Prevent with antimigraine medications.
   3. **Pyloric Stenosis -** narrowing of the pylorus preventing emptying of the stomach causing **non-bilious projectile vomiting** and continual hunger, poor weight gain, "**olive-shaped** mass", and signs of dehydration; TX: IVFs and prep for surgery to dilate pylorus.
   4. **Intussusception** – **telescoping** of one segment of bowel into another; most often seen in infants; **episodic pain** with **currant jelly stools** and bloody mucus; "sausage-shaped palpable mass in RUQ; diagnose and treat with **air or barium enema**; may require surgery.
   5. **Volvulus (Malrotation)** – bowel rotation resulting in strangulation; typically, in first month of life; **bilious vomiting** with abdominal distension, blood stools, and visible peristaltic waves; prepare for surgery.

L. **Abdominal Trauma**
   1. Initial diagnostic test is the **FAST exam** (focused assessment sonography for trauma).
   2. **Spleen - LUQ pain radiating to the left shoulder (Kehr's Sign)**, graded I-V. Nonoperative treatment preferred versus splenectomy (immunocompromised). Monitor H & H.
   3. **Liver - RUQ pain**, tachycardic, hypotensive, **Cullen's sign** – ecchymosis around umbilicus, graded I-VI. TX: Allow permissive hypotension (SBP 70-80 max), damage control surgery, massive transfusion protocol.
   4. Bowel injury seen more in gunshot wound or stab wound to left side, possible **evisceration** – cover with **sterile dressing** until surgery.
   5. Pancreas – epigastric pain radiating to the back since pancreas sits retroperitoneal, flank ecchymosis (Grey-Turner's). Monitor amylase, **lipase**, and glucose.

**Genitourinary Emergencies**
A. **Urinary retention** – inability to completely empty the bladder from urethral strictures, enlarged prostate, renal calculi, neurogenic bladder, or **side effects of antihistamines** (parasympathetic effect of OTC cold medicines); S/S: bladder distension and lower abdominal pain; DX: by ultrasound bladder scan; TX: insert an indwelling catheter (Coude catheter for benign prostatic hyperplasia BPH).
B. **Urinary tract infections** – most *E. coli* in women since short urethra, male from BPH; S/S: dysuria, burning, **urgency, and frequency**; suprapubic pressure and low back pain; **altered mental status in elderly**; DX: urinalysis for WBCs and hematuria; TX: antibiotics, NSAIDS and **phenazopyridine (urine bright orange)** for pain, increase fluid intake.
C. **Pyelonephritis -** inflammation or infection (bacterial) of kidneys that can lead to urosepsis; S/S: severe **costovertebral (CVA) pain**; fever and chills; N/V; urinary symptoms; DX: urinalysis for **pyuria** and hematuria, BUN and creatinine, renal ultrasound; TX: **antibiotics** and encourage fluids; **admit if pregnant.**
D. **Prostatitis** – inflammation of the prostate gland; S/S: sudden onset of **dysuria, frequency, and urgency**; hematospermia (blood in semen); tender prostate; DX: possible elevated PSA; urinalysis; TX: antibiotics (fluoroquinolones) and increase fluid intake.
E. **Testicular torsion** – twisting of the spermatic cord, surgical emergency. Peaks in infancy and peripubertal ages. S/S: **sudden onset of severe inguinal pain** and nausea; lack of cremasteric reflex; **worsens with elevation** and ice. DX: **color doppler ultrasound**. Manual detorsion may be attempted, but surgical intervention required.
F. **Epididymitis** – gradual onset of scrotal pain, urinary frequency and urgency, urethral discharge (**Chlamydia**). Pain relieved with elevation (Prehn's sign) and ice. D/C teaching on **safe sex practices** and treating partner too.
G. **Orchitis** – inflammation of testicle from STI or **mumps**; TX: NSAIDs and ciprofloxacin.

H. **Sexually Transmitted Infections/Vaginal Infections**
    a. **Chlamydia** –**frequently concurrent with gonorrhea**; S/S: 75% **asymptomatic**; thin, mucopurulent discharge; DX: cervical cultures; TX: Levofloxin 500 mg once daily for 7 days, **Azithromycin 1 gram PO once** or Doxycycline 100 mg BID for 7 days; DC instructions: abstain from sex for 7 days.
    b. **Gonorrhea** –leading cause of PID and can cause infertility and ectopic pregnancy; S/S: **UTI symptoms and mucoid discharge**; DX: cervical cultures; TX: **Ceftriaxone (Rocephin) IM** once, Azithromycin PO once or Doxycycline for 7 days (Chlamydia).
    c. **Syphilis** – S/S: **painless chancre with primary infection, rash on palms and soles** in secondary infection, dementia in tertiary syphilis years later; DX: **VDRL** (venereal disease research lab test) & RPR (rapid plasma reagin test) **blood tests**; TX: Penicillin IM once, or Doxycycline or Tetracycline for 14 days.
    d. **Genital Herpes Simplex** – **incurable STD (disease)** with recurrence 5-8 times per year; S/S: burning, **painful grouped vesicles** or crusted lesions on genitalia and flu-like symptoms; TX: **antiviral therapy** (Zovirax or Valtrex – daily suppression); DC instructions: **abstain from sex 24 hours prodromal until lesions crusted over**, protected sex always, C-section may be scheduled for pregnancy/delivery to avoid transmission.
    e. **Vulvovaginal candidiasis** – common in diabetics, IUD, antibiotics; S/S: vulvar irritation, **pruritic, cottage-cheese-like** white vaginal discharge; DX: wet prep for budding yeast; TX: intravaginal azole nystatin creams for 1-7 days or oral Fluconazole (Diflucan – prolongs QT) PO once (contraindicated in pregnancy).
    f. **Trichomonas vaginalis** – S/S: pruritis, vulvar irritation, **dyspareunia** (painful intercourse), malodorous **"fishy"** odor, yellow or **green discharge**; DX: "Strawberry cervix" wet prep; TX: **Metronidazole (Flagyl) PO** once or Tinidazole (Tindamax); DC: **no alcohol with Flagyl (severe vomiting)**, frequent coinfection with gonorrhea.
    g. **Bacterial vaginosis** – S/S: thin **"fishy" odor, grayish discharge**; DX: clue cells, pH > 4.5, + "whiff test" (KOH); TX: Metronidazole (Flagyl) PO for 7 days or gel for 5 days or Clindamycin cream for 7 days; DC: no alcohol with Flagyl, treat sexual partners, avoid douching and bubble baths, **Clindamycin weakens condoms.**
    h. **Genital warts** – increased **neoplastic risk** in both sexes, prevent with Gardasil vaccine at 11-12 years of age (as early as 9 years of age); cauliflower-like warts on vulva or penis.
    i. **Discharge teaching** – Take medications as prescribed, consistently use condoms; inform sexual partners and treat past partners. **Patients with Herpes must notify future partners**.
    j. **Pelvic Inflammatory disease (PID)** – S/S: abdominal pain and dyspareunia with vaginal discharge and **cervical motion tenderness** "chandelier sign"; TX: IV or IM **antibiotics**, analgesics, **admit if pregnant**; Complications: **increased risk of ectopic pregnancy** and infertility.
I. **Phimosis** – inability to fully retract foreskin over glans penis; TX: manual reduction, consider circumcision or dorsal slit. **Paraphimosis** – retracted foreskin is entrapped causing ischemia to penis; TX: small incision and consider **circumcision**.
J. **Priapism** – prolonged painful erection causes a **true urological emergency** from **sickle cell**, leukemia, spinal cord injury, **psychotropic (Trazodone)** or erectile dysfunction medications (phosphodiesterase inhibitors); DX: penile Doppler or arteriography; TX: urology consult; sedation and/or analgesia; injection of epinephrine, phenylephrine, or terbutaline; irrigation of corpora with NS and **aspiration of clot.**
K. **Renal calculi**
    - S/S: **sudden onset of severe, colicky, flank** (CVA-costovertebral angle) pain that may radiate to the groin; restlessness and pacing; urgency, frequency, dysuria, and hematuria; diaphoresis.
    - DX: urinalysis for hematuria; helical CT to **rule out AAA.**
    - TX: IVFs, NSAIDs, antiemetics, increase fluid intake, opioids, **strain urine for analysis** of stone type (most calcium). **Hospitalize if unable to keep down PO fluids.**

L. **Renal Trauma**
   - **Penile fracture** – rupture of tunica albuginea or corpus cavernosa of penile shaft due to torque (direct trauma or fall, sexual activity); report of "pop"; penile pain and **immediate loss of erection**; urethral bleeding; edema and ecchymosis; DX: penile Doppler; TX: immediate **surgical repair.**
   - **Renal trauma** – lacerations, contusions, or vascular injury associated with posterior rib fractures; S/S: flank or back pain and ecchymosis (**Grey-Turner's Sign – turn over**) with **hematuria**; TX: bed rest and increase fluid intake if stable, repair lacerations, **monitor urine output closely.**
   - **Urethral/Bladder** – contusions or rupture caused by straddle injuries, genital trauma, or foreign bodies; associated with **pelvic fractures**; S/S: urge to, but inability or difficulty voiding, blood at urinary meatus, high-riding prostate. DX: Cystogram for bladder, **retrograde urethrogram** for urethra. TX: **do not catheterize if suspected transection**, catheter (suprapubic) for 7-10 days placed by urologist.

**Gynecology Emergencies**
A. **Dysfunctional uterine bleeding** – fewer than 21 days between bleeding, typically painless; DX: CBC, bleeding times, pelvic or transvaginal ultrasound; TX: **low-dose oral contraceptive therapy**, iron supplements, treat hypovolemia.
B. **Vaginal foreign "lost" bodies** – IUD – **abdominal US** to determine position, remove with IUD hook or ring forceps; Diaphragm – remove with ring forceps.
C. **Bartholin cyst** – painful cystic mass; TX: **warm compress**, incision, and drainage. D/C education on warm compresses.
D. **Ruptured ovarian cyst** – pockets on the ovaries (Mittelschmerz mid-cycle); S/S: acute pain with sex or exercise, **sharp unilateral pain**; TX: analgesia, possible surgical intervention.
E. **Toxic shock syndrome** – sepsis from retained tampons or sponges, or secondary to necrotizing fasciitis; S/S: sudden onset of **high fever**, N/V, **sunburn-like rash on palms and soles those peels (desquamation)**; TX: contact **isolation**, ABCs, identify and remove source of infection, immediate antibiotic administration (sepsis protocol).
F. Sexual Assault – **chain of custody to document integrity – never leave kit unattended.**

## Sexual Assault Evidence Collection

- Safety and treating severe injuries is the priority!
- Place a sheet on the floor. Place paper sheet from kit on top of sheet to prevent debris from floor (send with evidence).
- Have patient take off or cut off clothing one piece at a time, taking care **not to cut through holes or stains.**
- Package each piece of clothing separately in **paper bags.**
- Wet speculum with tap water or water-soluble lubricant. **Air dry (no heat)** the evidence.
- Double fold the edge of the bags and apply tape (no staples) from one end of the fold to the other to completely seal. Initial across the tape for tamper-resistant seal. Follow **chain of custody.**

**Obstetrical Emergencies**

A. **Normal variances of pregnancy** – increased risk of aspiration, **compensated respiratory alkalosis** ($CO_2$ 27-32), increased circulating blood volume leading to increased pulse and decreased BP (**supine vena cava hypotension syndrome**), increased clotting factors (risk of HELLP). Normal **FHT's 120-160** (some manuals 110-160).

B. **Hyperemesis gravidarum** – S/S: intractable nausea, vomiting, and dehydration leads to electrolyte imbalances and malnutrition; TX: IVFs, **electrolyte, and vitamin replacement**, antiemetics, possible total parental nutrition.

C. **Fetal distress** – **fetal tachycardia is first sign of distress** (FHT > 160 bpm), loss of variability (heart rate increased with contraction), decreased fetal movement.

D. **Spontaneous abortion** - death or expulsion of fetus or products of conception before age of viability (15-20%), **threatened – cervical os closed, inevitable – os open.**
   a. S/S: brown or bloody discharge to profuse vaginal bleeding with passage of tissue or products of conception.
   b. DX: HCG, blood type and Rh, transvaginal ultrasound.
   c. TX: oxytocin, suction curettage, **RhoGAM to Rh – mothers**, psychosocial care for **both parents (partners).**
   d. DC Instructions: bed rest as much as possible for 2 days, avoid douching, tampons, and intercourse for at least 2 weeks, monitor body temperature twice a day for 5 days, seek medical attention if fever > 37.7 C (100 F), bleeding more than heavy period, clots > a quarter.

E. **Ectopic pregnancy** – embryo plants outside the uterine cavity, most in fallopian tube, rupture at 6-12 weeks; S/S: sudden onset of severe unilateral pelvic pain, **radiating to shoulder**, signs of shock, possible vaginal bleeding; DX: hCG +, CBC, TXM, transvaginal ultrasound; TX: IVFs, **RhoGAM if Rh -,** prepare for surgery or **Methotrexate** IM (no signs of bleeding, compliant about f/u).

F. **Placentae Previa** – implantation of placentae over cervical os, hemorrhage may occur as uterus expands; S/S: sudden, **painless, bright red** bleeding with signs of shock; TX: OB consult, **turn onto left side 15-30 degrees**, treat shock, **no vaginal exam until ultrasound completed**, prepare for emergency C-section.

G. **Abruptio placentae** – placental separation from uterine wall rupturing arterial vessels leading to hemorrhage and shock; S/S: painful contractions and **backache** with uterine rigidity; **frank, dark red** vaginal bleeding or concealed; abnormal FHT (normal 120-160); TX: OB consult, continuous fetal monitoring, **turn onto left side 15-30 degrees**, treat shock with **blood products STAT, prepare for emergency C-section.** High risk of **HELLP** syndrome.

H. **Preeclampsia (Gestational or Pregnancy-induced HTN)** – disorder leading to decreased oxygenation and perfusion, associated with coagulopathies, gestational **HTN**, edema, and **proteinuria** (can be present **postpartum**); TX: OB consult, continuous fetal monitoring, support maternal ABCs, minimize stimulation, admit to OB, antihypertensives, **Magnesium** loading dose and infusion (**monitor respiratory effort**, LOC, BP, and patellar reflexes – **Calcium gluconate** 10ml of 10% over 10 minutes as antidote for Magnesium).

I. **Eclampsia** – preeclampsia progressed to convulsive state (**seizures**), at risk for up to 3 weeks postpartum; TX: same as above plus **benzodiazepines** to stop seizures and emergent C-section.

J. **HELLP syndrome** – associated with preeclampsia with **RUQ pain**, HELLP = hemolysis, elevated liver enzymes, low platelets (DIC – disseminated intravascular coagulation).

K. **Prolapsed cord** – umbilical cord precedes the neonate out of vagina; TX: place mother in **knee-to-chest position**, insert sterile gloved hand into vagina to **elevate the presenting part off cord so pulsating** (prevent fetal anoxia) and leave hand in place, wrap **exposed cord in saline gauze, emergent C-section.**

L. **Emergent delivery** – S/S: bloody show, **rupture of membranes**, frequent contractions, desire to bear down, "baby is coming", crowning of head; TX: place in low-fowler with knees bent up, clean perineum if time permits, ask mother to "pant", assess for presentation and nuchal cord, gently guide head **to prevent perineal tears**, and deliver shoulders and body.

M. **Neonatal resuscitation** – **thoroughly dry and warm** (radiant warmer); gentle stimulation (back rub, foot tapping); place newborn in **sniffing position**; suction mouth, then nose, clamp and cut cord between clamps 30-60 seconds after cord stops pulsating; measure **APGAR at 1 and 5 minutes** (7-10 good outcome, 4-6 moderate outcome, 1-3 poor outcome); **assist breathing if HR < 100**; two-thumb encircling chest compressions at ½ AP diameter of chest if HR < 60 despite PPV; medications: epinephrine and glucose per NRP Guidelines; naloxone (Narcan) is not indicated; IVF bolus for **newly born is 10 ml/kg.** $SpO_2$ takes 10 minutes to increase.
N. **Postpartum hemorrhage** – excessive vaginal bleeding after delivery or abortion and up to 6 weeks postpartum; S/S: bright red bleeding, signs of shock, boggy uterus; TX: **fundal massage** with suprapubic pressure, treat shock with **blood products** STAT, **Oxytocin (Pitocin)** to stimulate uterine atony (contraction).
O. **Postpartum infection** – up to 10 days postpartum; S/S: fever, tenderness, foul-smelling lochia; TX: sepsis protocols, IVFs, **STAT antibiotics.**
P. **Obstetric Trauma**
    a. General concepts – mechanism of injury – MVCs, **falls, interpersonal violence.**
    b. Treatment: monitor FHT (**normal 120-160**) and fundal height (**above umbilicus – viable fetus** 20-24 weeks); ABCs, **turn onto left side** 15-30 degrees, or **tilt backboard,** or **manually displace uterus to side (supine vena cava syndrome)**, shield uterus for radiographic studies or bedside ultrasound, IVFs, **STAT C-section.**
    c. **Preterm labor** – most common OB complication following trauma; regular contractions every 10 minutes or less at < 37 weeks gestation, possible vaginal bleeding.
        i. TX: assist with pelvic examination, continuous fetal monitoring, **tocolytics (stop labor) such as Magnesium or Terbutaline** and admit to OB.
    d. **Uterine rupture** – rare, mostly seen after **sudden deceleration injury**; usually results in fetal demise.
        i. S/S: sudden onset of severe abdominal pain, vaginal bleeding, **fetal parts palpated outside of uterus**, fetal bradycardia/asystole, maternal shock.
        ii. TX: Blood products STAT, ABCs, emergency **C-section/hysterectomy.**

**Mental Health Emergencies (11 items)**

A. **Aggression/Violence**
   1. **Risk** – those who fear for personal safety, history of abuse, alcohol or drug intoxication, delusions of persecution, acute mania.
   2. **S/S:** Pacing, loud voice, clenched fists.
   3. **TX:** always **be aware of personal safety (have a clear exit plan)**; keep unobstructed access; **calm patient through empathetic yet firm verbal means**; appear calm, unthreatened, in control; speak calmly; **avoid confrontation. Priority is safety, exit and scream for help.** Call security, and **report threats to law** enforcement.

B. **Anxiety** – a feeling of nervousness about an imminent event or something with an uncertain outcome.
   1. **Situational crisis** – anxiety due to a life event, such as sudden illness, injury, or **death of a family member**; grieving varies by culture, personality, and coping skills. Stages of grief – **shock and denial, anger**, and bargaining may all occur in the ED (allowing family presence decreases denial and anger).
   2. **Panic attack** – abrupt onset of **intense fear**; S/S: sensation of **choking** or breathlessness, palpitations, chest pressure, trembling, paresthesia, feeling of "going insane."
      - **TX for both:** maintain a calm appearance, use therapeutic communication, **provide a supportive (non-judgmental) environment, and show acceptance**, encourage **slow breathing**, reassure patient they are "not crazy"; administer benzodiazepine (Clonazepam, Lorazepam, Diazepam) as ordered.
   3. **Post-traumatic stress disorder** – S/S: re-experiencing the traumatic incident (flashbacks, nightmares), avoidance behaviors, difficulty concentrating, **hyper arousal and hypervigilance (startle, tense)**; TX: provide a **low stimulus area** and counseling.

C. **Bipolar disorder** – chronic, recurring cycles of depression and elation (mania). S/S: major **depressive episode followed by inappropriate elation**, increased energy (**highest risk of harming themselves and others**) and insomnia, pressured speech, grandiose notions, poor judgement, racing thoughts, impulsivity, risk-taking behavior, and promiscuity; TX: provide **safety, minimize external stimuli**.
   1. Medications: **Lithium to control severe mood swings (toxicity: SAD LITH - S**eizures, **A**taxia – impaired balance, **D**ystonia – muscle contractions, **L**ethargy/Leukocytosis, **I**nsipidus (DI), **T**remors, **H**ypothyroidism), Carbamazepine (Tegretol).

D. **Psychosis** – mental disorder evidenced by **bizarre thinking**, often accompanied by sensory **hallucinations** (illusions) and delusions (misconceptions of belief). **Priority is safety, then medical clearance.** DX: rule out brain tumors (**head CT**), use of psychoactive drugs (LSD), sepsis, etc. Treat with **Haldol (risk of neuroleptic malignant hyperthermia) or Geodon.** Both **prolong QT interval, get ECG** when safe.

E. **Schizophrenia** – bizarre behavior including inability to care for self or manage activities of daily living, **typical onset in early 20's**; S/S: **delusions, hallucinations, disorganized speech.**
   1. **TX:** orient to reality **for safety**; use short, concrete sentences (avoid figures of speech); administer antipsychotic medications and **watch for extrapyramidal symptoms (dystonic reactions** from **neuroleptic medications** like **Haldol and Thorazine.** TX: of EPS - **diphenhydramine** (Benadryl), benztropine (Cogentin), trihexyphenidyl (Artane). Treatment effective when muscles relax.

G. **Neuroleptic Malignant Syndrome** – life-threatening condition that can be caused by antipsychotic medications (**Haldol**, Thorazine), manifested by **hyperthermia, muscle rigidity**, and **autonomic instability** (fluctuations in BP); TX: ABCs, **reduce temperature** with **cooling blankets** and ice packs.

H. **Depression** – symptoms that interfere with the person's ability to work, sleep, and actively participate in life; S/S: loneliness, lack of energy, sleep disturbances, weight changes, decreased libido, decreased interest in usual activities; **ask directly about thoughts of suicide and plan.**

I. **Suicide**
   a. **Risk** –increased risk if Caucasian, family history of attempts; behavioral health history; substance abuse; history of abuse; prior attempts; **chronic physical illness; gender identity crisis.**
   b. **S/S:** feeling worthless, hopeless, and helpless; indifference; social isolation.
   c. **TX:** undress patient and remove anything that may pose danger, **encourage communication**, involve family and friends as appropriate, look for positives in life and demonstrate worth.
   d. D/C instructions: **Antidepressants take weeks** for full effect, **contact someone if thoughts** of hurting yourself.

J. **Toxicology/ Ingestions/GI Decontamination**
   a. Activated charcoal with sorbitol (cathartic) every 4-6 hours for 12-24 hours for extended-release or **enteric-coated medications;** commonly used for acetaminophen overdose.
   b. Gastric lavage only for toxic, symptomatic patient with **recent ingestion** (< 1 hour); risk of esophageal perforation.
   c. **Whole bowel irrigation** with Go-lytely or MiraLAX for **body packers** (cocaine packs).

K. **Overdose and intentional ingestions**
   a. **Iron (FE$^+$)**
      - S/S: N/V and abdominal pain early, **hematemesis.**
      - TX: **No charcoal** - Iron does NOT bind to charcoal. Desferal **(Deferoxamine) - chelating agent** that binds free iron, it is excreted renally – rust, pink or **"vin rose"** urine color expected.
   b. **Acetaminophen – toxic to liver**
      - DX: quantitative level at **4 hours** from ingestion, monitor LFT's.
      - TX: Consider lavage and **activated charcoal, N-acetylcysteine (Acetadote)** within 8 hours for best response.
   c. **Salicylates**
      - S/S: tachypnea to compensate for **metabolic acidosis**, N/V, abdominal pain, **tinnitus**, hypoglycemia.
      - TX: **sodium bicarbonate** for urine alkalization, **dextrose for hypoglycemia**, hemodialysis.
   d. **Tricyclic Antidepressants (TCAs) Elavil, Tofranil – 3 C's**
      - S/S: altered LOC (Coma), ventricular tachycardia (Cardiac dysrhythmias), seizures (Convulsions).
      - TX: cardiac monitoring, intubation, **sodium bicarbonate** for urine alkalization, lidocaine, and **magnesium sulfate** if polymorphic ventricular tachycardia develops.

## Emergency Antidote Chart

| | |
|---|---|
| Acetaminophen | N-acetylcysteine (Acetadote) |
| Tricyclics (TCAs) | Sodium Bicarbonate |
| Opioids | Narcan (Naloxone) |
| Benzodiazepines | Romazicon (Flumazenil) |
| Ca Channel blockers | Calcium, Glucagon, Insulin |
| Beta blockers | Glucagon, Insulin |
| Organophosphates | Atropine/2-PAM |
| Ethylene glycol | Fomepizole (Antizol) |
| Iron | Deferoxamine |
| Sulfonylureas | Dextrose, Octreotide |

**Medical Emergencies (14 items)**

A. **Allergic reactions and Anaphylaxis**
   1. Hypersensitivity (allergic) reaction – exposure to allergen, IgE antibodies produced, histamine (urticaria) and leukotriene react, results in **vasodilation** and mucus production.
      - Causes: shellfish, Hymenoptera sting (**bee**)
      - S/S: **hives, urticaria**, itchy eyes, sneezing, runny nose
   2. **Anaphylaxis** – acute, rapidly progressive systemic reaction.
      - S/S: urticaria, pruritus, **angioedema.**
      - TX: airway management and oxygen (**possible surgical airway**), **Epinephrine 1mg/ml 0.2-0.5 mg IM** (SQ uneven absorption), progress to IV epinephrine **infusion,** if necessary, **diphenhydramine** (Benadryl) + H$_2$ blockers (Cimetidine, Ranitidine, Famotidine), Albuterol, methylprednisolone (no immediate effect), IVF's.
   3. **Anaphylactic Shock** – hypotension, decreased end-organ perfusion, multiple organ dysfunction (**distributive shock/maldistribution**).

B. **Hematologic disorders**
   1. **Hemophilia** – hereditary genetic disorder that impair the body's ability to control blood clotting; Hemophilia A (**Classic Factor VIII** – most common) & B (Factor IX) are recessive sex-linked, so occur in males; **Von Willebrand** is **in men and women (most common)**.
      - S/S: **decreased LOC if head injury (get CT)**; bleeding of soft tissues, muscles, or **joints (hemarthrosis),**
      - TX: **Replace clotting factor or administer cryoprecipitate or FFP**, ice, compression, immobilization, and elevation of joints; **topical thrombin for lacerations and observe for 4 hours post suturing**; hold pressure on venipunctures for at least 5 minutes, no IM injections.
      - DC teaching: wear medic-alert bracelets, **avoid aspirin and NSAIDs**, always keep factor VIII with you, extra protection – helmets, elbow pads, etc.
   2. **Disseminated intravascular coagulation (DIC)** – abnormal activation of the body's coagulation cascade from trauma, **sepsis**, pancreatitis, HELLP in OB.
      - S/S: bruising, petechiae, purpura, hematuria, end-organ failure.
      - DX: prolonged coagulation times (PT, PTT), **elevated D-dimer and fibrin degradation products**; low hemoglobin, hematocrit, platelets, fibrinogen.
      - TX: treat underlying cause, control bleeding, antifibrinolytic agents (aminocaproic acid – Amicar and tranexamic acid – TXA), platelet transfusion.
      - **Treatment plan effective if platelets increasing**.
   3. **Idiopathic Thrombocytopenia Purpura (ITP)** – low platelet count with normal bone marrow function. Causes: autoimmune disorder seen after a viral infection seen in **children 2-4 years** old and spontaneously resolves; or chronic in adults. S/S: indications of bleeding – bruising, **petechiae, purpura**, epistaxis, bleeding gums; bleeding from minor injuries is prolonged; brain hemorrhage.
   4. **Anemia** – low hemoglobin from blood loss, low iron, low vitamin B12, or low folic acid; TX: stop blood loss, oral **iron replacement** (dark stools, constipation), vitamin B12.
   5. **Polycythemia** – excess blood cells.
      - **Secondary polycythemia** – increased RBC in response to high altitudes and hypoxia seen in COPD, **increased blood viscosity, aspirin for clotting risk,**
      - Polycythemia Vera – overactive bone marrow results in increase in RBC, WBC, and platelets; hematocrit over 55%, hepatosplenomegaly (enlarged spleen and liver), increased blood viscosity.
      - TX: phlebotomy to remove whole blood and infuse NS, chemotherapy to decrease blood cell production.

6. **Sickle cell disease** – congenital (gene from both parents) hemolytic anemia (SS) causing "sickling" of RBCs. Patients take Hydroxyurea to decrease sickling and produce more Hgb.
   - **Triage 2 (high risk)** for sickle cell crisis. **Acute chest syndrome** of chest pain and dyspnea is the main killer. **Sequestration** of cells in spleen causes abdominal pain. **Vaso-occlusive crisis** – most common, **priapism**.
   - Triggers – low oxygen saturation, infection, **dehydration, exposure to cold.**
   - S/S: sudden **explosive pain** in abdomen, chest, back, and joints; splenic ischemia increases risk of infection; cardiac ischemia seen in acute chest syndrome.
   - DX: CBC to detect infection, reticulocyte count.
   - TX: **high-flow O$_2$**, IVFs for rehydration, antibiotics for infection, **opioids for pain**; early stem cell transplantation is goal.
   - D/C education: avoid triggers, take Hydroxyurea as prescribed to decrease sickling and produce Hgb.
7. **Neutropenia** – low WBC count, increasing the risk of infection (**Triage level 2**)
   - Causes: immunosuppressive therapy (chemotherapy or radiation) or leukemia - bone marrow manufactures leukemic (abnormal) immature WBCs, that do not function properly, **nor provide adequate protection from infection**.
   - S/S: low-grade fever with **low neutrophil count**, fever may be absent, recurrent infections.
   - TX: **protective (reverse) isolation**; avoid invasive procedures; **early antibiotics**; avoid raw and undercooked meat, well water, and unwashed produce; bone marrow stimulants (Filgrastim - Neupogen).

C. **Electrolyte/fluid imbalance**
   1. **Dehydration** – fluid resuscitation based on severity; IV isotonic (NS or LR) crystalloids 1-2 L in adults, **20 ml/kg boluses in children**, 10 ml/kg in neonate.
   2. **Hyperkalemia (> 5.0 mEq/L)** - Seen in renal failure, burns, crush injuries, ACE inhibitors, rhabdomyolysis. EKG: **Peaked T waves** early, widening of QRS, loss of P waves, Sine wave.

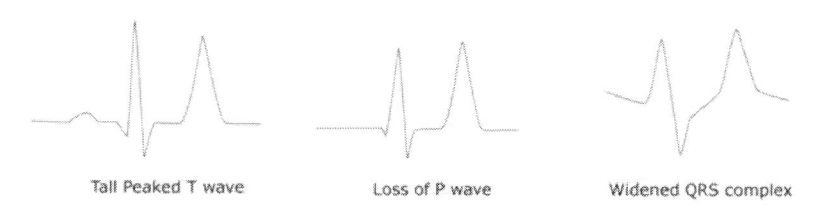

Tall Peaked T wave   Loss of P wave   Widened QRS complex

### Hyperkalemia TX "C BIG K Drop"

- **C** Calcium gluconate 10% - 10 ml IV over 10 mins (cardiac stabilizer)
- **B** Beta agonists – Salbutamol 10-20 mg in 4 ml NS nebulized over 10 mins OR Bicarbonate 8.4% (50meq) IV over 5 mins (intracellular shift)
- **I** Insulin 10 units IVP (intracellular shift)
- **G** Glucose D50W 1 ampule over 5 mins (maintain glucose)
- **K** Kayexylate 15-30 g IN 15-30 ml (70% sorbitol) PO for GI removal (for chronic renal failure)
- **D** Diuretics – Furosemide 40-80 mg IVP (renal removal)
- **rop** Renal unit for extracorporeal removal

3. **Hypokalemia (<3.5 mEq/L)** - Seen in metabolic alkalosis, overuse of diuretics, acute alcoholism, cirrhosis, **intestinal tract diseases (malabsorption).**
    - S/S: muscle weakness, N/V, **paralytic ileus**/abdominal distension/gas, shallow respirations, mental depression, leg cramps; EKG: tachycardia, **flat T waves, possible U wave**, ventricular irritability.
    - TX: Replace K+, correct alkalosis (K+ low = pH high), correct hypomagnesemia too, increase K+ in diet.
4. **Hypercalcemia (> 10.5 mg/dl)** - Seen in renal disease, prolonged immobility, malignancies, hyperparathyroidism. S/S: Lethargy, DTR's decreased, constipation, "metallic taste", **risk of kidney stones.** TX: IVF's, furosemide, glucocorticoids to decrease GI absorption of Ca+, dialysis
5. **Hypocalcemia (<8.5 mg/dl) (Need albumin)** - Seen in **pancreatitis**, hypoparathyroidism, low albumin, burns, malignancy, and hyperventilation.
    - S/S: **Chvostek's sign – spasm of lip and cheek, Trousseau's sign – carpopedal spasm;** tetany, confusion.
    - **Prolonged QTI - risk of Torsades VT** (polymorphic VT).
    - TX: Replace Calcium, Vitamin D, and parathyroid hormone (as needed), increase calcium in diet.
6. **Hypernatremia (>145 mEq/L) (Serum osmolality 2x Na+ > 295)**
    - Seen in renal failure = sodium and water excess, treated with diuretics and dialysis.
    - Hypovolemic hypernatremia seen in DKA, HHS, Diabetes Insipidus.
    - S/S: Thirst, dry membranes, orthostatic, hypotension.
    - TX: Treat cause and correct slowly with D5W or .45 NS to prevent cerebral edema, sodium restriction; vasopressin (ADH) for DI.
7. **Hyponatremia (<135 mEq/L) (Serum osmolality < 275 – 2 x sodium)**
    - Hypovolemia from vomiting, diarrhea, or burns treated with 0.9% NS replacement.
    - Hypervolemic hyponatremia seen in fluid overload, SIADH, excessive water ingestion.
    - S/S: fatigue, diarrhea, **risk is seizures.** TX: **Hypertonic saline, water restriction.**
8. **Hypermagnesemia (>2.5 mEq/L)**
    - Seen in renal failure and laxative abuse.
    - S/S: **Respiratory depression**, bradycardia, hypotension, decreased DTR's.
    - TX: Stop magnesium if infusing, furosemide, **calcium gluconate** 10 ml or 10% over 10 minutes, dialysis.
9. **Hypomagnesemia (< 1.5 mEq/L)**
    - Seen in **acute and chronic alcoholism** (most common), malnutrition, malabsorption, thiazide (HCTZ) and loop (Lasix) diuretics.
    - S/S: Ventricular dysrhythmias like **polymorphic ventricular tachycardia (Torsades de pointes)**, agitation, hyperreflexia.
    - TX: **Magnesium sulfate administration** – 1-2 grams IV (rapid if emergency, over 2 hours if non-emergent) or IM depending on severity (monitor for respiratory depression, hypotension, decreased DTR).

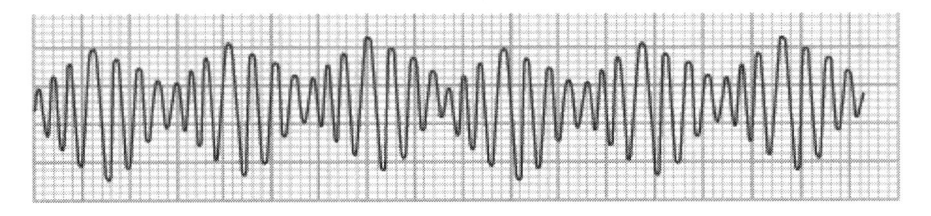

D. **Endocrine disorders**
   1. **Adrenal glands** – control the release of epinephrine (adrenalin) for fight-or-flight response; a tumor of the adrenal medulla – **Pheochromocytoma** stimulates release of adrenaline, resulting in tachycardia and hypertensive crisis. TX: alpha-blocking agent like **Phentolamine (Regitine)**, nitroprusside (Nipride), or labetalol. Beta-blocker without alpha blockade is contraindicated.
   2. **Cushing Syndrome** – elevated levels of glucocorticoids (Decadron) resulting in moon face, buffalo hump, fat above clavicles, Hirsutism, insomnia; TX: **taper off glucocorticoids.**
   3. **Acute Adrenal Insufficiency (Adrenal Crisis) – Addison's Disease (chronic)**
      - Causes: **sudden discontinuation of glucocorticoids**, infection, trauma, surgery, burns. S/S: signs of shock (tachycardia and **hypotension**), **hyponatremia** and **hypoglycemia, hyperkalemia.** DX: **cortisol level**, CMP.
      - TX: Treat **hypovolemic shock** with **0.9% NS** (treats hyponatremia and dilutes potassium too), replace glucocorticoids (**hydrocortisone**) and mineralocorticoids (dexamethasone) immediately, **dextrose** for hypoglycemia, insulin/dextrose for hyperkalemia.
   4. **Thyroid Storm**
      - Severe hypermetabolism from an **overactive thyroid gland (Grave's Disease)**, excessive production or secretion of hormones, or ingestion of hormones.
      - S/S: Extreme hyperthermia, **tachydysrhythmias**, agitation, tremors, mania, goiter, exopthalamus (protuberant eyes).
      - Labs: **T3 & T4 high**, thyroid stimulation hormone (TSH) low.
      - TX: Decrease heart rate with **beta-blockers**, administer antithyroid drug propylthiouracil (PTU) to block hormone synthesis, Iodine to block conversion of T4 to T3 and hour after PTU, **manual cooling** and acetaminophen to reduce temperature, **NO aspirin**.
   5. **Myxedema Coma**
      - Severe complication of hypothyroidism with decreased metabolism and progressive mental deterioration. MC is more common in older females during cold weather. Mortality rate as high as 60% even with treatment.
      - S/S: Fatigue, weight gain, tongue swelling (macroglossia), confusion to coma or "Myxedema Madness".
      - DX: Decreased T3 and T4 with elevated TSH.
      - TX: Protect airway and support breathing, rewarm, rehydrate, and IV Levothyroxine (T4).
   6. **Hypoglycemia** – blood sugar < 60 mg/dl in adult, < 40 mg/dl in infant
      - S/S: **early signs** are hunger, cool, diaphoretic skin, **tachycardia**, and tremors; **later signs** are slurred speech and disorientation (**beta-blockers mask signs**).
      - TX: Conscious - 15 grams of rapid-acting oral glucose, repeat as needed; follow with complex carbohydrate. Unresponsive – IV dextrose, **no higher than 25% dextrose in children (half-strength D50% - 25 cc of each)**, no higher than 12.5% in infants. Consider $D_5W$ boluses as alternative to D 50% for all ages.
   7. **DKA** – (**D**iabetic) blood sugar increased, **K**etones, **A**cidosis (pH < 7.35)
      - Most common in type 1 diabetes mellitus (DM), **develops rapidly.**
      - S/S: signs of **dehydration/shock** – tachycardia, N/V, abdominal pain, rapid, deep respirations (**Kussmaul** respirations), **acetone** odor of breath, mental status changes
      - DX: blood glucose typically <600 mg/dl, elevated BUN, **ketones** in urine, **pH< 7.35 (metabolic acidosis)**, monitor **potassium** carefully.
      - TX: Treat **hypovolemic shock** with **0.9% NS, IV insulin infusion** (no bolus) (if K+ 3.5 or >). **Add dextrose-containing fluid when blood sugar < 250 mg/dl**, replace electrolytes

(**potassium**), treat with sodium bicarbonate only if pH < 7.0 despite IVF's and insulin. **Continue insulin until you close the anion gap**, resolving ketosis and acidosis.
8. **Hyperosmolar Hyperglycemic Syndrome (HHS/HHNK)** – blood sugar > 600 mg/dl
    - Presents in unknown diabetics and type 2 DM, develops **slowly.**
    - S/S: significant volume depletion (**hypovolemic shock**), acute mental status changes (lethargy, **coma**), seizures.
    - DX: blood glucose > 600 mg/dl, **extremely elevated BUN**, glucose in urine but **no ketones, normal pH.**
    - TX: **Treat hypovolemia with 0.9% NS** (lots), IV insulin infusion (less than in DKA) (if K+ 3.3 or >) until blood sugar < 300 mg/dl (then $D_5 0.45$ NS), replace electrolytes.

| DKA | HHS |
|---|---|
| • Type I DM | • Type II DM |
| • Blood Sugar >250 mg/dl | • Blood Sugar > 600 mg/dl |
| • **Acetone** breath | • No fruity smell |
| • **Ketones** in urine | • Minimal or no ketones |
| • pH < 7.35 | • Normal pH, no acidosis |
| • **Kussmaul's respirations** | • Shallow breaths |
| • Develops rapidly | • Develops slowly |
| • Nausea, vomiting, abdominal pain | • Severely altered LOC |
|  | • **Profound dehydration** |

| DI | SIADH |
|---|---|
| • **Low ADH** | • **High ADH** |
| • **High UO** (polyuria) | • Water intoxication |
| • High sodium | • **Low UO** (oliguria) |
| • High serum osmality from dehydration | • **Low sodium** (dilutional) |
| • Risk: **Hypovolemic shock** | • Low serum osmolality |
| • TX: DDAVP (ADH) | • Weight gain |
| • Better if decreased UO | • Risk: **Seizures** |
|  | • TX: Hypertonic Saline, Dilantin |
|  | • Better if sodium increases |

9. **Diabetes Insipidus (DI)** – low levels of antidiuretic hormone (ADH)
    - Neurogenic from **head injury**, brain tumors, meningitis, **phenytoin, lithium.** Nephrogenic from pyelonephritis and familial genetic disorder.
    - S/S: polydipsia and **polyuria (increased urine output).**
    - DX: **hypernatremia** and increased serum osmolality despite polyuria, low urine specific gravity and urine osmolality.
    - TX: **aqueous vasopressin** IV or SQ, lysine vasopressin spray, **DDAVP (desmopressin)**; then fluid replacement, but monitor for cerebral edema.
10. **Syndrome of Inappropriate Antidiuretic Hormone (SIADH)** - high levels of ADH
    - SIADH causes – head trauma, infections (**meningitis**), malignancies (oat cell lung cancer), oral hypoglycemic and psychotropic medications, general anesthetics.
    - S/S: decreased urine output, **water intoxication**, cerebral edema.
    - DX: **dilutional hyponatremia (risk of seizures)**, increased specific gravity.
    - TX: **hypertonic saline** or IV NS and furosemide, **water restriction.**
E. **HIV/AIDS** – HIV is a retrovirus (RNA) that spreads through infected blood or body secretions; if untreated, may progress to AIDS.
    1. S/S of HIV: **swollen lymph glands**, fever, fatigue, diarrhea, weight loss, **oral candidiasis** (thrush); **shingles**. S/S of AIDS: CD4+ cell count < 200 cells/ul, CD4+ < 14% of all lymphocytes, or an AIDS-related condition is present (Kaposi's, TB).
    2. TX: antiretroviral medications to **keep virus from replicating, treat opportunistic infections**, vaccine on the horizon.
F. **Acute Renal Failure** – rapidly progressive loss of renal function (< 400 mL per day in adults, or < 0.5 ml/kg/hour in children) (prerenal failure is most common).
    1. Prerenal - cause **not kidneys, typically hypoperfusion from hypovolemic shock**

- DX: BUN: Creatinine ratio – 20-40:1 (Example: **BUN 90**, Creatinine 2.8); low urine sodium (<20 mEq/L), **high specific gravity** (>1.020) and urine osmolality. TX: **IV crystalloids** to increase circulation – increasing urine output.
      2. Intrarenal (kidney damage – progresses to chronic renal failure)
         - Causes: acute kidney injury (AKI), glomerulonephritis, acute tubular necrosis (ATN). from **rhabdomyolysis**. BUN: Creatinine ratio – 10-15:1 (Example: BUN 50, **Creatinine 11**); high urine sodium (> 20 mEq/L), low specific gravity (<1.010) and low urine osmolality. TX: Cessation of nephrotoxic drugs, **dialysis.**
      3. Postrenal (obstruction in the flow of urine)
         - Causes: renal calculi, urethral blockage (prostate stricture or BPH), neurogenic bladder, tumor. TX: remove obstruction.
G. **Chronic Kidney Disease**
   1. S/S: HTN, volume overload, **hyperkalemia**, metabolic acidosis, anemia, uremic syndrome, bruises, pruritus. TX: Correct electrolyte and fluid imbalances, dialysis, CCRT if unstable.
H. **Sepsis and Septic shock**
   1. **Systemic Inflammatory Response Syndrome SIRS** (2 or more) WBC > 12,000 (> bands) or < 4,000; Temperature > 38 C (100.4 F) or < 36 C (96.8F); Heart rate > 90 bpm; **Respiratory rate > 20 breaths/minute.**
   2. **Sepsis** –presence or suspicion of infection with 2 or more SIRS criteria.
   3. **Septic shock** – hypotension (SBP < 90, MAP < 65) **unresponsive to fluid** resuscitation, **requires vasopressors.**
   4. **MODS** – multiple organ dysfunction syndrome; elevated BUN and creatinine > 2.0 (kidneys), elevated ammonia and bilirubin > 2.0 mg/dl (liver), $CO_2$ elevated (lungs), thrombocytopenia, coagulopathy.
   5. DX: CBC, **lactate**, ABG, procalcitonin, BMP, cultures prior to antibiotics, chest x-ray.
   6. TX: early fluid resuscitation at **30 ml/kg of isotonic crystalloids** and **antibiotics** have been shown to improve outcomes; remove source of infection; **vasopressors. (Norepinephrine preferred)**; mechanical ventilation; glucose control < 150 mg/dl.
I. **Substance use and abuse**
   a. **Sympathomimetic/Stimulants** - Illegal street drugs (**cocaine**, amphetamines, methamphetamine). Illicit **designer**/synthetic drugs (MDMA – ecstasy, Molly for enhanced sensory perception), bath salts, salvia plant, synthetic cannabinoids (Spice, K2), peyote, psilocybin tea (altered time perception), over-the-counter cold agents (DXM) and dietary supplements containing ephedrine, and Imodium at large quantities. Prescription drugs: albuterol, Ritalin, Adderall, etc.
      - S/S: severe HTN, tachycardia, **hyperthermia, dilated pupils (mydriasis),** hallucinations, paranoia.
      - Risks: **ventricular arrhythmias**, MI, aortic dissection, **rhabdomyolysis.**
      - TX: patient sedation with **benzodiazepines**, control BP and HR, **manual cooling.**
   b. **Sedatives/ Benzodiazepines end in "pam" or "lam"** - Diazepam (Valium), Alprazolam (Xanax), Lorazepam (Ativan).
      - S/S: **respiratory depression**, hypotension, bradycardia, and hypothermia.
      - TX: **aspiration risk, intubation, Flumazenil (Romazicon) for acute benzodiazepines toxicity, not chronic use (risk of seizure).**
   c. **Opioids (Heroin, Morphine, Oxycodone)**
      - S/S (classic triad) - **respiratory depression**, CNS depression, miosis (pinpoint pupils); along with hypotension, bradycardia, and hypothermia.
      - TX: **assist breathing**, intubation, Naloxone (Narcan - opioid antagonist) dose **only to produce adequate respirations**. Duration of action is 30-60 minutes. **Buprenorphine** (Suboxone) for withdrawal/detoxication.

- d. **Phencyclidine (PCP)** - Dissociative anesthetic = decreased awareness of surroundings and decreased pain sensation. S/S: **Combative behavior, increased physical strength, lack of pain sensation.** TX: Reduce stimulation, protect patient from harming themselves or others, benzodiazepines for agitation, antihypertensives for HTN.
- e. **LSD** - S/S: Euphoria, panic, **hallucinations**, paranoia, psychosis; TX: **reduce stimulation**, benzodiazepines for agitation, **Haldol for psychosis.**
- f. **GHB/Rohypnol (salty water)** - S/S: Depressed LOC; blackout, amnesia of event, so **inquire about a sexual assault exam.**
- g. **Cholinergic Crisis**
  - Examples: **organophosphate (OP) pesticides**, chemical warfare agents (Sarin), Tensilon or Mestinon.
  - S/S: **SLUDGE** – Salivation, Lacrimation, Urination, Defecation, GI distress, Emesis; plus **bronchorrhea (increased bronchial secretions).**
  - TX: **Atropine until bronchial secretions dry**, Pralidoxime (2-PAM), benzodiazepines.
- h. **Anticholinergics**
  - Examples: antihistamines, TCAs, Jimson weed.
  - S/S: "Blind as a bat, Mad as a Hatter, Hot as Hades, Dry as a bone", HTN, **tachycardic**, flushing, **delirium**, hallucinations.
  - TX: Sedate with benzodiazepines, **Haldol**, cool patient, **Physostigmine IV slowly.**

9. **Cardiac medications**
   - Calcium-channel blocker – TX: Calcium is priority, treat bradycardia.
   - Beta-blocker – TX: Glucagon is priority, also helps increase blood glucose.
   - Digoxin – TX: Digi Fab or Digi Bind, treat arrythmias.

J. **Alcohol abuse**
   - a. Methanol "snow field vision" (windshield wiper fluid, may lead to **blindness**).
   - b. Ethylene glycol **(antifreeze)** – **calcium oxalate crystals** cause fluorescence. TX: **IV ethanol or Fomepizole (Antizol).**
   - c. Alcohol withdrawal – starts around 6-8 hours post last drink, starts with tremors. Treat with acamprosate (Campral) to reduce cravings and disulfiram (Antabuse) as deterrent.

# Musculoskeletal and Wound Emergencies (13 items)

A. **Neurovascular Assessment - 6 Ps:** Pain, Paresthesia, Pallor, Pressure, Paralysis, Pulselessness
B. **Nerve Assessment**
   1. Radial – motor - extend wrist or thumb (hitchhike or thumbs up), sensation to thumb.
   2. Median – motor - oppose thumb to fingers, sensation of index finger.
   3. Ulnar – motor - abduct (fan) fingers, sensation to 4th and 5th fingers.
C. **Tetanus toxoid (active immunity)** – revaccinate q 10 years for minimal contamination; revaccinate q 5 years for grossly contaminated, **add 250 units of IM immunoglobulin** (TIG) if no or unsure of initial vaccination with gross contamination (migrant farm worker). **Tetanus – trismus, lock jaw.**
D. **General concepts** – splint injury as it lies on padded splint, **immobilize above and below the joint**, avoid ice packs directly on skin.
E. **Crutch walking** – fit with wearing shoe on unaffected side, **arm pieces 2 inches below axilla**, elbow at **30-degree angle**, keep crutches 6 inches to side for stable gait, stairs - uninjured (good leg) first ascending (going up), injured (bad leg) first descending (going down). D/C education: return demonstration.
F. **Abrasions** "friction burn" – consider pain control prior to cleansing with soap and water, apply **non-adherent dressing. Avulsion** – peeling of skin from underlying tissue; degloving injury is avulsion where skin is pulled away from the scalp, hands, digits, foot, and toes; apply **non-adherent dressing.**
G. **Foreign bodies**
   1. Retained object in wound, caused by dirt, debris, gravel (tattooing), glass, wood, metal etc.
   2. DX: Radiography based on the material, tempered glass seen on x-ray, vegetative requires MRI.
   3. TX: **remove vegetative material (thorn) ASAP, do not soak or it swells**, tetanus, antibiotics.
H. **Lacerations**
   a. **Avoid** xylocaine with **epinephrine** on ears, nose, fingers, toes, and penis (hose) - decreased circulation to distal areas **increases risk of infection.**
   b. **Do not shave eyebrows, uneven regrowth.**
   c. Leave adhesive tape strips until they fall off on their own (**7-10 days**) – avoid petroleum ointments or weakens glue. Staple scalp, remove in 10-14 days.
   d. Wound bonding agents leave a waterproof bandage, slough off in **5-10 days** – avoid petroleum ointments. **Suture removal – Face is 3-5 days**; Scalp/Trunks 7-10 days; Arm/Leg is 10-14 days; Over Joint is 14 days.
I. **Traumatic amputation**
   1. Poor outcomes with crush injuries, contamination, comorbidities, age, poor nutrition.
   2. TX: ABCs, bleeding control (**pressure or tourniquet to stump**), immobilization, antibiotics, tetanus
      a. Prepare early for transfer to applicable facility for replantation.
      b. Lightly brush off gross material, **rinse gently with sterile saline** (avoid iodine).
      c. Wrap amputated part in saline moistened gauze; **do not soak in saline or part swells.**
      d. Place amputated part in sealable plastic bag, label with patient info.
      e. Place bag on separate bag of ice; **avoid direct contact between amputated part and ice.**
J. **Compartment syndrome**
   1. Excessive pressure develops within a body cavity enclosed by fascia; as pressure increases, circulation decreases, and edema increases; leading to ischemia and necrosis.
   2. Most common in **lower leg and forearm**; irreversible damage after **4-6 hours of ischemia.**
   3. Causes: fractures; external compression from **circumferential burns**, casts, splints, ace bandages, edema, soft tissue, or vascular injury (**crush injury**, bleeding, hemarthrosis, recent surgery).
   4. S/S: **early sign - severe pain disproportionate to the injury, unrelieved by narcotics; pulselessness is a late sign (permanent damage).**
   5. DX: measure compartment pressure with compartmental pressure monitoring device - normal: < 10 mm Hg, 20 (high)-30 close observation.

6. TX: **elevate to level of heart (neutral position)**, remove any external compression, surgical decompression - **fasciotomy at > 30 mm Hg.**

K. Fractures
- **Open fracture** - risk is hemorrhage and infection, so irrigate with NS and administer antibiotic.
- **Closed fracture** - risk is compartment pressure.

1. **Clavicle (fracture of scapula is rare)**
   - Assess for axillary nerve as well as damage to subclavian or axial artery, may have associated **pneumothorax/hemothorax or great vessel injury.** TX: Ice, sling & swath, Figure of 8.
2. **Humerus – assess for brachial nerve injury.**
   - TX: Sling & swath for **proximal**, sugar tong splint if **mid-shaft humeral** fracture, surgery for distal humerus fracture.
3. **Forearm (Radius/Ulnar)**
   - FOOSH – fall on outstretched hand, **Colles (silver fork deformity** – distal radius**)**, Monteggia's (dislocation of radius, fracture of ulna), or Smith fracture (arms full).
   - Assess for **median** nerve damage. TX: Splinted with elbow flexed 90 degrees, sling to support arm.
4. **Scaphoid**
   - S/S: Pain in **anatomic snuff box.** TX: Splint with thumb abduction (**thumb spica splint**).
5. **Boxer's "Amateur Boxer" fracture (4th or 5th metacarpal fracture)**
   - S/S: depression of knuckles. TX: Apply a **posterior ulnar splint.**
6. **Pelvic fracture**
   - Stable (fall – one point broken) versus unstable (MVC – multiple points broken).
   - Assess: **gentle inward compression and down over symphysis pubis** if no obvious injury, **only once so you do not dislodge clot.**
   - Risk: **hypovolemic shock,** associated **urethral damage and bladder rupture.**
   - TX: **apply pelvic binder over greater trochanter ASAP for pelvic ring fractures, massive transfusion protocol** (10 units of PRBCs plus plasma and platelets), permissive hypotension, prepare for embolization (REBOA) or surgery, **post-op risk: DVT/PE/Fat emboli.**
7. **Femur fracture**
   - Femoral head fracture seen in falls especially in elderly with osteoporosis; femoral shaft fractures seen in high-energy forces.
   - S/S: **shortened leg, external rotation**, swollen thigh.
   - TX: **traction splint** for mid-shaft fractures to **reduce blood loss** and pain; ORIF for femoral head fracture; highest risk of **fat emboli (12-48 hours after injury).**
8. Additional fracture information
   - **Patella/knee fracture** - fall on knee, **knee into dashboard**; TX: surgery, long leg splint/cast.
   - **Tibia/fibula** - sports injuries, axial loading (fall from height); **monitor for compartment syndrome.**
   - **Ankle/malleolus** – eversion injury; immediate reduction if dislocated.
   - **Foot metatarsals – short leg walking cast.**
   - **Foot phalanges – buddy tape** to adjacent toes if non-displaced.
   - **Calcaneus** – fall from height – assess for associated **lumbar spine** injuries, compression dressing and crutches.

L. Dislocations
1. **Anterior shoulder dislocation**
   a. Direct blow to shoulder or a fall on extended arm, inability to raise arm or adduct.
   b. Reduce (may require sedation to overcome muscle spasms), **apply sling & swath.**
2. **Posterior shoulder (rare, may be seen after seizure)**
   a. Seizure or blow to anterior shoulder, arm held in **adduction** close at side.

b. Reduce, apply sling & swath or **shoulder immobilizer.**
3. **Elbow**
   a. Fall on outstretched arm, elbow swelling, neurovascular compromise. Immediate reduction, sling.
4. **Child Elbow (Radial head subluxation or Nursemaid's elbow)**
   a. Children are jerked up, refuses to use arm, **limited supination.**
   b. Easily reduced by manual reduction by supination/flexion or forced pronation.
5. **Hip**
   a. Fall or front seat MVC dashboard injury - Posterior – adducted, internal rotation; Anterior – abducted, external rotation.
   b. Reduce emergently within 6 hours to prevent **femoral head necrosis.**
6. **Patella/Knee**
   a. Blow or fall on knee, may damage peroneal and **popliteal artery.**
   b. Extend leg to reduce, compression, place in a **knee immobilizer.**
7. **Ankle**
   a. Frequently involves leg fractures. Splint in neutral position, prepare for open reduction due to blood vessel and nerve impingement.

M. **Sprain/Strain** - RICE – avoid use of limb, **ice for 20-minute sessions** for first 48 hours, compression during day (take off at night), **elevate above level of heart** for first 24 hours.

N. **Gouty Arthritis**
   1. Etiology: Acute arthritis with **uric acid crystals** in synovial fluids, mostly male.
   2. S/S: Intolerable pain **in toes**, increased at night. TX: Colchicine, Allopurinol, steroids, NSAIDs.
   3. DC teaching: **avoid high purine diet** (heart, herring, mussels, salmon, sardines, anchovies, veal, bacon, organ meats). Caution with aspirin, alcohol, and thiazide diuretics. Increased risk of **kidney (uric acid) stones**.

O. **Bursitis**
   1. Excessive fluid in or infection of the bursa. Etiology: **overuse, repetitive movements**, inflammatory disease, infection, trauma. S/S: pain, **redness, warmth**, swelling, decreased ROM. TX: NSAIDs, analgesia, bursal aspiration. D/C teaching: RICE, decrease movement of extremity.

P. **Joint effusion**
   1. Collection of fluid in joint space; **knee** is most common from trauma or overuse. S/S: pain, **redness, warmth**, swelling, stiffness, decreased ROM. TX: NSAIDs, RICE, **arthrocentesis.** DC teaching: RICE, decrease movement of extremity.

Q. **Osteomyelitis**
   1. **Infection of the bone** and surrounding tissue; may lead to sepsis.
   2. Etiology: open fractures, infection in area of fracture, **puncture wounds (hand from fight bite or wound on bottom of foot).**
   3. S/S: pain, malaise, fever, redness, swelling, warmth.
   4. DX: **blood cultures.** TX: analgesia, **IV antibiotics**, specialty consults.

R. **Rhabdomyolysis**
   1. Breakdown of skeletal muscle, resulting in release of **myoglobin, CK, and potassium.**
   2. Etiology: **prolonged immobilization, stimulant drug use, statins (Lipitor), heatstroke, and crush injuries.**
   3. S/S: malaise, fever, **myalgia (muscle soreness), dark brown urine (tea colored), increased K$^+$, myoglobin, and CK.**
   4. TX: ABCs, **Large volumes of IV fluids (6-12 liters in 24 hours) to produce urine output > 100 -200 ml/hour**, 1-2 amps of sodium bicarbonate in NS (**urine alkalization pH > 6.5**), loop diuretics, mannitol, hemodialysis.
   5. Treatment effective if increased clear urine. Complication: **Acute tubular necrosis** (renal failure).

- S. **Achilles' tendon rupture**
    1. A tear in the Achilles tendon from a sudden, **unexpected dorsiflexion**; **sprinter** or basketball ballplayer who hears "pop" when pushing off. Higher risk if on **fluoroquinolones** (Cipro, Levaquin), especially for older patients. **DX by MRI**, TX: Surgery.
- T. **High Pressure Injection Injuries (grease gun, paint gun, hydraulics)**
    - Cause **massive underlying tissue trauma**, carries high risk for complications such as **compartment syndrome** and infection; hydraulics, paint and grease can travel down through hand, leading to major damage. **TX: Requires immediate surgical intervention.**
- U. **Injection Injuries**
    - Penetrating injuries related to guns & industrial incidents; **appearance of wound may not reflect actual tissue damage; DO NOT REMOVE impaled objects.**
    - TX: ABCs, bleeding control, **stabilize any object**, preserve any forensic evidence, projectile path can be unpredictable, most chest and abdominal **require surgical intervention.**

## Maxillofacial and Ocular Emergencies (11 items)

- A. **Peritonsillar abscess**
    a. Collection of pus beyond the into the neck and chest tonsils.
    b. S/S: severe throat pain, **deviated uvula**, fever, halitosis, pain that radiates to ear, erythematic tonsils.
    c. TX: throat culture, IV fluids, analgesics, **antibiotics, steroids, aspiration incision and drainage** (I&D).
- B. **Ludwig's Angina**
    a. Bacterial infection submandibular after a tooth abscess.
    b. S/S: difficulty swallowing, **drooling**, swelling and redness of neck, **tongue swelling.**
    c. TX: **maintain airway, antibiotics.**
- C. **Avulsed tooth**
    a. TX: preserve tooth by placing back **in socket** or between in cheek/gum or under tongue **only** if patient alert and adult. If altered LOC, concurrent injury, or child, place tooth in saline, **milk** or in **a calcium-based solution;** replant tooth within 6 hours if possible. Hold by crown, do not touch root.
- D. **Lip laceration – consider** specialty consultation to suture if laceration is through **vermillion border**. First stitch prior to xylocaine due to swelling to approximate.
- E. **Epistaxis**
    a. Anterior is most common, bright red blood caused by picking nose.
    b. Posterior is more serious, caused by **HTN and coagulopathies** - heaver bleeding, darker red, drips out of nares and down throat, leads to clots, **monitor airway.**
    c. TX: **elevate HOB, suction available,** IV fluids, pinch nostrils firmly for 10-15 minutes for anterior, progress to cauterizing with silver nitrate or electrocautery, nasal packing soaked in TXA, phenylephrine, or lidocaine with epinephrine). **Monitoring airway is most important, so may need to admit.**
    d. DC teaching: BP management for posterior; avoid blowing/picking nose and cool mist humidifier for anterior bleed.
- F. **Bell's Palsy**
    a. Unilateral facial paralysis due to cranial nerve **VII (facial)** inflammation.
    b. S/S: tears, drooling, **unable to blink or close affected eye, facial drooping,** ipsilateral loss of taste, **increased sensitivity to sound (hyperacusis).**
    c. DX: Rule out stroke and meningitis.
    d. TX: antivirals and **corticosteroids** to shorten progression, analgesics, and **eye lubricants.**

- e. DC teaching: wear sunglasses/eye protection to help with eye irritation, moist heat from humidifier, **artificial tears** during awake hours, **facial massage** can help prevent permanent contractures/paralysis. Most resolve in 3-6 months.

G. **Trigeminal neuralgia (tic doloureux)**
  a. Causes: Compression of **CN V** from tumor, AV malformation, trauma, or multiple sclerosis
  b. S/S: Sudden, unilateral, severe, **stabbing pain** on one or more of branches of **CN V** (Trigeminal); facial twitching that is provoked by brushing teeth or chewing.
  c. TX: **Tegretol** (carbamazepine), phenytoin, valproic acid, gabapentin, lamotrigine, clonazepam.

H. **Nasal Foreign Body** – most common in pediatrics, monitor for **aspiration.**
  a. S/S: pain in nasal/sinus cavity, unilateral **purulent nasal drainage**, recurrent epistaxis, fever. TX: Use **least invasive means possible – decongestants or pressor agent prior to removal to decrease swollen tissue;** occlude unaffected nostril and ask child to **blow nose**, or ask mother to blow in mouth, or use BVM; **wall suction**, forceps as last resort.
  b. **Alkaline button batteries dangerous, cause saponification of tissue quickly.**
  c. DC teaching: education on dangers of small objects with children, choking hazards.

I. **Ear Foreign Body**
  a. S/S: pain, **anxiety/fear (increased with live insects)**, bleeding, hearing loss on affected side, N/V, **dizziness**, purulent drainage from ear.
  b. TX: **flying insects may fly to the light. Suffocate live insect with viscous lidocaine or mineral oil**, then irrigate and **attach wall suction**. Use alcohol base solution in irrigation of organic material (bread, peas, beans). Last resort - consider sedation, then use forceps to remove object, without pushing deeper in canal.

J. **Otitis externa (Swimmer's Ear; outside tympanic membrane)**
  a. Infection (typically bacterial) of external auditory canal.
  b. S/S: pain with movement of **tragus or auricle**, possible periauricular cellulitis, hearing loss, drainage from ear, swelling, erythema. TX: analgesics, antibiotics, warm otic drops.
  c. DC teaching: apply warm compress, **keep ear dry**, no objects in ear, earplugs while swimming/bathing.

K. **Otitis media**
  a. Infection of inner ear canal; blocked Eustachian tubes causing fluid to build up behind TM; common 6 months – 3 years old, after an URI.
  b. S/S: sharp ear pain, **pulling at ear**, fever, hearing loss, sensation of fullness, **bulging of TM**, history of URI.
  c. TX: analgesics, possible systemic antibiotics, antipyretics.

L. **Sinusitis** - bacterial infection of mucosa of paranasal sinuses
  a. S/S: pain, **nasal congestion**, purulent drainage, malaise, fever, facial swelling, **decreased transillumination of sinuses.**
  b. DX: frontal view of maxillary sinus, orbits & nasal structures (Water's View X-ray).
  c. TX: oral antibiotics, analgesia, antipyretics, limited use of nasal decongestants.
  d. DC teaching: **monitor BP for HTN from antihistamines, limit nasal sprays.**

M. **Mastoiditis**
  a. Complication of otitis media that erodes mastoid and affects surrounding structures.
  b. S/S: history of otitis media, pain & swelling in mastoid area, ear pain, fever, possible TM rupture, headache, hearing loss.
  c. TX: prepare for admission, **IV antibiotics**, analgesics, surgical intervention.

N. **Labyrinthitis**
  a. Inflammation of inner ear (labyrinth) from **recent infective process** (fluid), **treatable.**
  b. S/S: **nystagmus, vertigo, tinnitus** (ringing in ear), pain in ear (otalgia), N/V, hearing loss.

      c. TX: **corticosteroids, meclizine for motion sickness**, antihistamines, fall risk.
- **O. Meniere's Disease (acute attack)**
  - a. Unknown etiology, more common in **women 40-60 years old.**
  - b. S/S: **recurring episodes of nystagmus, vertigo, tinnitus,** hearing loss, N/V.
  - c. TX: **corticosteroids, meclizine (Antivert) for motion sickness**, antihistamines, diuretics, anticholinergics.
  - d. DC teaching: bed rest, **slow position changes to avoid falls**, limit activity and sodium/sugar intake; avoid caffeine, nicotine, and alcohol.
- **P. Maxillary Le Fort Fractures – Mainstay of treatment is suctioning and maintaining airway!**
  - a. **Le Fort I:** "A man with a MUSTACHE"
    - Transverse detachment of the entire **maxilla above the teeth** at the level of nasal floor; **Free-floating maxilla.**
    - S/S: malocclusion, **lip laceration**, fractured teeth, swelling to area.
  - b. **Le Fort II:** "goes to the PYRAMIDS"
    - **Pyramidal shaped fracture** with transverse detachment of maxilla (base of pyramid), fracture at bridge of nose (top of pyramid), fracture through lacrimal & ethmoid bones (sides of pyramid).
    - S/S: **nasal fracture**, epistaxis, malocclusion, **lengthening of face.**
  - c. **Le Fort III:** "and takes off his Halloween MASK"
    - Free-floating segment of mid-face; **craniofacial disjunction** - involves maxilla, zygomatic arch, orbits, & cranial base bones.
    - S/S: commonly **unresponsive**, malocclusion, **immense swelling** "beach ball", severe hemorrhage.

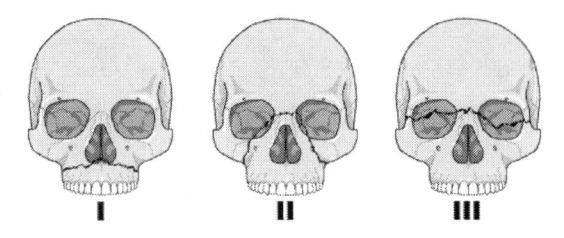

- **Q. Mandibular Fracture**
  - a. S/S: malocclusion, trismus (lockjaw), edema, ecchymosis, **numbness (paresthesia) of lower lip**, pain.
  - b. TX: **secure airway (loss of tongue control)**, elevate HOB, suction frequently, ice, surgery, analgesics, antibiotics.
- **R. Orbital Wall Fracture** - fracture of orbit - holds eye in proper placement.
  - a. S/S: ecchymosis, **ocular entrapment (unable to look up with affected eye CN 3)**, diplopia, swelling, subconjunctival petechiae, infraorbital hypesthesia (reduced sensation).
  - b. TX: elevate HOB, **ice pack** (not chemical) to reduce swelling.
  - c. Education: ophthalmic follow-up; ice packs to face; **avoid valsalva maneuver, straining, and blowing nose.**
- **S. Zygomatic Fractures**
  - a. Typically seen with orbital wall fracture.
  - b. S/S: **TIDES** = **T**rismus: reduced ability to open jaw related to muscle spasm; **I**nfraorbital hypesthesia: abnormal loss of sensation to heat, cold, touch, or pain; **D**iplopia: double vision; **E**pistaxis: nosebleeds; **S**ymmetrical abnormality (asymmetry); also, **loss of cheekbone (malar) eminence**.
  - c. TX: elevate HOB, ice pack (not chemical) to reduce swelling, EENT consult.
  - d. Education: ophthalmic follow-up; ice packs to face; **avoid valsalva maneuver, straining, and blowing nose.**

**Ocular Emergencies**

A. **Corneal Abrasions** - scratching of cornea, most common eye injury seen in ED.
   1. S/S: ocular pain, sensation of foreign body, photophobia, tearing, blurred vision.
   2. DX: visual acuity, **topical anesthetic** (Tetracaine), **fluorescein staining.**
   3. TX: ophthalmic antibiotics drops, nonsteroidal agents for eye, systemic analgesics.
   4. DC teaching: **No patching required since there is consensual movement of eyes.**

B. **Ocular Burns - true ocular emergency** from chemicals, radiation, or thermal
   1. **Alkali (lye, cement, ammonia, drain cleaner) - deep penetration until neutralized (requires large amounts of irrigation),** liquification or saponification; Acid - limited penetration.
   2. S/S: severe pain, photophobia, decreased visual acuity, tearing, involuntary spasms/closing of eyelid (**blepharospasm**).
   3. TX: **Immediately irrigate** (do not delay for assessment or visual acuity), **Tetracaine** and irrigate with NS or LR **until pH is 7.0-7.4,** tetanus, ophthalmology consult.
   4. DC teaching: **ophthalmic appointment within 24 hours,** dark environment.

C. **Ocular Foreign bodies**
   1. Welder - metal may leave **rust ring** if not removed immediately.
   2. Organic material (wood chips) can cause infection, so remove quickly.
   3. S/S: pain, photophobia, sensation of "something in eye," tearing, blurred vision.
   4. TX: analgesics (tetracaine) before exam, remove object with cotton tipped applicator or 25-27 g needle, examine cornea for rust ring, treat as corneal abrasion after removal.

D. **Acute Angle Closure Glaucoma**
   1. Normal IOP < 20 - Aqueous humor cannot move into anterior chamber; **increase in intra ocular pressure (IOP),** compression of **CN 2 Optic Nerve**; blindness within hours if left untreated.
   2. S/S: pain, decreased peripheral vision **"tunnel vision"**, **halos around light**, N/V, headache, reddened eye, **dilated, fixed pupil, cloudy cornea, firm feeling globe**, shallow chamber due to pressure.
   3. TX: HOB elevated, **miotic drops (pilocarpine), topical beta blockers (timolol maleate), carbonic anhydrase inhibitors (acetazolamide),** antiemetics, opioids for pain.
   4. DC teaching: ophthalmology follow-up, **no lifting** > 5 pounds, avoid coughing/straining, **do not lower head below waist.**
   5. Treatment effective if IOP < 20.

E. **Central retinal artery occlusion (CRAO)**
   1. Loss of perfusion to the retina; circulation must be **restored within 60-90 minutes** to prevent blindness, causes: emboli (**atrial fibrillation** increases risk), thrombosis, HTN, temporal (giant cell) arteritis.
   2. S/S: sudden onset of painless loss of vision, **"curtain or shade came down over eye"**, cherry red spot, **Amaurosis fugax** (transient episodes of blindness), DX: **increased IOP.**
   3. TX: **high triage priority**, digital massage by MD, topical **beta blocker**, acetazolamide, **sublingual nitroglycerin** to dilate vessel, fibrinolytic therapy, hyperbaric (HBO).

F. **Conjunctivitis (Pink eye)**
   1. Inflammation of membrane that lines the eyelid and sclera (conjunctiva).
   2. Causes: bacterial, viral, or fungal infection, allergic reaction, chemical irritation.
   3. S/S: **crusty eyelids**, sensation of foreign body, **conjunctival erythema**, discharge (bacterial = purulent; allergic/viral = serous), pruritus with allergic reaction.
   4. TX: antibiotics (systemic if gonococcal), antivirals, **compresses** and decongestants for allergic reaction. DC teaching: **avoid contact lenses and eye make-up, compresses.** Avoid spread – no swimming pools and hot tubs, do not share linens, hand washing.

G. **Iritis (Uveitis)**

1. Inflammation of iris, ciliary body, and choroid (middle portion of eye), from infection, trauma, rheumatic dx, syphilis, lupus. S/S: pain, **redness around the outer ring of iris**, blurry vision, photophobia, tearing, decreased visual acuity, irregular shaped pupil. TX: cycloplegics, **warm compresses**, ophthalmology consult.

H. **Retinal detachment**
   1. **Tear in retina** allowing vitreous humor to leak and reducing blood flow to retina so true ocular emergency, sudden from trauma.
   2. S/S: sudden decrease or loss of vision, **veil or curtain effect, flashes of light (photopsia), floaters** or specks in vision. TX: ophthalmic referral, prepare for surgical intervention.

I. **Hyphema**
   1. **Blood in anterior chamber** from trauma increases intraocular pressure (IOP); S/S: pain, **reddish hue to vision.**
   2. TX: analgesia, steroids, **maintain HOB elevated 30-45 degrees.**
   3. DC teaching: **avoid NSAIDs and aspirin**, protect **eye with rigid shield**, keep HOB elevated 30 degrees, minimize activities to increase intraocular pressure, follow up to monitor for rebleed (**most common 3-5 days post event**).

J. **Eyelid lacerations** - ice packs (not chemical) to reduce swelling, **specialty consultation** if through lacrimal gland.

K. **Globe rupture (ruptured globe)**
   1. Loss of integrity of the globe related to trauma; penetrating - knife, scissors, nail; blunt - ruptures related to increased IOP (burst).
   2. S/S: **tear-drop shaped pupil,** visual disturbances, evisceration of aqueous or vitreous humor, **decreased intraocular pressure.**
   3. TX: **secure protruding objects, DO NOT instill topical meds**, protect with **rigid shield**, ophthalmology consult.

L. **Corneal Ulcerations**
   1. Inflammation of epithelium of cornea; caused by trauma, bacterial, fungal, parasitic or viral infection; contacts, trauma, immunosuppression increases risk for infection.
   2. S/S: pain, photophobia, sensation of FB, tearing, blurred vision, eyelid swelling, will see "**white spots**," purulent drainage.
   3. TX: **antibiotics**, antifungals, antivirals, cycloplegics.

M. **Keratitis (Exposure to UV light – snow blindness, glare off water, welding)**
   1. Inflammation of cornea caused by **exposure to UV light - snow sports/welders**.
   2. S/S: pain, **photophobia**, red sclera, decreased vision, purulent drainage.
   3. TX: antibiotics, antifungals, antivirals, **cycloplegics**, systemic analgesics.
   4. DC teaching: **dark environment, warm compresses.**

N. **Orbital cellulitis** – inflammation of eye, eyelid redness and swelling, painful and limited eye movement. Complication: Meningitis or cavernous sinus thrombosis.

O. **Retrobulbar hematoma** – increased pressure in orbit from blunt trauma or valsalva maneuver. S/S: Proptosis from increased IOP (ocular compartment syndrome). TX: **lateral canthotomy** or Mannitol to decrease pressure STAT or may have permanent vision loss.

**Environment and Toxicology Emergencies, and Communicable Diseases (14 items)**
A. **Burns**
   1. **Burn Assessment**
      - Airway patency: edema, hoarse voice, **carbonaceous sputum**, and **stridor** indicates oral burns (not just singed nasal hairs) – **intubate immediately.**
      - **Escharotomy if circumferential chest burn, and you cannot ventilate.**

2. **Fluid resuscitation for burns**
   - **LR fluid of choice**
   - **American Burn Association** Recommendations **(2 adult, 3 peds, 4 electrical)**
     o Begin LR at **2 ml/kg** X TBSA for thermal burns, 3 ml/kg x TBSA for pediatrics, 4 ml/kg x TBSA for electrical burns.
     o Calculate based on partial and full thickness, **not superficial.**
   - Parkland Formula - 4 ml/kg instead of 2 ml/kg for adult thermal burn.
   - **1st half of the total volume of fluid over the 1st 8 hours from time of burn injury**; remaining half over the next 16 hours.
   - Monitor urine output to get **0.5-1.0 ml/kg/hour** (1-2 ml/kg/hour for pediatrics), **at least 75-100 ml/hour for electrical burns.**
3. **Electrical burns**
   - **Risk of rhabdomyolysis, so increase IVF's. ECG monitoring** for 24 hours for electrical burns, risk of **ventricular fibrillation**.

B. **Lightning** – Lichtenberg feathering, ruptured tympanic membrane.
C. **Chemical exposure**
   1. **Brush off dry chemicals first** (lime powder).
   2. Decontaminate outside of facility if fumes. Consider inhalation injury and support oxygenation and ventilation.
   3. **Asphalt** – cool and apply emollient to loosen if ordered by burn professional.
   4. **Phenol (carbolic acid) burns** - copious irrigation with 50% PEG (MiraLAX) and water.
   5. **Hydrofluoric acid** (rust remover) - irrigate for at least 30 min, until pain relief, then apply **2.5% calcium gluconate gel.**
   6. Alkalis (lye, cement, ammonia) cause **liquefaction or saponification** (destroy tissue) so require large volumes of irrigation.
D. **Carbon monoxide poisoning**
   1. Carbon monoxide (CO) poisoning can develop with exposure to smoke. When you breathe CO in, it attaches to and replaces the oxygen on the hemoglobin molecule, resulting in carboxyhemoglobin and reducing the oxygen content of the blood "silent killer".
   2. S/S: headache, nausea, vomiting at 10-20%; confusion and lethargy at 20-40%; **ST segment depression from hypoxia,** arrhythmias, seizures at 40-60%; death > 60%, cherry red skin.
   3. DX: **serum Carboxyhemoglobin, do not trust SpO$_2$.**
   4. TX: Treat with **100% high-flow O$_2$** via tight-fitting mask until level **< 10%, consider hyperbaric oxygenation HBO for pregnant patient (fetus most vulnerable).**
E. **Cyanide**
   1. Burning of **plastics or carpets**, interferes with cellular respiration (shifts oxyhemoglobin curve to left – hemoglobin holds onto O$_2$).
   2. Signs: smell of **bitter almonds** on breath, headache, dizziness, seizures.
   3. Treatment: Cyanide Kit - **inhaled amyl nitrite** (causes methemoglobinemia), IV sodium nitrite, IV sodium thiosulfate or Cyanokit: **Hydroxocobalamin** (vitamin B12) – turns urine pink.
F. **Envenomation emergencies**
   1. **Spiders**
      i. **Black Widow** – red hourglass on abdomen of female.
         1. S/S: Immediate sting, dull ache in 20 minutes, then **abdominal cramping**, muscle spasms, HTN, tachycardia, nausea & vomiting, weakness.
         2. TX: Ice, elevate, **analgesics and benzodiazepines** to control muscle spasms, antivenin cautiously.
      ii. **Brown Recluse (Fiddle-Back)** – "violin-shape"

2. S/S: - Painless bite; pruritus, redness, blister in 1-3 hours, **bluish ring**
   i. Fever, chills, nausea, vomiting, malaise within 24 hours of bite.
   ii. **Necrotizing ulcerating wound (tissue sloughing)** over time.
3. TX: Wound care, **removal of necrotic tissue**, hyperbaric oxygen therapy, antibiotics, steroids.

4. Snakes
   A. **Pit vipers (Crotalid) – hemotoxic (bleed)**
      1. Venomous: diamond-shaped (triangular) heads; vertical, elliptical pupils; fang(s); single row of caudal plates. Rattlesnakes, copperheads, & water moccasins (cotton mouth).
      2. Most snake bites are dry bites, do not require antivenin. Signs of envenomation: pain, redness, swelling to site, **progressive edema, blood-filled vesicles (candidates for antidote).**
      3. TX: 2 large-bore IV's, **remove constrictive clothing** and jewelry, immobilize limb, **antivenom (antivenin) if severe hemorrhagic swelling**, repeated until swelling subsides; **NO ICE.**
   B. **Coral snakes (Elapidae)** "Red on yellow, kill a Fellow. Red on black, venom lack."
      - Neurotoxic venom causing **respiratory paralysis.** S/S: respiratory distress, local paresthesia, diplopia, ptosis, difficulty swallowing, increased salivation. TX: Supportive care, possible antivenom.

5. Aquatic organisms
   A. **Stingrays -** Venom-coated barbed stingers create severe pain and swelling at site. TX: **Immerse in warm water** (110 degrees F) for up to 2 hours **until relief of pain**, removal of barbs with hemostats.
   B. **Jellyfish -** Nematocysts are stinging darts that fire producing severe pain and reddened welts. TX: Rinse in normal saline and remove tentacles using forceps. Water stimulates venom.

G. **Dog bites -** associated with underlying **crush injury**, 5 – 15% become infected, leave open and consider rabies prophylaxis or watch dog closely for signs of rabies.

H. **Cat bites - highest rate of infection** of animal bites because long fangs penetrate deep into tissue, saliva contains **Pasteurella** which can cause cellulitis or osteomyelitis; **leave wound open unless on face, prophylactic antibiotics.** (Excrement toxoplasmosis)

I. **Human bites**
   - Human saliva carries 10 bacteria per milliliter, and can also transmit **Hepatitis B.**
   - Require **copious irrigation** and debridement, **usually left open and a bulky dressing is applied to decrease movement, prophylactic antibiotics.**

J. **Submersion injury**
   1. **Decompression Sickness/Arterial Gas Embolism**
      a. Inadequate decompression after exposure to increased pressure resulting in bubbles growing in tissue that causes local damage known as **"the bends;" body absorbs nitrogen during ascent**, if ascent is too quick the nitrogen forms bubbles.
      b. S/S: **SOB**, creptitus, numbless, tingling, diplopia, **petechial rash, seizures,** joint discomfort, pain.
      c. TX: oxygen administration, fluids, analgesia, **position patient on left side in trendelenberg, hyperbaric oxygen therapy,** heliox.

K. **Temperature-related emergencies**
   1. **Heat cramps** – sweat-induced electrolyte depletion causes muscle cramps. TX: with rest in a cool environment and **fluid/electrolyte replacement.**
   2. **Heat exhaustion** – prolonged exposure to heat leads to heat cramps, anorexia and vomiting, headache, syncope. TX: with rest in a cool environment and **fluid/electrolyte replacement.**
   3. **Heat Stroke** – young and elderly more vulnerable
      a. Medication risk: Thyroid meds, Haldol, antihistamines, anticholinergics.
      b. S/S: Core body temperature above 41 C (105.8 F) affects CNS and cardiac.
         - Tachycardia, tachypnea, hypotension, **hot dry skin, decreased level of consciousness.**
         - **Rhabdomyolysis** from muscle breakdown – dark brown urine.
      c. TX: - **Cool patient quickly** to 102 F

- Remove clothing, evaporation, not immersion. Cover with wet sheets & blow fans on patient. **Cool IV fluids, and correct electrolyte (sodium) imbalances.** Prevent shivering with benzodiazepines.
4. **Hypothermia Core body temp < 95F (35.3C) is mild; 33-35 is moderate; < 33 severe.**
    a. S/S: hypoventilation, altered mental status, shivering (mild), hypotension, cardiac dysrhythmias (**Osborn or J wave**), bradycardia (< 90 F) to V Fib with severe hypothermia).
    b. TX: Severe (< 33) – **active core rewarming** (warmed IVF's, heated humidified oxygen, warm peritoneal, gastric, or colonic lavage, hemodialysis). Rewarm core prior to periphery to **prevent rewarming shock** – may cause ventricular fibrillation.
    c. Passive external like warmed blankets for mild (< 36); active external with warming devices for moderate hypothermia.
5. **Frostbite**
    a. TX: **Pain medication and quickly rewarm** the affected part for 15 to 30 minutes in 40–42 °C (104–107 °F) water; avoid any friction or rubbing; **continue narcotics.**

L. **Vector-borne illnesses**
1. **Rabies** - Viral disease transmitted through the bite of an infected animal (**bats, raccoons, foxes**)
    i. S/S: **delirium, hallucinations, excessive salivation.**
    ii. TX: early, **aggressive wound management**; **infiltrate rabies immunoglobulin (RIG)** 20 U/kg in the wound if possible. **Rabies vaccine** given 1 mL IM (**deltoid in adult** or **vastus lateralis** in young children) on days 0, 3, 7, and 14 for those never vaccinated. **Vaccine provides active immunity.**
2. **Tick-borne** – remove tick with forceps, do not squeeze.
    a. **Lyme disease** (Borreliosis)
        1. S/S: non-pruritic, target-like, circular **bulls-eye rash;** flu-like symptoms (malaise and headache). TX: **antibiotics (doxycycline)**, risk if untreated: **facial paralysis, arthritis, and myocarditis.**
    b. Rocky Mountain Spotted Fever (Rickettsia) - S/S: non-pruritic, **non-blanching** macules on the **palms, wrists, forearms, soles, and ankles;** nausea & vomiting; fever and chills. TX: antibiotics (doxycycline).

M. **Communicable Infections**
1. **Measles (Rubeola)** – highly contagious; **incubation period of 8-12 days.**
    - S/S: **3 C's** – **c**onjunctivitis, **c**oryza (rhinitis), **c**ough; fever, eyelid edema; **Koplik spots** rash first– small specks on buccal mucosa (near molars "grains of salt"); maculopapular rash from **head** to trunk to lower extremities.
    - TX: supportive care, immunizations for patient's family/contacts.
2. **Mumps (Parotitis)** – contagious 16-18 days, swollen salivary glands leads to **puffy cheeks** and swollen jaw.
3. **Rubella (German or 3-day Measles)** – contagious up to a week prior to symptoms and a week after rash. Rash starts on face. Complication is birth defects and arthritis.
4. **Pertussis (Whooping cough)** – highly contagious, attaches to the respiratory tract and limits the child's ability to clear secretions. Incubation period of 7-10 days. Pertussis Stages
    - Catarrhal – coryza, sneezing, low-grade fever.
    - **Paroxysmal – unremitting paroxysmal bursts of coughing "whoop", petechial rash above nipple line from burst blood vessels.**
    - Convalescent – gradual recovery.
        o DX: Dacron swab in posterior nasopharynx.
    - TX: Supportive care, **macrolide antibiotics**, antitussives, antipyretics, treat family with antibiotics, pertussis vaccination.

5. **Chickenpox (Varicella)** – **virus becomes latent** after primary infection (may become shingles). Infectious for **48 hours** before rash appears, **contagious until all skin lesions are crusted over. Airborne precautions.**
    - S/S: purulent **vesicular rash starts on trunk,** fever, pruritus, **urticaria.**
    - TX: symptomatic care, antiviral agents, **antihistamines**, antipyretics
        - **NO aspirin containing products** should be administered since associated with **Reye's syndrome** (liver dysfunction – **increased ammonia**).
    - Prevention: varicella zoster vaccine
6. **Shingles** – reactivation of dormant varicella virus, lesions follow path of **nerve dermatomes.** S/S: pain develops first, followed by vesicular lesions (typically does not cross the body's midline), **severe nerve pain.** TX: Antivirals, **pain control** with analgesics, xylocaine patches, and nerve blocks. Prevention: varicella zoster vaccine.
7. **Diphtheria**
    - Incubation 1-8 days. S/S: Sore throat; low-grade fever; **thick, gray, membranous** (pseudo membrane) **covering on tonsils and pharynx.** Complications: **airway obstruction.** DX: throat culture and gram stain. TX: **Erythromycin** STAT, diphtheria antitoxin counteracts toxin produced by bacteria.
8. **Mononucleosis** – Epstein-Barr virus, spread by body fluids, especially saliva (Kissing Disease, college students).
    - S/S: fatigue, myalgia, **lymphadenopathy**, abdominal pain.
    - Complications: **splenomegaly - so watch for splenic rupture (avoid strenuous activities and return for LUQ and left shoulder pain),** hepatomegaly.
    - DX: **Monospot** (+ 2nd week of illness), CBC, LFTs.
    - TX: Analgesics; corticosteroids; warm salt gargles.
9. ***C. difficile*** – gram +, anaerobic, bacillus; **antibiotic-associated diarrhea.**
    - S/S: profuse, frequent diarrhea; abdominal cramping and pain; fever; loss of appetite; dehydration.
    - Standard and **contact isolation.** TX: **stop antibiotics**, IVFs, antiemetics, Metronidazole (Flagyl), fecal transplant for chronic infection.
10. **Multidrug-Resistant Organisms (contact isolation)**
    - MRSA "spider bite" – incision and drainage (I&D), treat with mycins or tetracycline.
    - VRE – remove source of infection. Consult infection control and wound care.
11. **Active Pulmonary Tuberculosis (TB)** – most TB infections are latent, 10% progress to active disease, pulmonary TB 90% of time, but sometimes spreads outside lungs.
    a. S/S: **chronic cough, night sweats, fever, chills,** hemoptysis, weight loss, anorexia, fatigue.
    b. DX: Chest x-ray, **sputum culture for acid-fast bacilli.**
    c. Isolation: standard and airborne precautions (**Negative pressure room STAT**)
    d. TX: **6 months** of combination antibiotic therapy – **rifampin, isoniazid.**
    e. DC teaching: **importance of medication compliance**, containment of respiratory secretions (zip lock bags), avoidance of close contact with others until medically cleared (work), **rifampin stains body fluids bright orange (no contacts).** Prevention: TB vaccine

**Professional Issues (14 items)**
1. **Caregiver Burnout**
    - Causes: significant deaths, chronic short staffing, violence.
    - **Recognize burnout** & post-traumatic stress **in yourself and others.**
    - **Take a Break:** self-reflection, self-monitoring, build resilience.
2. **Ethical Principles**
    - Autonomy – right to make one's own choices and have choices respected (DNR).
    - Beneficence – duty to help others, **care for unresponsive patient, report suspected abuse.**
    - Nonmalficence - duty to do no harm, report discharge of unstable patient.
    - Justice – to be fair and impartial, **treat all equally (alcoholics/addicts).**
    - Utilitarianism – benefit of the majority (disaster triage).
3. **Drug diversion** – Prevention is the key, train staff to "see something, say something." If you suspect a nurse is diverting drugs, report to supervisor first. Report to drug enforcement agency (DEA) if you witness a nurse tampering with controlled substances.
4. **Just culture – blame-free reporting** to increase reporting to uncover the source of the error.
5. **Discharge planning**
    - Keep instructions short and **concise**, immediately understandable.
    - Reinforce with **written** discharge instructions, in patient's language if non-English speaking. Review with family if illiterate, **explain to elderly due to decreased vision to read instructions**.
    - **Assess effectiveness of D/C teaching**.
        - Ask patient to **restate important details in their words,** ask questions?
        - **Return demonstration** (pulse checks, capillary refill, crutch-walking, peak flow, inhaler, NTG, safe sex practices, miscarriage instructions).
6. **End of life issues**
    - **Organ and tissue donation**
        - Determination of death – irreversible cessation of circulatory and respiratory function or brain death.
        - Notification of the local organ procurement organization **as soon as potential candidate identified**. HIV positive cannot donate.
        - **Corneal donation** – elevate head 20-30 degrees, instill artificial tears and **tape eyelids shut with paper tape**, **apply ice over eyes**.
        - Post-Transplant Emergencies – Risk of rejection.
7. **Advance directives**
    - Written guide detailing a patient's wishes; prepared when a patient is competent; **enacted when the patient loses decision-making capacity.**
    - **Living Will - a**llows an individual to declare what treatments an individual does and does not want; applies only to terminal illness or a vegetative state.
    - Durable **power of attorney for health care** - designates a **surrogate decision maker** when an individual is unable to make their own decisions.
    - **Physician orders for life-sustaining treatment (DNR) -** may limit CPR or intubation but **does not withhold comfort** measures such as pain relief or oxygen.
8. **Palliative care -** To alleviate physical, psychological, emotional, and spiritual suffering and to promote quality end of life (for patient and family).
9. **Family presence**
    - Gives closure, reduces questioning of events and care, obtain patient history.
    - Decreases shock and anger.

- Death notification (Delivering bad news)
    - Physician and nurse (never deliver bad news alone).
    - Sit down and **ascertain the family's knowledge** of the event (they may already know).
    - Use simple, clear terms; **use the words died or dead.**
    - Give the family the opportunity family to see patient, **encouraging them to touch and talk to their loved one.**
- Postmortem care
    - Leave tubes in place for **coroner cases** and circle unsuccessful IV stick sites too.
    - Be sensitive to family needs (female, allow washing of body and prayer).

10. **Forensic evidence collection**
    - Use "quotation marks", **document statements verbatim.**
    - Avoid judgement, document **facts** only.
    - **Do NOT cut through any clothing tears, rips, holes, or stains.**
    - Place all evidence in **paper bags** or cardboard boxes, do NOT use plastic (mold).
    - Double fold the bag and tape across, **do not staple.**
    - Place **paper bags over patient's hands** if suspected of recently discharging a firing arm (gunshot residue).
    - Do not remove bullet with metal instrumentation, **use gloved fingers or rubber-tip hemostats.**
    - Do **not label wounds** as entrance and exit wounds; **label as wound 1 and wound 2.**
    - **Chain of custody** - Court evidence must be accompanied by documentation that **demonstrates the item's location and responsible party** to prove integrity of evidence.

11. **Pain management and procedural sedation**
    - Pain must be accurately assessed using an **appropriate pain scale.**
        1. N-PASS or NIPS for neonates.
        2. **FLACC for children up to 7 (can be used for adults) since they cannot correlate a number or face to pain.** Faces, Legs, Activity, Cry, Consolability.
        3. Numeric scale for acute pain in children > 7 and adults.
        4. PAIN-AD for dementia.
    - TX: local (xylocaine), systemic, non-opioid (Acetaminophen and Ibuprofen), and opioid; **adjuvant medications** (antiemetics, antidepressants, corticosteroids).
    - Nonpharmacological interventions: position of comfort, **distraction (TV, cell phone**, IPADS) relaxation (deep breathing), aromatherapy, music, pets.
    - **Procedural Sedation**
        1. Used for minor procedures not requiring general anesthesia.
        2. Trained staff and appropriate equipment available, constant monitoring.
        3. **Reversal agents** readily available
            a. Naloxone (Narcan) – **opioid antagonist** for reversal of opiates (half-life of Narcan shorter than most opiates). **Flumazenil** (Romazicon) – reversal of benzodiazepines (use caution when administering to patients with a known dependence of benzodiazepines).
        4. Post procedure criteria: awake, able to ambulate, able to swallow, vital signs within range of normal/baseline vitals.

12. **Patient and Staff Safety**
    - **Promote a culture of safety, avoid a culture of blame, report near misses.**
    - Technology of safety - EMR, order entry, smart pumps, barcode-enabled point of care, standardized order sets.

- Pediatric medication errors - **weight based errors (Kg)**, limit dose strengths available.
- **Violence in the Emergency Department**
    - Causes: Long waiting times, overcrowding, staff shortages, behavioral health disorders, drug use, and alcohol use. Be alert for potential violence – pacing, getting louder. Be aware of environment, **all staff trained in crisis intervention**, controlled access doors, panic buttons.
13. **Transfer and stabilization**
    A. The **transferring facility is responsible** for determining the best mode of transport, equipment needed in route, and qualified personnel based on patients' needs.
    B. Consider access, time, distance, weather, special needs.
    C. Ground may take longer but allows for **more room.**
    D. **Rotor-wing** (helicopter) allows **rapid point to point transfer**, but **cabin not pressurized** and small (air expands, vibration).
    E. **Fixed wing** (airplane) is pressurized and can fly in inclement weather.
    F. Considerations prior to transport
        - **Decompress the stomach** with a gastric tube prior to rotor wing transport to decrease risk of aspiration.
        - Assure patent **intravenous sites** (a minimum of two are preferred).
        - Consider an indwelling urinary catheter for longer trips.
        - **Air splints will expand and are NOT appropriate** for rotor-wing, use regular splint.
        - **May place chest tubes for smaller pneumothorax if rotor-wing.**
14. **Cultural considerations/ Interpretive services** - Use **hospital approved translation services**; do not use family members unless true emergency.

- **System**
    1. Delegation of tasks to unlicensed personnel – **nurse retains accountability. Do not delegate assessment.**
    2. Patient leaving AMA – assess and document **mental competence.** Can leave if competent and not in abusive environment.
    3. False imprisonment – keeping a mentally competent person against their will.
    4. **Professional Negligence -** 4 elements must be present to establish malpractice.
        - Duty - the nurse has a duty to perform care.
        - Breach of duty - the person failed to complete/ adequately complete the duty.
        - Proximate Causation – the breach caused damage (physical, emotional, psychological, or social).
        - Damages - damages exist.
    5. **Handoffs** – safe transition of care, use a **standardized tool** like (SBAR).
        - Communicate chief complaint, results of testing, care provided and response to care, diagnosis, **care remaining to be completed.**
        - **Bedside reporting** increases safety.
    6. **HIPAA -** Health Insurance Portability & Accountability Act (HIPAA)
        A. Enacted to prevent/ limit access to personal health information.
        B. Facilities are required to secure electronic medical records.
        C. Sharing of patient history **can only occur with patient's consent. Do not leave chart open so others can see.**
        D. Do not access charts of patients **when you are not involved** in their care.
        E. Assures patients will have access to their personal medical records (with the option to amend them).
    7. **EMTALA**
        A. **Congress-enacted National Law** - Consolidated Omnibus Budget Reconciliation Act (COBRA) and Emergency Treatment and Active Labor Act (EMTALA) are meant to **protect patients from**

"dumping" practices in which hospitals transferred patients based on their ability or lack of ability to pay.
- B. COBRA applies to any patient "who comes to the emergency department requesting examination or treatment for a medical condition". These patients must be provided with a **medical screening exam** performed by a "qualified medical provider".
- C. If a patient is **to be transferred**, the following must be secured in advance:
- D. The patient has been **stabilized** to the extent possible by the transferring facility. A **receiving hospital must be secured**. The receiving hospital must have the following: the services and capacity to care for the patient. Have an **accepting physician** qualified to care for the patient.
- E. The patient and/or legal representatives for the patient **must be notified** by the transferring physician of the risks and benefits of transfer and must have signed a certification that the benefits outweigh the risks (the transferring physician must certify that the benefits of transfer outweigh the risks). **This certification must accompany the patient on the transfer.**
- F. The transferring hospital must send appropriate medical records, reports, and consultation records (or copies) with the patient. The **transferring facility must arrange appropriate transportation** with adequate life support equipment and assure trained personnel are on board suitable for the patient's condition.

8. **Patient consent**
   - A. **Implied** – allows appropriate treatment in an emergency, as in unresponsive patient.
   - B. Express – agreement to treatment, signs paperwork.
   - C. Informed – patient understands **risks and benefits** of the proposed treatment, is not under the influence, and has **legal capacity** to make the decision.
   - D. Involuntary – ensuring needed treatment when an individual refuse care, i.e., suicidal, delusional, dementia.
   - E. Federal consent allows treatment of minor who is pregnant, has STI, requesting rehabilitation, suicidal.

9. **Symptom surveillance of a biologic** – be aware of **clusters of symptoms** in triage, isolation precautions, report symptoms to public health authorities.
   - **Ricin** – made from castor bean; latent 8 hours, then flu-like symptoms.
   - **Anthrax** – Black eschar with cutaneous anthrax (infected animal hides).
   - **Viral hemorrhagic fever (Ebola)** – fever, petechiae, bleeding. Most arise in Africa, so inquire about travel.
   - **Nerve agents** – Sarin or VX gas. Decontaminate, **Atropine** until bronchial secretions dry, 2-PAM, benzodiazepine.
   - **Botulism** – Ptosis, flaccid paralysis, blurred vision.

10. **Triage**
    - Use ESI triage and ABCD for prioritization questions. Free to download at ENA.org under education.
    - **Level 1** – requires **life-saving interventions** immediately (overdose with respiratory rate of 8, unresponsive with blood sugar of 20, cardiac or respiratory arrest, trauma requiring fluid/blood).
    - **Level 2** – **high-risk situation** (pulmonary embolus risk, suicidal patient, victim of assault, sickle cell crisis, testicular torsion).
    - Levels 3-5 based on resources.

11. **Disaster Triage**
    - **START Triage** based on ambulation "Green", then RPM 30-2-can do (respiration between 10-30, perfusion of capillary refill < 2 seconds, mental status follows commands. Priority is to determine **"Red"** and get them treated ASAP. "Yellow" are delayed. "Black" are expectant to die.
    - **JumpSTART** is pediatric disaster triage. Give child 5 positive-pressure breaths before moving to "Black" tarp.

- **Decontamination** – patient flow is opposite of wind direction. HazMat gear in hot zone to provide life-saving treatment only. Decontamination occurs in warm zone. Care in "Cold" zone.

12. **Disaster Management Phases**
    1. **Mitigation** – to prevent or minimize potentially adverse effects (Hazard Vulnerability Assessment).
    2. **Preparedness** – Emergency training (NIMS, HICS), mutual aid agreements, stockpile supplies.
    3. **Response** – Evacuation, shelter, disaster triage (START, jump START).
    4. **Recovery** – Restoring systems, replenish supplies, dispose of waste, CISM.

13. **Abuse**
    a. **Neglect – failure to provide basic needs** - medical, physical, and/or educational. Physical – intentional injury (maltreatment). Sexual - inappropriate sexual contact. Emotional – mental anguish. Financial – mostly seen with **developmentally disabled** and **elderly** who require caregivers.
    b. **Physiologic mimics of abuse** - Cultural practices – cupping and coining; coagulation disorders; Mongolian spots (dark spots); Osteogenesis imperfecta "brittle bone".
    c. **History (High Index of Suspicion)**
        - Does the story match the injury/illness? **Description conflicting or improbable**? Answers vague? Delay in seeking treatment or bypass of closer ED?
        - Tension between caregivers? Caregiver demanding? **Describes patient as clumsy or accident-prone.** Refuses to leave patient alone with providers.
    d. **Signs/Symptoms of Pediatric Abuse – Priority is SAFETY.**
        - **Fractures** in various stages of healing, in a child < 3 year of age, or fingers in non-mobile child.
        - **Burns** bilateral with **lines of demarcation** "sock-like".
        - **Bruises in various stages of healing**, shape of identifiable object, human bite marks.
        - **Triad** of subdural hematoma, rib (posterior) fractures, and retinal hemorrhages **- probable shaken impact syndrome** (shaken infant).
    e. **Interview/Documentation of abuse and contact child protective services.**
        - Interview multiple caregivers separately.
        - Watch interactions between caregivers and patient.
        - Be nonjudgmental/nonaccusatory.
        - Document statements **verbatim** in "quotation marks".
        - Use body diagrams to document injuries.
        - Use medical terms, **NOT legal terms** like alleged.
    f. **Fabricated Illness**
        - Adult caregiver (typically Mother) fabricates or creates child's illness.
        - Illness is unexplained, extremely rare, recurrent, unresponsive to treatment, or occurs only when caregiver present. Caregiver overly knowledgeable about the illness, uses medical terms, overly interactive with providers. Caregiver not concerned about painful procedures for child (requests an LP).
        - Believes ill child will improve relationship with partner, **gains attention.**

14. **Human trafficking**
    a. Person accompanying has all identification documents, refuses to leave patient, and answers all questions.
    b. Patient is fearful, has signs of abuse, and possible tattoos of numbers, bar codes, or dollar signs.

15. **Gender equity**
    a. Sexual assignment at birth based on external genitalia.
    b. Gender identity is internal sense of gender.
    c. Transgender patient identifies with gender other than one assigned at birth. Ask what pronoun the patient would like to be referred to by and note it in the medical record.

# PDB Nurse Education, LLC CEN References

1. American Heart Association, Manual of Advanced Life Support (ACLS), 2020.
2. American Heart Association, Manual of Pediatric Advanced Life Support (PALS), 2020.
3. Emergency Nurses Association (ENA). *CEN Review Manual,* 5th ed., Jones & Bartlett Learning, 2020.
4. Emergency Nurses Association (ENA). *Emergency Nursing Pediatric Course,* 5th ed., Jones & Bartlett Learning, 2020.
5. Emergency Nurses Association (ENA). Sheehy, S. *Sheehy's Emergency Nursing: Principles and Practice*, 7th ed. Elsevier, 2020.
6. Emergency Nurses Association (ENA). *Trauma Nursing Core Curriculum,* 8th ed., 2019.

*This Study Guide is registered with the Board of Certification for Emergency Nursing (BCEN®); however, they do not endorse any resource or have a proprietary relationship with any publishing company.*

# PDB Nurse Education, LLC CEN Key Points

## Cardiovascular Emergencies (19 Items)

1. Preload is volume measured by CVP (right atrial pressure), Afterload is pressure measured by SVR (systemic vascular resistance). **Afterload is low only in distributive shock**. Volume increases preload, **diuretics (Lasix) decrease preload**. NTG and Nipride decrease afterload. Vasopressors increase afterload.
2. Vasopressor extravasation – **Phentolamine (Regitine)**.
3. Identify rhythms strips – possibly one of **AV heart blocks**, Atrial Fibrillation (risk of stroke), **Ventricular Pacemaker with failure to capture**, Ventricular Tachycardia.
4. Treatment of Ventricular Tachycardia –If pulse, but unstable - **synchronize cardioversion** on R wave (Peds wattage 0.5-1 j/kg). **If stable – Adenosine for monomorphic**, then choice of Amiodarone, Sotalol, or Procainamide. If pulseless VT- BLS and defibrillation at 120-200 joules (Peds start at 2-4 j/kg).
5. Cardiac arrest – Get $ETCO_2$ > 10 in quality BLS. Point of care ultrasound (POCUS) to assess H & T's, epinephrine 1 mg, amiodarone 300 mg, Lidocaine 1 – 1.5 mg/kg, Sodium bicarbonate 1 mEq/kg.
6. Symptomatic bradycardia – Try atropine 1.0 mg, then try transcutaneous pacing – set rate at 60-80 & turn up milliamps until capture (Do not assess carotid pulse). Next, Dopamine or Epinephrine infusion.
7. No Atropine needed for **transplanted heart, treat with Isoproterenol (Isuprel)** instead.
8. **Wolff-Parkinson-White (WPW)** is an accessory pathway disorder – Delta wave = short PR interval, wide QRS on upstroke of QRS, WPW risk - tachycardia.
9. **R on T phenomenon** (PVC) occurs when an electrical impulse (R) is to too close to the resting phase of the ventricle (T), leading to **ventricular tachycardia** or ventricular fibrillation.
10. **Prolonged QTi** from medication (Erythromycin, **Haldol**, TCA's, etc.) or **hypomagnesemia/hypocalcemia**. (Not all-inclusive list)
11. ST segment elevation in leads **II, III, AVF - Inferior MI (right coronary artery)**; V1-V4 - Anterior MI **(LAD artery)**; and **Leads I, AVL, V5 & V6 in Lateral MI** (circumflex).
12. **Inferior MI** (II, III, aVF) – epigastric pain, **bradycardia, hypotension**, heart block; **get right side ECG to look at V4R.**
13. **Right Ventricular MI** – V4R at 5th intercoastal space, right MCL; cautious with preload-reducing agents like NTG and morphine, give IVF 250 cc bolus or **Dobutamine (Dobutrex) for hypotension (positive inotrope increases contractility). Treatment plan effective if BP increasing**.
14. **Anterior MI** (V1-V4) – **crushing chest pain, dyspnea**, ventricular dysrhythmias, cardiogenic shock (crackles, S3). Difficult to detect in left BBB. TX: NTG (caution with phosphodiesterase inhibitors).
15. **Reperfusion dysrhythmias (AIVR**, V Tach) common with fibrinolysis (TPA).

16. **Hypertensive crisis** –Mean arterial pressure (MAP) is equal to [(2x DBP) + SBP] divided by 3. **Decrease MAP by 20-25% over 1-2 hours** with Nipride (preload and afterload reducer – protect from light). Consider arterial line, do Allen's test for radial arterial line.
17. Dissecting **Aortic Aneurysm** – **BP difference of 20 mm Hg** between arms, **ripping or tearing chest pain into back**, pulsatile mass, lower extremity weakness with **decreased peripheral pulses** with AAA. Increased risk if **Marfan's** and Ehrler Danlos. TX: IV x 2, IVF's/blood, **lower HR to 60-80 and lower BP to 100-120 mm Hg with beta-blocker.**
18. **Traumatic aortic dissection** at ligamentum arteriosum **seen with 1st and 2nd rib fractures – widened mediastinum** and obscured aortic knob seen on chest x-ray.
19. **Blunt cardiac injury** – cardiac contusion injuries the right ventricle so **ST with PVC's**. Monitor cardiac rhythm and get an echocardiogram.
20. **Pericardial (Cardiac) Tamponade** – Muffled heart tones, JVD, hypotension = **Beck's Triad**; also see **pulsus paradoxus** and electrical alternans. Assist with pericardiocentesis left xyphoid process. Patient better if BP increasing.
21. **Pericarditis** – Pleuritic **retrosternal chest pain**, worse with inspiration and supine position. **Global (diffuse, widespread) concave ST segment elevation** on ECG. Friction rub heard best at left sternal border with diaphragm. Treat with **NSAIDs** and allow to lean forward. **Steroids** if refractory to NSAIDs.
22. **Endocarditis** – **IV drug abuser**, tattoo, piercing. Fever, pleuritic pain, **new onset murmur,** Janeway lesions, Roth spots. May see JVD if tricuspid valve. Treat with **antibiotics** STAT.
23. **Left heart failure** (lungs) – S3 heart sound, nocturnal dyspnea, and pulmonary edema; treat with loop **diuretics (venodilator Lasix), NTG, NIPPV.**
24. **Right heart failure** (rest of body) from **Cor pulmonale** (COPD, pulmonary HTN) - **JVD**, ascites, and peripheral edema.
25. LVAD – get manual BP with Doppler to hear MAP, **keep MAP 70-90**, contact LVAD coordinator.
26. AICD not firing in VF – defibrillate patient.
27. Peripheral venous insufficiency - **intermittent claudication** calf pain, red, hot, and swollen. Risk of **DVT**, which may lead to pulmonary embolus.
28. Arterial clot (popliteal artery most common)– S/S: pain at rest, pale, cyanotic, cold. **DX: ankle brachial index**, normal 0.9-1.2, severe if < 0.5. TX: embolectomy.
29. **Hypovolemic hemorrhagic shock** – hold direct pressure to site, replace blood loss with MTP blood products at 1:1:1. Beta-blocker's mask early signs of hypovolemic shock like tachycardia and diaphoresis. Allow permissive hypotension in abdominal trauma and pelvic fracture.
30. Cardiogenic shock is left ventricular function, seen post anterior MI. TX: Decrease preload and afterload, increase contractility.
31. **Obstructive shock is cardiac tamponade, tension pneumothorax**, abdominal compartment syndrome, supine vena cava syndrome. TX: Relieve the obstruction with needle decompression, pericardiocentesis, etc.
32. **Pediatrics cardiovascular**
    a. Hypotension is a late sign of shock (30% blood loss) in pediatric patients.
    b. Minimum SBP - [70 + (2 x age)] up to age 10.
    c. Bradycardia is an ominous sign in pediatrics. **Hypoxemia is most common cause** of pediatric arrest.
    d. **Defib 2-4 joules/kg first shock**, up to 10 j/kg. Cardioversion 0.5-1.0 joules/kg, up to 2 j/kg.
    e. **Replace volume at 20 ml/kg boluses of isotonic crystalloid,** 10 ml/kg of packed cells.

## Respiratory Emergencies (18 Items)

1. Tracheal intubation/mechanical ventilation – listen for placement over **epigastrium first**, then lung fields. Assess by **ETCO₂ capnography (35-45 mm Hg is normal)**. Use DOPE (displaced, obstructed, pneumothorax, equipment failure) if patient deteriorates.
2. **No succinylcholine** (Anectine) if history of **malignant hyperthermia**, penetrating eye injury, increased ICP, conditions that precipitate hyperkalemia (72 hours post burn, crush injury, renal failure).
3. **ABG interpretation** based on pH (nl 7.35-7.45), CO₂ (nl 35-45), Bicarb (nl 22-26). CO₂ = Respiratory component, Bicarb = Metabolic component. Low pH = acidosis. High pH = alkalosis.
    a. Metabolic acidosis – **DKA**, diarrhea, **shock, alcoholic ketoacidosis** (ethylene glycol ingestion).
    b. Metabolic alkalosis – vomiting.
    c. Respiratory acidosis – hypoventilation, **compensated respiratory acidosis in COPD**.
    d. Respiratory alkalosis – hyperventilation, pulmonary embolus.
4. Patient hyperventilating – Priority is to assess for **pulmonary embolus**, head injury with increased ICP, toxicological ingestions (Methanol, Ethylene Glycol), or **DKA from compensation**.
5. **Pulmonary embolus** risk "Virchow's" Triad, most from **DVT**'s. Dyspnea and tachypnea lead to **respiratory alkalosis**. Common S/S are tachycardia and **tachypnea**, with **sense of impending doom**; accentuated S2 heart sound. DX with spiral CT, pulmonary angiography, and elevated d-dimer. Massive PE is obstructive shock.
6. **Active pulmonary tuberculosis** (TB) – S/S: **hemoptysis**, fever, chills, and night sweats. **Negative pressure room is priority since airborne and droplet precautions**, surgical mask on patient when outside room. TX: **Isoniazid** (INH) contraindicated with Dilantin. **Rifampin** stains body fluids orange.
7. **Croup** (LTB) – Upper airway obstruction, stridor, **seal-like cough**, low-grade fever, **steeple sign** on chest x-ray. TX: **Racemic epinephrine** and humidification.
8. **Epiglottitis** – **Drooling**, tripod position, **thumb print sign** on lateral neck x-ray. Bacterial (**HIB**) infection, so high fever, **priority is airway**. Let caregiver hold, do not start IV or draw blood. "If they cry, they die!"
9. **Bronchiolitis (RSV)** – Infant with runny nose, cough, and fever. Teach caregivers how to **suction nares** and good hand washing.
10. Acute bronchitis – nonproductive, dry cough. No antibiotics required.
11. **Asthma** – dyspnea, tachypnea, **expiratory wheezing**; treat with short-acting **bronchodilators** (SABAs) like albuterol. Perform **peak flow before and after** each nebulizer. **Discharge education** on peak flow meter and understanding inhalers, spacers, and nebulizers.
12. **COPD** – Emphysema "Pink Puffer", increased AP diameter. Bronchitis "Blue Bloater" - secondary polycythemia, prone to clots. **Low levels of oxygen only** or decrease respiratory drive. Encourage pneumonia and influenza vaccines.
13. **Pleural effusion** – Prepare for thoracentesis to remove fluid or pus (empyema).
14. **Spontaneous pneumothorax** – increased risk with smoking, **Marfan's** and COPD. S/S: tachypnea, and decreased breath sounds and **hyperresonance** on affected side. Apply oxygen, insert chest tube, improved if decreased respiratory rate and effort to breathe.
15. **Hemothorax** – Massive blood loss so transfuse and consider **autotransfusion** in blunt injury. Autotransfusion: all blood products, warmer, no risk of reaction or disease transmission.
16. **Tension pneumothorax** – dyspnea, absent or reduced breath sounds on injured side, **tracheal shift away from injured side**. Emergency treatment is **needle decompression** mid-clavicular line of affected side, then insert small chest tube.
17. **Rib fractures** – Fractures of 1-2 – suspect aortic disruption, 4-9 – pulmonary contusion and blunt cardiac injury, 9-12 – liver if right side, spleen if left. **Rib fractures are painful** – xylocaine patches, nerve blocks.
18. Inhalation injury – immediate intubation if **carbonaceous sputum and stridor**. Monitor for **carbon monoxide poisoning** – get **COHb** level, apply **100% high-flow oxygen**.

19. **Tracheobronchial injury** – clothes-line type blunt injury, **SQ emphysema**, dyspnea, tachypnea; prepare for fiberoptic bronchoscopy so you do not tear trachea during intubation. Laryngeal – dysphonia.
20. **Open pneumothorax** - cover open chest wound with **occlusive dressing taped on 3 sides at end-exhalation**, so ask patient to exhale prior to application. Take dressing off if patient deteriorates, risk of **causing a tension pneumothorax**.
21. Pulmonary contusion – judicious use of IVFs to decrease risk of ARDS.
22. ARDS – shunt defect leads to **refractory hypoxemia**. Mechanical ventilation and prone position.

## Neurological Emergencies (18 Items)

1. **Cluster headache** – **lacrimation (excessive tearing)**. Treat with oxygen.
2. Migraines – **Unilateral, pulsating headache** with sensitivity to light and sound. **Ask the patient to journal to find triggers to avoid,** requires lifestyle changes. Propranolol may be used to prevent migraines. If using Depakote, female must be on BCP, risk of birth defects.
3. **Temporal arteritis** – severe stabbing pain in temporal area, **palpable cord-like artery**. Treat with **steroids**.
4. **Ischemic stroke** – Get "last time well" and FAST exam in triage, NIH Stroke scale (**https://www.stroke.nih.gov/resources/scale.htm**) for assessment. TX: of ischemic stroke – **r-TPA at 0.9 mg/kg, 10% bolus**, rest over 1 hour; peripheral within 4.5 hours on onset of symptoms. **Monitor LOC during fibrinolytic infusion and stop if decreased LOC**. Know exclusion criteria. (Bleeding diathesis – **low platelets**). Antihypertensives such as labetalol to lower **BP <185/110** only.
5. **Meningitis** – fever and neck stiff (**nuchal rigidity**), Kernig's and Brudzinski's sign (bend chin to chest and legs bend). Irritability and inconsolability in infants with arched back. **Glucose low in CSF if bacterial**. If scenario has purpuric, non-blanching **rash – isolation is priority**.
6. **Seizures** – (bicycling movement in infant), check **blood sugar and sodium**. No alcohol if on Keppra for seizures (lowers seizure threshold). **Benzodiazepines are the priority to stop the seizure**. Dilantin mixed in NS only, slow or stop infusion if cardiac dysrhythmias or hypotension.
7. **Epidural Hematoma (EDH)** – Hit to temporal brain, **middle meningeal arterial bleed** so rapid bleed. **Classic presentation**: unresponsive, **period of lucidity**, then secondary unresponsiveness. Uncal herniation - **ipsilateral pupil dilation**.
8. **Subdural Hematoma (SDH)** – **Venous** bleed, so **steady decline in LOC**, fixed and dilated pupil. 3 scenarios – infant from **shaken impact syndrome**, alcoholic, and elderly on anticoagulant.
9. Subarachnoid hemorrhage (SAH) – "Worst HA of my life" or explosive headache. TX: with **calcium-channel blockers** for aneurysm rupture vasospasm, no steroids needed.
10. **Basilar skull fracture** – Raccoon's eyes (periorbital ecchymosis), Battle's sign (mastoid ecchymosis), CSF (rhinorrhea, otorrhea), bizarre behavior – halo sign (bloody drainage) or glucose testing (clear drainage). **Do not pack nose let it drain, just sterile nasal drip pad**. Complication is infection.
11. Normal ICP = <15, increased ICP if sustained over 20 mm Hg. Early sign of increased ICP – restlessness. TX: Keep head in neutral position and **head of bed up at least 30 degrees**. Reduce stimulus, limit visitors, remove cervical collar. **Mannitol** (osmotic diuretic) effective if increased urine output and improving LOC. Monitor for **hyponatremia and low serum osmolality**.
12. Later signs of increasing ICP – **"Cushing's Triad"** – Increased systolic BP with decreasing diastolic BP **(widened pulse pressure)**, profound bradycardia, altered respiratory pattern (Cheyne-Stokes).
13. **Concussion** patient – DC instructions – acetaminophen only for pain, no narcotics or NSAIDs; **cognitive rest** (no electronics); **medical clearance and graduated return to play** for sports to prevent secondary impact syndrome.
14. Fall onto feet – calcaneus fracture plus **axial loading** compression injury to spine, so x-ray spine too.
15. Use NEXUS (neuro deficit, spinal tenderness, alcohol, distracting injury) criteria for spinal immobilization.
16. Get **MRI if suspected SCIWORA** (spinal cord injury without radiographic abnormality) in child.
17. **Incomplete spinal cord injury** (will have sacral sparing)

a. **Brown-Sequard** is a transverse (lateral) hemisection from **penetrating injury** – loss of motor function on side of injury(ipsilateral). Great rehabilitation potential.
   b. Anterior - loss of motor function but retains proprioception, so like complete transection. Poor prognosis for rehabilitation.
   c. **Central cord – more weakness in arms than legs**. Scenario of alcoholic or older adult, so extensive rehabilitation.
18. **Neurogenic shock** – Loss of SNS stimulation leads to profound **bradycardia**, hypotension, **skin warm and dry** below level of injury, **priapism**, poikilothermy. Augment vascular **tone with fluids, vasopressors (Norepinephrine), and inotropes (Dopamine).** (Increased ICP has increasing SBP).
19. Autonomic Dysreflexia – Severe HTN, blurred vision, nasal congestion. **Treat by relieving trigger** (impaction, full bladder, infection) and BP control.
20. **Guillain-Barre – classic sign is ascending symmetrical paralysis** after viral illness and tingling in extremities. **Monitor respiratory effort** due to diaphragm paralysis.
21. Myasthenia gravis - Ptosis – perform **Tensilon** test. Have Atropine at bedside in case of cholinergic crisis.
22. **Thiamine** prior to dextrose in malnourished to prevent **Wernicke's encephalopathy**.


### Gastrointestinal Emergencies (18 Items with GU, GYN, OB)

1. Rehydrate pediatric patient with mild gastroenteritis with **small sips (3-5 ml) of oral pediatric rehydration fluid frequently. Infuse 20 ml/kg isotonic crystalloid IV boluses over 5-10 minutes** for severe dehydration/shock.
2. **Appendicitis** – Periumbilical to **right lower quadrant** abdominal pain (**McBurney's point**) with rebound tenderness (**Rovsing's sign**), nausea, anorexia. Start assessment on LUQ. Keep NPO.
3. **Cholecystitis** – RUQ pain after fatty meal radiating to right shoulder, **costal margin tenderness (Murphy's sign)**. Increased risk in 5 F's (fat forty female), post bariatric surgery patients, and postpartum.
4. **Pancreatitis** – sudden, sharp **epigastric pain radiating to back. Amylase (early) and lipase (most specific) elevated, calcium decreased. Complication: exudative pleural effusion** to ARDS, so monitor breathing effectiveness.
5. **Diverticulitis** – from low fiber diet. LLQ pain from large intestine; alternating diarrhea and constipation; TX: bowel rest initially, then **increase fiber and water** in diet to prevent exacerbations.
6. **Hepatitis** – Vowels (A and E) from the bowels (fecal-oral route) – fluid resuscitation (Missionary trip scenario) – **teach handwashing.** Hepatitis B from body fluids (sexually transmitted or IV drug abuser). C from circulation (blood). **Vaccine for A, B.** No vaccine for Hepatitis C. S/S: **jaundice**, tiredness. TX: for chronic – Interferon.
7. **Liver failure/Cirrhosis** – elevated **LFT's and direct bilirubin**, jaundice (icterus eyes), ascites, asterixis, spider angiomas. **Risk of GI bleed from portal HTN and esophageal varices, administer Octreotide (Sandostatin) or vasopressin. Lactulose for elevated ammonia** levels due to hepatic encephalopathy. Treatment effective if increase in LOC and decreased ammonia levels.
8. Bowel obstructions early S/S is **hyperactive high-pitched bowel sounds** - Small Bowel obstruction – **fecal vomiting**, with minimal distention. Large Bowel obstruction – gross distention. Patient is in **hypovolemic shock**.
9. Mesenteric infarction – severe abdominal pain, but abdomen soft, history of atrial fibrillation.
10. **Intussusception** (telescoping of bowel) – infant inconsolable, drawing up legs, then periods of decreased LOC. Vomiting, and may palpate sausage-shaped mass and see **currant-jelly** (red mucus) stool. **Air or barium enema if stable**, or surgical repair.
11. **Pyloric Stenosis – non-bilious projectile vomiting** and continual hunger, olive-shaped mass, requires dilation of pylorus.
12. **Volvulus** – malrotation **requires immediate surgery**.

13. **FAST exam first** to diagnose abdominal injury (spleen and liver), next CT of abdomen.
14. **Liver injury** – Suspect with right lower rib fractures, RUQ pain, **Cullen's sign** (ecchymosis of umbilicus). Prepare for massive transfusion protocol (MTP) and damage control surgery.
15. **Splenic injury** – Suspect with left lower rib fractures. LUQ pain to left shoulder (**Kehr's sign**). Encapsulated, so may see hours after injury. Manage nonoperatively is goal.
16. **Ruptured diaphragm** – Peristaltic gurgling sounds audible in the left lower to mid chest, **progressive scaphoid abdomen**. Requires immediate surgical repair (laparotomy).
17. **Duodenal (hollow organ) injury** and **Chance fracture** (T12-L2) seen more in children from **lap restraint injury** – Prepare for OR due to contamination.


## Genitourinary, Gynecology, Obstetrical Emergencies

1. Renal injury – **monitor urine output**. Suspect ruptured bladder if **urge to urinate** but inability to void, esp. with pelvic fracture.
2. Suspect urethral trauma (frequently with pelvic FX) if **blood at urinary meatus – no urinary catheter or cause more damage**. Obtain a retrograde urethrogram.
3. **Testicular Torsion** – sudden onset of severe **inguinal pain** and nausea; lack of cremasteric reflex; worsens with elevation and ice. **Triage as level 2 urological emergency**, get **Doppler US** that shows decreased blood flow. Prepare for emergency surgery.
4. Epididymitis – urinary frequency and urgency, urethral discharge (**Chlamydia**). Pain relieved with elevation and ice. D/C teaching on **safe sex practices using condoms, treat partners**.
5. Pyelonephritis – costovertebral angle (CVA) flank tenderness with pyuria, **admit if pregnant**.
6. **Vaginal discharge**
    a. BV and Trichomonas – fishy-smelling, treat with **Flagyl (no alcohol intake)**.
    b. Candida – **cottage cheese-like discharge and pruritis**, treat with nystatin or Diflucan.
    c. Chlamydia – mucopurulent – treat with **Doxycycline (sunburn risk)** or azithromycin.
    d. Gonorrhea – Ceftriaxone
    e. D/C instructions on signs of **worsening infection – may be PID** (increases ectopic pregnancy risk). Clindamycin cream weakens condoms, so use other form of birth control.
7. **Herpes** – painful blisters, **Acyclovir (Valtrex) does not cure**, just reduces flare-ups.
8. **Syphilis** – Serology testing VDRL and RPR. Treat with penicillin.
9. **Sexual assault** – ESI triage level 2, priority is to **treat major injuries and keep patient safe**. Evidence-collection focuses on keeping evidence in **paper bags** (plastic molds, degrading DNA). Never leave kit unattended. Morning after pill – side effect is nausea.
10. Fetal Heart tones normal 120-160 beats per minute. First sign of distress is fetal tachycardia and loss of variability.
11. Threatened abortion (miscarriage) – vaginal OS is closed. Bedrest 1-2 days except bathroom, nothing in vagina. Inevitable abortion – prepare for D&C surgery.
12. **Pregnancy-induced HTN (Gestational HTN)** – HTN, proteinuria, HA, diplopia, and edema. Treat with **magnesium sulfate** to decrease seizure threshold and HTN, and position patient on left side. **Risk of HELLP syndrome – pain in RUQ**.
13. Eclampsia – **seizures, treat with benzodiazepines**. Monitor for **respiratory depression** while on Magnesium infusion. Calcium gluconate is antidote.
14. **Ectopic Pregnancy** – abdominal pain referred to shoulder, **orthostatic hypotension**, more common with history of PID. Methotrexate IM.
15. **Placenta Previa** – Painless, bright-red bleeding. Position on side, no pelvic exam until US.

16. **Abruptio Placenta** – severe, **knife-like abdominal pain** radiating into back, No pelvic exam until ultrasound. Turn on **left side** to increase circulation and venous return, gets weight of fetus off vena cava. (Supine vena cava syndrome). If on spine board, place towels under board on right side. Risk of HELLP.
17. **Newborn resuscitation** – Warm, dry, stimulate, O2. Assist ventilation at 40-60 breaths/minute if HR < 100 bpm (cardiac monitor). CPR if HR < 60 at 3:1. **Goal is to get heart rate > 100**. Pre-ductal (right wrist) $O_2$ sat at 1 minute is 60-65%, 90% in 10 minutes. Medications are last resort (Epinephrine), **Narcan is NOT indicated initially**. APGAR at 1 and 5 minutes (not immediately at birth).
18. **Fundal massage** for **post-partum hemorrhage** to enhance **uterine atony**, then Pitocin (oxytocin).
19. Prolapsed cord – position patient in **knee to chest position** and relieve pressure on the umbilical cord to prevent fetal anoxia.
20. OB trauma – order a Kleihauer-Betke (KB) test to detect fetal RBCs in maternal circulation.

**Mental Health Emergencies (11 Items)**

1. Recognize **signs of maltreatment** - child with **bruising on face or torso** (normal to have bruising over knees and elbows), fractures in various staging of healing, **burns with lines of demarcation** (sock-like), **shaken impact syndrome** (SDH, retinal hemorrhage, posterior rib fractures). Keep child safe and contact child protective services immediately.
2. Risk factors for **suicide potential** – feeling of hopelessness. **Ask directly and encourage communication to find purpose and plan.** SSRI and SNRIs increase the risk of suicide initially, take 1-4 weeks to increase mood. Keeping patient safe is the priority of care.
3. Gender-identity struggle – **increased risk of suicide** in adolescents. Cutting to "feel something" not high risk for suicide.
4. Always **rule out organic cause (medical clearance) of bizarre behavior** (delirium – sudden onset) such as drug withdrawal, increased ICP from head injury, hypoglycemia, hypoxia, electrolyte imbalance, seizure disorder.
5. **Neuroleptic malignant syndrome (Thorazine)** – severe hyperthermia, so cool patient.
6. **PTSD** – flashbacks, nightmares, hypervigilance, difficulty concentrating. Do not startle, **low-stimulus area**. Announce yourself before entering room.
7. Treat **dystonic reactions (EPS)** from **neuroleptics** with **diphenhydramine** (Benadryl) initially.

**Medical Emergencies (14 Items)**

1. **DKA** – Patient is in **hypovolemic shock**, so **fluid resuscitation** with an isotonic solution is **THE priority**. DKA causes metabolic acidosis, so see Kussmaul's respirations to compensate by blowing off $CO_2$. Ketones in urine and BUN elevated due to dehydration. **Monitor glucose and potassium level closely**. Insulin infusion only when potassium stable, no insulin bolus to avoid risk of cerebral edema. Add **dextrose-containing solution when glucose reaches 250 mg/dl. Do not stop insulin infusion gap is closed**. Improved if respiratory rate decreases, pH > 7.3, $HCO_3$ increased, showing resolution of acidosis and ketosis.
2. **HHS** – Higher blood sugars since gradual increase in glucose, and **severe dehydration**. No ketones or acidosis. Require more fluids, but less insulin. **Risk of renal failure and DVT** since severe dehydration.
3. **Thyroid storm** – tachycardic, restless, and in pulmonary edema. **TSH low, T3 and T4 elevated. No aspirin** or elevates T4 higher. Treat with **beta-blockers** initially, then PTU, then iodine an hour after PTU.
4. **Adrenal crisis** – See in Addison's disease or **sudden discontinuation of steroids**. Labs: hyponatremia, **hypoglycemia**, and **hyperkalemia**. Treat with NS and glucocorticoids (Florinef). Improved if BP increasing, since patient is in hypovolemic shock.

5. **Diabetes Insipidus** – See in **head injury**, lithium and dilantin. Lose volume, but **hypernatremia**. Treat with desmopressin (DDAVP) or aqueous **vasopressin** (ADH), then **fluid resuscitation**.
6. **SIADH** – Seen in head injury or oat cell carcinoma. Volume overload with **hyponatremia**, so risk of **seizures**. Treat with **hypertonic saline and Lasix**, fluid restriction.
7. **Hyperkalemia** – **Tall, tented T waves** initially on EKG, then widened complex, then **Sine wave**. Treat initially with **Calcium gluconate** (cardiac stabilizer), **insulin and dextrose** (to shift K+).
8. **Hyponatremia** – **Risk is seizures**, treat with saline (0.9% or hypertonic 3% saline).
9. **Hypocalcemia** – Seen commonly in pancreatitis, S/S: **Chvostek's & Trousseau's** (carpal pedal spasm) **signs, prolonged QTi**. TX: calcium gluconate.
10. Hypomagnesemia – **risk of Torsades**, administer **Magnesium sulfate**.
11. **Hemophilia** (sex-linked) – scenario of patient with injury – **hemarthrosis (bleeding in joint)**, so elevate, ice, and immobilize affected joints. **If altered LOC, get head CT immediately** due to risk of brain hemorrhage. Replace **Factor VIII** for Type A and Von Willebrand's (male and female, most common). Monitor post laceration repair.
12. **DIC** (Disseminated intravascular coagulation) – **Petechiae and purpura** since over coagulating. Labs: **decreased platelets, fibrinogen**, hemoglobin, hematocrit. **Increased fibrin degradation products**, D-dimer, and bleeding times (PT, PTT). Treat the cause, i.e., sepsis. Better if platelets increasing.
13. **Sepsis/septic shock** (distributive shock) - keep **MAP 65 or greater** with **fluids (30 ml/kg initially), vasopressors, and inotropes**, **STAT antibiotics**.
14. **Sickle cell anemia** – **Triage as level 2**. Labs: increased retic count. Treat with $O_2$, IVFs to dilute blood, narcotic pain control. **Acute chest syndrome** is most common cause of death in SCD – chest pain, dyspnea, hypoxemia.
15. **Immune-compromised** (neutropenia due to chemotherapy or leukemia) – Aseptic technique, **reverse (protective) isolation so triage as ESI level 2**.
16. **Anaphylactic shock** (distributive shock) – **Priority is oxygen and epinephrine IM**. Seen with Hymenoptera sting (hives, urticaria from histamine release), or suspect if food fried in peanut oil if patient has peanut allergy.

## Musculoskeletal and Wound Emergencies (13 Items)

1. To assess radial nerve injury, assess motor (thumbs up, hitch hike) & sensory (feel thumb) nerve assessment. Medial – thumbs to opposing fingers (Colles fracture). Ulnar – fan out fingers.
2. **Scaphoid (navicular) fracture** – Pain at anatomic "snuff box". Splint with thumb spica splint.
3. **Metacarpal (Boxer's) fracture** – 5th metacarpal fracture, apply ulnar splint. Look for "fight bite".
4. **Colles (land on palm) or Smith fracture** – from fall on outstretched hand. Apply a double sugar-tong.
5. **Spiral fracture** more indicative of child maltreatment. **Worst fractures go through epiphyseal plate** (growth plate) – Salter Harris classification in pediatrics, V is worst.
6. **Pelvic fracture** - Gentle **compression inward and downward** to assess for pelvic fracture, no pelvic rock. Only assess once, do not dislodge clot. **Apply** pelvic binder **over greater trochanters to decrease bleeding**. Allow permissive hypotension and follow massive transfusion protocol (MTP) at 1:1:1 with platelets, plasma, pRBC's for hemorrhagic shock. Associated bladder and urethral injury.
7. **Nursemaids Elbow** – **subluxation** of radial head, no sedation needed.
8. Posterior hip dislocation most common with **knee to dashboard** in MVC from intrusion injury.
9. **Traction splint for mid-shaft femur fractures** to decrease bleeding, muscle spasms and relieve pressure on nerves. Assess pulses prior and after splint application.
10. **Crush injury** – Monitor for **compartment syndrome** - may require fasciotomy. Monitor for **rhabdomyolysis** - dark, tea-colored urine is myoglobinuria.

11. **Compartment Syndrome** – Pain **disproportionate to injury** on passive movement, despite analgesia. Monitor with intracompartmental device. Typically, lower leg or forearm. Remove cast. Keep in **neutral position**. Increased pressure > 20, may require multiple **fasciotomies.**
12. **Rhabdomyolysis** – from heat stroke, crush injury, stimulants, prolonged immobility, electrical burn. **CK and K+ elevated on labs. Myoglobin in urine – dark urine. Massive IVF's and urine alkalization to prevent acute tubular necrosis.** Monitor urinary output, **effective if increased UO 9100-300 ml) and clearer urine**.
13. **Fat embolism** – 12-72 hours post **long-bone (femur) fracture**. Dyspnea, altered LOC, tachypnea, transient **petechiae (axilla)**. Treat with oxygen first.
14. **High pressure injection injury – OR ASAP** to prevent saponification of tissue.
15. **Amputation** – **tourniquet to stump**. Gently rinse amputated part, wrap in saline-moistened gauze. Keep **amputated part on top of ice**, do not let it freeze.
16. Gouty arthritis – great toe pain, **increased uric acid**. Risk if on thiazide diuretics. **Avoid high purine diet** - protein, seafood, and alcohol.
17. **Achilles' rupture** – popping sound upon **sudden dorsiflexion injury**, more common after taking **fluoroquinolones** like Ciprofloxin.


## Maxillofacial and Ocular Emergencies (11 Items)

1. **Peritonsillar abscess – deviated uvula**, prepare for aspiration incision and drainage.
2. **Ludwig's Angina – drooling**, submandibular swelling, triage as level 1 and prepare for surgical airway.
3. Remove alkaline batteries quickly due to necrosis.
4. **Bell's palsy** – unilateral facial nerve (VII) paralysis, **cannot close affected eye,** ipsilateral impaired taste, hyperacusis, tinnitus, flattening of forehead. Treat with **steroids, protect eye from injury**, use artificial tears, and do facial massage.
5. Labyrinthitis – inflammation of inner ear from recent infection, causing hearing loss, dizziness, and vertigo.
6. **Meniere's Disease** (recurrent) – vertigo, visual disturbances, tinnitus. Treat with meclizine (Antivert) and antihistamines. Avoid smoking, caffeine, chocolate, alcohol, and salt. Fall risk, so slow movements.
7. **Maxillary** Fractures (Le Fort) – **airway is the priority for all**. Le Fort 1 with lip laceration, 2 with nasal fracture, 3 complete craniofacial separation.
8. **Mandibular** Fracture – **malocclusion**, paresthesia of lower lip, trismus, **airway compromise** due to tongue.
9. Zygomatic fracture – TIDES mnemonic – trismus, infraorbital hypesthesia, diplopia, epistaxis, not symmetrical; **loss of malar eminence**.
10. Iritis/Keratitis – Excessive tearing from bright light, tanning bed, or **snow blindness**. Keep in dark environment, **wear sunglasses**, warm compresses.
11. **Ocular burns – Alkaline burns (cement) worse,** immediate copious irrigation until pH 7.4
12. Corneal abrasion - tetracaine for pain, **do not patch**.
13. **Acute angle glaucoma** – sudden onset of unilateral eye pain and **halos** (angel) around eye. Treat with **beta-adrenergic antagonist drops (timolol), miotic drops, and diuretics** (Diamox).
14. **Central Retinal Artery Occlusion – painless, unilateral loss of vision** without injury and prior episodes of blindness (Amaurosis Fugax). Consult ophthalmology. Risk of stroke.
15. Eyelid laceration – assess cranial nerve 2 and 3. Anticipate specialty consultation. **Rigid shield if suspect globe rupture.**
16. **Retinal Detachment** – painless unilateral decreased vision, curtain, or veil closing, most from trauma, **flashes of light (photopsia), floaters in vision**.
17. Orbital fracture – limited upward gaze (CN III) after injury.
18. **Hyphema – blood in anterior chamber**, keep HOB up 30 degrees. Highest chance of rebleed is in 3-5 days. Avoid NSAIDs.

19. **Ruptured globe** - extrusion of vitreous humor, decreased IOP, **tear-drop shaped pupil**. Do **NOT instill medications**. Protect affected eye with **rigid shield**, patch over unaffected to **stop consensual movement.**
18. Retrobulbar hematoma – prepare for **lateral canthotomy**.

## Environmental, Toxicological, and Communicable Diseases Emergencies (14 Items)

1. Heat Stroke – **Altered LOC** so **rapid cooling** until 102 (38.9) degrees, administer benzodiazepines to reduce shivering, replace electrolytes. Heat exhaustion – cool patient through evaporation.
2. **Frostbite** – **narcotic pain control** since rewarming is painful, rapidly rewarm but do not rub area; apply bulky dressing.
3. **Severe hypothermia** – see **Osborne "J" wave on EKG**. Rewarm from core "active internal" with warmed oxygen and warmed fluids. Monitor core temperature. Cardiac arrest V Fib – shock again every 1-2 degree C increase in temperature.
4. **Cat bites** – Risk of **Pasteurella** from long thin fangs so **prophylactic antibiotics**. Risk of toxoplasmosis – do not change cat litter when pregnant.
5. **Rabies** – mostly from **bats** or raccoons, so **infiltrate RIG** 20 U/kg in the wound if possible. **Rabies vaccine** given 1 mL IM (deltoid or thigh in children) on days 0, 3, 7, and 14 for those never vaccinated.
6. Venomous **Pit viper** bites – **no ice** on bite. Antivenom CroFab/Anavip only if intense **hemorrhagic swelling**. CroFab/Anavip not indicated for coral snakes.
7. Black widow spider – **abdominal cramps**, treat with pain medication and **benzodiazepines**.
8. Brown recluse spider – "Red, white, and blue", then **tissue sloughing**, wound care consultation.
9. **Lyme disease (bull's eye-shaped rash)** from deer ticks, treat with Doxycycline. **Complication – Bell's (facial) palsy**.
10. Hymenoptera (Bee, hornet) sting – **histamine release** causes allergic response – **hives, urticaria**. Treat with diphenhydramine (Benadryl).
11. Aquatic animals - jellyfish sting – alcohol or vinegar. Sting ray – immerse in **hot water until pain relief**.
12. Air embolism from rapid **ascent** while scuba diving – position on **left lateral decubitus in trendelenburg**.
13. **Thermal burns** – Hypovolemic shock, so LR based on ABA guidelines - **2** ml/kg/BSA for adult, **3** if pediatric. Fluids based on partial and deep thickness, not superficial burn. May be Parkland formula **4** ml/kg/BSA for adults.
    a. **Half of the total amount given in first 8 hours** from time of burn.
    b. Keep warm during transport.
14. **Circumferential chest burn** patient intubated, but unable to ventilate – perform an **escharotomy**.
15. **Carbon monoxide** (CO) poisoning – cherry red skin, check **carboxyhemoglobin, high-flow oxygen until < 10%.** Do not trust SpO$_2$. Consider hyperbarics for pregnant patient.
16. **Cyanide** from plastics burning, **odor of bitter almonds**; **Cyanokit (hydroxocobalamin)** is antidote, turns **skin and urine red** as it turns cyanide into Vitamin B12.
17. Electrical burns – **rhabdomyolysis**, so IVFs based on **urine output**. Risk of ventricular fibrillation.
18. **Chemical burns** – Don PPE. Brush off dry chemicals like lime powder.
    a. Decontamination with **copious irrigation is priority**.
    b. **Hydrofluoric acid in rust remover – antidote is calcium gluconate**.
    c. Asphalt/tar –**cool in water if hot tar** and contact burn center.
    d. **Alkalis (anhydrous ammonia, cement, lime powder) cause liquification (saponification) of tissues**, more damaging than acids.
19. Alcohol withdrawal – within 6-8 hours of last drink, starts with **trembling and tachycardia**. Treat with benzodiazepines based on CIWA scale. Improved if heart rate decreasing to normal rate.
20. Sympathomimetics (Cocaine) – Tachycardia, dilated pupils, hypertensive so administer **benzodiazepines**.

21. **Opioid (heroin, fentanyl) overdose** – Assist breathing, administer **opioid antagonist naloxone** (Narcan) in small increments to **adequate respiration only**, not to wake up or put in withdrawal. Naloxone half-life is 30-60 minutes.
22. Benzodiazepine overdose or poisoning (EX: Rohypnol - flunitrazepam) – Assist breathing, **flumazenil** (Romazicon) is antidote, but **risk of seizures** with chronic benzodiazepine use.
23. **Acetaminophen toxicity** – administer activated **charcoal initially**, antidote is **Acetadote (N-Acetylcysteine)** once 4-hour level is obtained. Monitor liver studies closely.
24. **Iron toxicity** – antidote is the chelating agent **Deferoxamine (Desferal), turns urine pink (vin rose) as iron is excreted**.
25. **Organophosphates** (pesticides) **cholinergic** toxicity – SLUDGE mnemonic (salivation, lacrimation, etc. plus **bronchorrhea**). **Decontaminate first**. Treat with **Atropine & 2-PAM** until bronchial secretions dry.
26. **Ethylene glycol** (antifreeze – calcium oxalate) and methanol toxicity– Antidote is 5-10% ethanol infusion or **Fomepizole** (Antizol). Methanol – "Snow blindness" visual changes.
27. **Digoxin Toxicity** – S/S: GI distress and **yellow-green halos** in vision. Treat with Digi Bind (Digi Fab).
28. Calcium-channel blocker toxicity – antidote is **calcium** and treat bradycardia.
29. **Beta-blocker toxicity** –**glucagon** to treat bradycardia and **hypoglycemia**.
30. **Clostridium difficile** – see after use of antibiotics or use of proton pump inhibitors. **Contact isolation**.
31. **Mononucleosis** – **No heavy lifting or contact sports** due to enlarged spleen and **risk of rupture** (Kehr's sign). If patient comes in complaining of left shoulder pain, get **FAST exam** ASAP.
32. **Mumps** (Parotitis) – swollen salivary and **parotid glands**, spread through respiratory droplets, symptoms appear weeks after infection. Complication – **orchitis in males** may lead to infertility.
33. **Pertussis** (whooping cough) – **paroxysmal spasms of coughing**, highly contagious through respiratory droplets. Treat with **mycins**.
34. Varicella (Chicken pox) – Airborne isolation. **Contagious until lesions crusted**. Shingles (herpes Zoster) follows dermatome, very painful, contagious until crusted over too.
35. **Diphtheria** – thick **grey pseudomembranous coating** in the back of throat. Treat with **penicillin**.
36. **Measles** (Rubeola) – **3 C's** - cough, coryza, conjunctivitis. Maculopapular rash (**Koplik spots** – bluish gray lesions) in mouth, then to face. Contagious 10-14 days before rash appears.
37. **Tuberculosis** – **hemoptysis**, fever, chills, night sweats. Spread by respiratory (**airborne**) route, place immediately in **negative pressure room**. Spreads fast in homeless, dormitories, nursing homes, prison, etc. TX: Isoniazid (INH) and rifampin.

## Professional Issues (14 Items)

1. Nursing ethics – Autonomy – right to make own health decisions; **Beneficence** – oath to help others (**unresponsive patient scenario, reporting abuse**); Nonmaleficence – do no harm; **Justice – treat all patients fairly (addict or alcoholic scenario)**.
2. **Evidence collection** – **paper bags** over hands if you suspect patient recently fired a handgun (gunshot residue, preserve evidence). Do not cut clothes through stains. Never leave evidence unattended.
3. Consents – Patient must understand risk for informed consent. **Unresponsive patient cared for under implied consent**. Federal consent for STI treatment, pregnancy care, substance abuse.
4. Use of translator/interpreter – **Talk directly to patient, best to use trained interpreter** instead of family.
5. EMTALA – anti-dumping laws; **medical screening exam required** and transfer criteria. **Transferring patient – stabilize to the best of your ability**. Pregnant patient delivers baby at free-standing ED – do not transfer until delivery of placentae too.
6. Transferring facility responsible for selecting best mode of transport, ground, rotor-wing, or fixed wing.
7. **HIPAA** – share patient information with their consent only. Violation if nurse accesses chart of patient not under their care or leaves chart open in hallway where others may see.

8. **ESI 5-level Triage criteria**. **Triage level 1 examples -** narcotic OD with decreased respirations, hypoglycemic patient who is unresponsive, severe respiratory distress. **Triage level 2 examples** – suicidal patient, violent patient, victim of assault, sickle cell crisis, patient requiring isolation).
9. Reportable conditions – homicide or suicide, child and vulnerable adult abuse, sexual assault (can be anonymous), communicable infections.
10. **Signs of child maltreatment** – inconsistent story, delay in care. Bruising on torso and head, normal to have bruising on lower legs. Sock-like burns with **line of demarcation**. **Shaken impact syndrome – triad of SDH, retinal, rib fracture**. Keep the **child safe** and report to child protective services if you suspect neglect or abuse.
11. Elder abuse – ask directly "Is someone hurting you?" Keep the patient safe and report to social services if you suspect neglect or abuse.
12. Monitoring patients undergoing procedural sedation – have resuscitation equipment and **reversal agents available, opioid antagonist naloxone and flumazenil (Romazicon)**. Propofol duration of action is 3-5 minutes.
13. **Disaster plan** –Mitigation – **hazardous vulnerability assessment**, Preparedness – Mutual aid agreements, stockpiling, training. Response during disaster like disaster triage. Recovery – restocking.
14. **Disaster START triage** based on **respiration, perfusion, mental status** at 30-2-can do. Jump START triage (pediatrics red if RR > 45; give 5 positive-pressure breaths before moving to black).
15. Weapons of Mass destruction or Chemical warfare (CWA) – TX: Cipro or Doxycycline for Anthrax (widened mediastinum); **2-PAM & Atropine for nerve agents** (Sarin gas).
16. **Discharge teaching** – Return demonstration for crutch-walking, peak flow, inhaler with spacer. **Ask patient to restate important components of instructions**. Written instructions at 6th grade reading level. Discuss instructions with older adult who may not be able to see to read sheet.
17. End-of-life care – Even if allow patient is allow natural death, provide **palliative (comfort) care**, symptom management for cough, secretions, pain, etc. Put a copy of AND/DNR paperwork on chart.
18. Leaving AMA - patient must be **mentally competent** to sign out against medical advice.
19. **Corneal donation – head of bed up 30 degrees**, dressing with paper tape and ice over eyes.
20. Stages of grieving – shock and disbelief are first stage, anger comes next. **Family presence reduces shock and anger**. Never deliver bad news alone.
21. **Patient satisfaction increases compliance** with treatment plan. Increased patient satisfaction - use distraction through TV, cell phone, etc.
22. Patient safety – **weight on pediatrics in kg's only for weight-based dosing, lock scale in kg's**. Give bedside report when appropriate.
23. Use appropriate pain scale like **FLACC** in children. Children cannot correlate a number or face to pain.

# PDB Nurse Education, LLC    CEN Post Test - Part 1

1. Which of the following injuries is most suspicious for child abuse in a 2-year-old child?
    a. A spiral ulnar fracture after reportedly falling off the bed.
    b. Bruises to the arms and legs in various stages of healing.
    c. A forehead hematoma after reportedly falling out of a stroller.
    d. Partial thickness burns to the palms after reportedly touching the inside of the oven while his mother was cooking.
2. The nurse assisting in the cardiac arrest of a 6-year-old is unable to locate the length-based, color-coded measuring tape. He calculates and anticipates the need for which size uncuffed endotracheal (ET) tube?
    a. 4.0 Fr
    b. 4.5 Fr
    c. 5.0 Fr
    d. 5.5 Fr
3. EMS transports a patient to the emergency department with a fragment of machinery in his thigh after a factory explosion. His injury is an example of which blast injury type?
    a. Primary blast injury
    b. Secondary blast injury
    c. Tertiary blast injury
    d. Quaternary blast injury
4. A patient with a blood pressure of 260/120 (MAP 167) is in hypertensive crisis and being treated with IV nitroprusside (Nipride). Over the next 60-120 minutes, the nurse expects to titrate the Nipride infusion to a mean arterial pressure (MAP) of:
    a. 150 mm Hg
    b. 125 mm Hg
    c. 100 mm Hg
    d. 80 mm Hg
5. Which of the following statements is INCORRECT regarding Hepatitis?
    a. Vaccines are available for Hepatitis A and B.
    b. Hepatitis D cannot occur without being infected with Hepatitis B.
    c. Hepatitis A is spread through food or water contaminated by feces.
    d. Prevention of Hepatitis E includes not sharing a needle, razor, or toothbrush with someone infected.
6. Which of the following is the preferred diagnostic test for testicular torsion?
    a. Abdominal CT
    b. Doppler ultrasonography
    c. Urethral swab for Chlamydia
    d. Urine C & S
7. A patient with a history of sickle cell disease taking hydroxyurea complains of chest pain and dyspnea. Which ESI triage level is appropriate for this patient?
    a. ESI triage level 2
    b. ESI triage level 3
    c. ESI triage level 4
    d. ESI triage level 5
8. EMS transports an 86-year-old female from a long-term care facility for new onset agitation and delirium. She is febrile, tachypneic, and tachycardic. What is the most likely cause of this patient's condition?
    a. Alzheimer's disease
    b. Parkinson's disease
    c. Drug intoxication
    d. Urosepsis
9. A potential sign/symptom of cyanide poisoning is:
    a. Painless skin ulcer.
    b. Smell of bitter almonds.
    c. Excessive lacrimation.
    d. Descending symmetrical paralysis.

10. The best method to effectively communicate with a non-English-speaking patient is:
    a. A member of the healthcare team fluent in the patient's native language.
    b. A member of the patient's family.
    c. A certified translator fluent in the patient's native language.
    d. A visitor who is fluent in the patient's native language.
11. After an airplane crash, a patient is unable to ambulate, has a respiratory rate of 20 breaths/minute, a capillary refill < 2 seconds, and follows commands. Using mass casualty START triage for adults, this patient is classified as:
    a. Green
    b. Yellow
    c. Red
    d. Black
12. A patient with a history of a recent heart transplant is transported to the emergency department after a syncopal episode. The patient's heart rate is 38 beats/minute, and the blood pressure is 74/40. The nurse anticipates administering which of the following medications?
    a. Atropine
    b. Procainamide
    c. Isuprel
    d. Labetalol
13. A 28-year-old female complains of double vision and difficulty swallowing. Assessment reveals ptosis and dysarthria, so the provider plans to perform a Tensilon (edrophonium) test. What medication should be readily available in case the patient develops cholinergic crisis?
    a. Atropine
    b. Lorazepam
    c. Magnesium
    d. Succinylcholine
14. A 50-year-old male with no past medical history presents after two days of abdominal pain and hematemesis. The patient denies alcohol abuse. Which of the following is the most likely reason for his symptoms?
    a. Esophageal varices secondary to portal hypertension
    b. Mallory-Weiss tear
    c. Small bowel obstruction
    d. Peptic ulcer disease
15. Which of the following chest radiograph findings is most seen in patients with anthrax?
    a. Diffuse pulmonary edema
    b. Mediastinal widening
    c. "Ground glass" opacities
    d. Pneumothorax
16. A 7-year-old male with a history of asthma presents with cough, tachypnea, and a prolonged expiratory time. What is the desired outcome of a nebulized albuterol treatment?
    a. Increased work of breathing.
    b. Increased peak expiratory flow reading.
    c. Pulsus paradox.
    d. Silent chest.
17. Migrant workers accidentally sprayed with pesticides present to the emergency department entrance with excessive tearing, salivation, and respiratory secretions. What is the nurse's first action?
    a. Don your personal protective equipment and decontaminate the patients.
    b. Administer 2 to 5 mg of Atropine IV, repeated every 3 to 5 minutes.
    c. Prepare for immediate intubation and mechanical ventilation.
    d. Administer pralidoxime (protopam chloride 2-PAM) IV.
18. EMS transports a patient from a housefire with burns to the face, neck, and chest. The patient has stridor and is coughing up carbonaceous sputum. What is the priority intervention?
    a. Calculate the total surface burn area for fluid resuscitation.
    b. Send blood to lab for a carboxyhemoglobin to assess for carbon monoxide toxicity.
    c. Assess the patient for the odor of bitter almonds to determine cyanide toxicity.
    d. Prepare for immediate intubation.

19. A patient eating steak presents to the emergency department complaining of "something stuck in throat". The nurse anticipates administering which of the following medications to move the impacted food bolus?
    a. Magnesium sulfate
    b. Glucagon
    c. Calcium gluconate
    d. Pantoprazole (Protonix)
20. Which medication should be avoided in thyroid storm?
    a. Ibuprofen
    b. Acetaminophen
    c. Aspirin
    d. Beta-blockers
21. The nurse has calculated the 0.9 mg/kg dose of tissue plasminogen activator (r-TPA) for the 60 kg patient as 54 mg total. What is the bolus dose to be administered over 1 minute?
    a. 2.7 mg
    b. 5.4 mg
    c. 10 mg
    d. 10.8 mg
22. Which type of shock is characterized by bradycardia?
    a. Hypovolemic
    b. Obstructive
    c. Anaphylactic
    d. Neurogenic
23. A patient with polyuria is diagnosed with diabetes insipidus (DI). Which laboratory value is expected in DI?
    a. Increased urine specific gravity.
    b. Increased serum osmolality.
    c. Increased urine osmolality.
    d. Decreased sodium level.
24. A patient in diabetic ketoacidosis (DKA) has a serum glucose of 450 mg/dL, pH of 7.20, and a serum potassium level of 4.6 mEq/L. IV fluid replacement is started at 20/mL/kg of NS and a continuous infusion of regular insulin at 0.1 units/kg/hour is started. What is the expected response of serum potassium to the treatment plan?
    a. Potassium will increase.
    b. Potassium will decrease.
    c. Potassium will remain unchanged.
    d. Potassium will drop, then spike due to resolution of acidosis.
25. A 55-year-old male complains of substernal chest pain and shortness of breath. The 12-lead ECG shows ST segment elevation in leads I, aVL, V5, and V6. Which area of the heart is damaged in this MI?
    a. Inferior wall
    b. Anterior wall
    c. Lateral wall
    d. Posterior wall
26. In which shock class would you expect to see the heart rate less than 100 beats per minute and a narrowed pulse pressure?
    a. Class I
    b. Class II
    c. Class III
    d. Class IV
27. Which of the following disorders would NOT cause obstructive shock?
    a. Tension pneumothorax
    b. Blunt cardiac injury
    c. Cardiac tamponade
    d. Massive pulmonary embolism

28. A 60-year-old female in pulmonary edema has dyspnea, tachypnea, and tachycardia. She is anxious and her skin is cool, pale, and moist. You auscultate crackles in the lungs and S3 and S4 heart sounds. The treatment plan of BiPAP, furosemide (Lasix), and morphine will provide which hemodynamic effect?
    a. Decrease preload.
    b. Increase contractility.
    c. Decrease heart rate.
    d. Increase afterload.
29. A 60-year-old male with chronic bronchitis exhibits nostril flaring, pursed lips, and use of accessory muscles. ABG's are expected to reveal which acid base imbalance?
    a. Metabolic acidosis
    b. Metabolic alkalosis
    c. Respiratory alkalosis
    d. Respiratory acidosis
30. A 25-year-old male kicked in the chest by a horse has chest wall ecchymosis. What is the most common cardiac dysrhythmia seen in blunt cardiac injury?
    a. Sinus tachycardia with PVC's.
    b. Left bundle branch block.
    c. Sinus bradycardia.
    d. Third-degree heart block.
31. Adenosine (Adenocard) may be used in the treatment of which cardiac dysrhythmia?
    a. Wolff-Parkinson White (WPW)
    b. Sick Sinus Syndrome
    c. Monomorphic Ventricular Tachycardia
    d. Polymorphic Ventricular Tachycardia
32. You are rewarming the frostbitten hands of a homeless patient in a gently swirling warm-water bath at 37 to 39 degrees Celsius (99 to 102 F) when the patient starts crying in pain. The nurse anticipates:
    a. Administering opioids for pain control.
    b. Cooling the water temperature since it is too hot.
    c. Removing the hands from water and wrapping in bulky dressings.
    d. Administering nonsteroidal anti-inflammatory drugs (NSAIDs) for pain control.
33. A 50-year-old female complains of sensitivity to sound and facial drooping for the past 2 days. She is unable to raise her eyebrow on the left side of her face and has a lack of forehead wrinkling. The remainder of her neurologic and physical exam is normal and brain CT is normal. The nurse expects a plan of:
    a. Doxycycline until the Lyme titers return.
    b. Neurology consult, and MRI to rule out stroke.
    c. Oral corticosteroids and antivirals for Bell's Palsy.
    d. Diphenhydramine for dystonic reaction.
34. A 35-year-old male presents to the emergency department with symmetrical ascending weakness and depressed deep tendon reflexes and is diagnosed with Guillain Barre syndrome. Which of the following is FALSE concerning the care of the patient?
    a. Perform pulmonary function tests.
    b. Keep the patient NPO until swallow studies are completed.
    c. Administer IV immunoglobulins.
    d. Administer IV methylprednisolone.
35. A 30-year-old female with a history of depression, anxiety, and migraines has a significantly high fever, agitation, and diaphoresis. Her neurological exam reveals hyperreflexia and rhythmic muscle spasms without rigidity. The head CT and lumbar puncture are unremarkable. What is the most likely diagnosis?
    a. Meningitis
    b. Serotonin syndrome
    c. Malignant hyperthermia
    d. Sepsis
36. A patient with right fourth and fifth rib fractures should be monitored closely for signs/symptoms of:
    a. Great vessel injury
    b. Brachial plexus injury
    c. Liver injury

d. Pulmonary contusion

37. A 24-year-old female complains of severe dizziness, nasal congestion, nausea, and decreased hearing in the left ear. Assessment reveals left side nystagmus. Vital signs are unremarkable, and he denies previous similar episodes. What is the most likely diagnosis?
    a. Trigeminal neuralgia
    b. Meniere's disease
    c. Labyrinthitis
    d. Otitis media

38. A 64-year-old male with a history of heart disease and hypertension presents to the emergency department with a complaint of severe pain the first metatarsophalangeal (MTP) joint. Which of the following statements is INCORRECT regarding gouty arthritis?
    a. Inflammation occurs when too much uric acid deposits in the joints.
    b. Hydrochlorothiazide (HCTZ) and aspirin can cause attacks.
    c. The patient should avoid organ meats, shellfish, red meat, and alcohol.
    d. The patient should stop their Allopurinol (Zyloprim).

39. A calcium channel blocker such as Nicardipine or Nimodipine is useful in the treatment of which neurological emergency?
    a. Cerebral aneurysm rupture
    b. Subdural hematoma
    c. Epidural hematoma
    d. Guillain-Barre Syndrome

40. The nurse anticipates administering oral iodine for thyroid storm in which sequence?
    a. Oral iodine should be the first medication administered.
    b. Administer oral iodine immediately after beta-blocker.
    c. Administer iodine at least one hour after the propylthiouracil (PTU) administration.
    d. Aspirin should be the first medication, then beta-blocker, PTU, and iodine.

41. A patient with a history of alcohol abuse complains of severe epigastric pain radiating to the back, fever, and vomiting. White blood cell count, amylase and lipase levels are elevated so the nurse suspects which disease process?
    a. Appendicitis
    b. Cholecystitis
    c. Pancreatitis
    d. Diverticulitis

42. A patient with a history of atrial fibrillation, hypertension, and heart failure is being treated for pneumonia. You notice a prolonged QTi on the cardiac rhythm. Which of the following orders should the nurse question before administering?
    a. Erythromycin
    b. Aspirin
    c. Labetalol
    d. Lisinopril

43. In hypokalemia the ECG may reveal:
    a. Flattened T-wave and prominent U-wave.
    b. Peaked T-waves and widened QRS.
    c. Delta wave with short PR interval and wide QRS.
    d. Osborn or J-wave.

44. A patient complains of fever, chills, a cough for the last three weeks, chest pain, coughing up blood, weight loss, and night sweats. You place the patient in a negative-pressure room since you suspect:
    a. Influenza
    b. Tularemia
    c. Tuberculosis
    d. Inhalational anthrax

45. Which of the following is an early sign/symptom of methanol ingestion?
    a. Mydriasis
    b. Cherry-red skin
    c. Bradycardia

d. "Snow field" vision

46. A patient with fever, chills, chest pain increasing with inspiration, and global ST segment elevation is diagnosed with pericarditis. The treatment plan includes the following, **EXCEPT**:
    a. Oxygen via nasal cannula
    b. Anti-inflammatory agents
    c. Nitroglycerin
    d. Corticosteroids

47. An elderly patient arrives in triage with abdominal pain. Early signs of a small bowel obstruction (SBO) include:
    a. Rovsing's sign
    b. Abdominal distention
    c. Hyperactive high-pitched bowel sounds
    d. Murphy's sign

48. A 60-year-old female complains of headache, abrupt onset of visual disturbances, and fever. The erythrocyte sedimentation rate and C-reactive protein are elevated. To prevent permanent vision loss, the nurse anticipates administering:
    a. Acetazolamide (Diamox)
    b. Corticosteroids
    c. Timolol (Timoptic)
    d. r-TPA (recombinant tissue plasminogen activator)

49. Hyperosmolar hyperglycemic syndrome/state (HHS) is characterized by:
    a. Metabolic acidosis and ketones in the urine.
    b. Kussmaul respirations and pulmonary edema.
    c. Hypokalemia and hypertension.
    d. Markedly elevated serum glucose and altered mental status.

50. A patient is experiencing crushing chest pain and shortness of breath. 12-lead ECG reveals ST segment elevation in V1-V4. He likely has an occlusion in which coronary artery?
    a. Left anterior descending (LAD)
    b. Right coronary artery (RCA)
    c. Circumflex artery
    d. Posterior descending artery

51. Four patients are transported via EMS and arrive in the department simultaneously. The experienced charge nurse knows the highest acuity patient is the:
    a. 15-year-old who dove into the pool hitting her head. She is immobilized on a spine board, awake, alert, and moving all extremities. Vital signs are stable, no bleeding is noted to the head. PERRL.
    b. 16-year-old tackled while playing football, with obvious deformity to his left lower leg. 2+ pedal pulses, toes are warm.
    c. 5-year-old struck by a car who is pale, tachycardic, and hypotensive.
    d. 5-year-old with hemophilia who fell off his bicycle hitting his knee, with obvious joint swelling.

52. Your patient is diagnosed with diffuse axonal injury. Which intervention is appropriate to decrease intracranial pressure?
    a. Keep the patient's head in a neutral midline position.
    b. Apply a rigid cervical collar to keep the head midline.
    c. Turn the patient on the left side to promote circulation.
    d. Elevate the head of the bed with the knees flexed.

53. A patient who overdosed on Diltiazem (Cardizem) exhibits tetanic muscle contractions, numbness and tingling of fingers, and hyperactive deep tendon reflexes. The ECG shows a prolonged QT interval. The nurse anticipates administering:
    a. IV hydration and loop diuretics.
    b. 2 grams magnesium sulfate IVP.
    c. 10% calcium gluconate over 10 minutes.
    d. Potassium chloride 20 mEq/hour.

54. A patient with a right ventricular MI becomes hypotensive. Which is the initial treatment to increase preload?
    a. Nitroglycerin infusion
    b. Dopamine infusion
    c. Dobutamine infusion
    d. Isotonic fluid boluses
55. Laboratory results reveal hyponatremia in a patient with lung cancer. Which of the following is the likely cause of the electrolyte imbalance?
    a. Elevated thyroid stimulating hormone (TSH).
    b. Elevated T3 and T4.
    c. Excessive antidiuretic hormone (ADH).
    d. Decreased cortisol levels.
56. Which opiate will more likely cause histamine release, resulting in skin rashes and urticaria?
    a. Fentanyl (Sublimaze)
    b. Hydromorphone (Dilaudid)
    c. Morphine
    d. Remifentanil (Ultiva)
57. A patient in DKA is receiving a continuous infusion of regular insulin and 0.9% NS with 20 mEq KCL at 125ml/hour. The serum blood glucose is now 240 mg/dl. The nurse anticipates an order to:
    a. Discontinue the insulin infusion.
    b. Administer a long-acting insulin.
    c. Administer a dextrose-containing solution.
    d. Recheck the blood sugar in 4 hours.
58. Your patient has esophageal varices from portal hypertension secondary to liver disease. Gastroesophageal variceal bleeding is treated with which of the following?
    a. Omeprazole (Prilosec)
    b. Octreotide (Sandostatin)
    c. Protonix (Pantoprazole)
    d. Sucralfate (Carafate)
59. Rhabdomyolysis may be seen in crush injury, prolonged immobility, hyperthermia, and drug or toxin ingestion. The following values may be increased in skeletal muscle destruction, **EXCEPT**:
    a. Potassium
    b. Blood urea nitrogen (BUN)
    c. pH
    d. Creatine kinase (CK)
60. A patient with a stick impaled in his eye has vitreous hemorrhage. The following are appropriate treatments, **EXCEPT**:
    a. Secure the stick in place and shield the eye.
    b. Patch the unaffected eye to minimize consensual movement.
    c. Instill tetracaine eye drops.
    d. Update tetanus immunization.
61. A 16-year-old male presents to the ED after cement is splashed in his left eye. The priority nursing intervention is:
    a. Measurement of bilateral ocular pH.
    b. Copious irrigation with NS or LR.
    c. Snellen chart visual acuity assessment.
    d. Contacting his parents for permission to treat.
62. A 34-week pregnant patient sustained blunt abdominal trauma in an MVC. She is complaining of severe back pain and is hypotensive. Which of the following interventions is **contraindicated** initially?
    a. Administering high-flow oxygen to keep oxygen saturation > 95%.
    b. Performing a pelvic exam to assess uterine injuries.
    c. Turn the patient 15 to 30 degrees to the side.
    d. Starting two large-bore IV's.

63. Discrepancy between blood pressure values and pulse strength, a loud systolic murmur, and mediastinal widening on a chest radiograph are symptoms of which traumatic injury?
    a. Diaphragmatic rupture
    b. Aortic disruption
    c. Traumatic asphyxia
    d. Flail chest
64. Which incomplete cord syndrome occurs from a hyperextension injury resulting in a greater loss of function in the upper extremities than in the lower extremities, and requires extensive rehabilitation?
    a. Anterior cord syndrome
    b. Central cord syndrome
    c. Posterior cord syndrome
    d. Brown-Sequard syndrome
65. Which facial fracture results in trismus, epistaxis, and loss of malar eminence?
    a. Maxillary fracture
    b. Mandibular fracture
    c. Orbital blowout fracture
    d. Zygoma fracture
66. An 8-year-old returned from summer camp with ear pain worsened by chewing, swelling, redness, and purulent drainage. Discharge instructions for otitis externa include:
    a. Use earplugs lightly coated with petroleum jelly to protect the ear from water.
    b. Take meclizine (Antivert) to control vertigo.
    c. Follow up with ENT for myringotomy tube placement.
    d. Use topical decongestants for 7 days.
67. Markers of cardiac reperfusion after fibrinolytic therapy include relief of chest pain, normalization of ST segment changes, and which of the following?
    a. Hypotension
    b. Reperfusion dysrhythmias such AIVR
    c. Normalization of pH
    d. Bradycardia
68. A 100-kg adult presents with extensive partial thickness & full-thickness burns from a housefire, measuring 50% body surface area (BSA) & requires fluid resuscitation. According to American Burn Association (ABA) guidelines, what amount of fluid should the patient receive in the first 8 hours after injury?
    a. 2000 ml
    b. 2500 ml
    c. 5000 ml
    d. 10,000 ml
69. An unresponsive 9-month-old child is brought into the ED by her parents who say the child fell off the bed onto the carpet below. The nurse assesses bilateral ecchymosis on the torso, retinal hemorrhages, and crepitus in the rib area. Which of the following is the likely cause of the child's presentation?
    a. Accidental injury
    b. Septic shock
    c. Shaken impact syndrome.
    d. Child neglect
70. You patient becomes unresponsive, apneic, and pulseless. You see the rhythm below on the cardiac monitor, what is the priority intervention?
    a. Prepare for immediate tracheal intubation.
    b. Insert an intraosseous needle into the humerus and administer Epinephrine 1 mg.
    c. Begin chest compressions and ask your team to prepare for defibrillation.
    d. Administer sodium bicarbonate 0.5 mEq/kg.

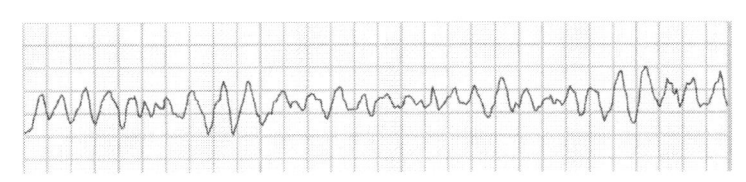

71. You notice the cardiac rhythm below on a patient who is apneic and pulseless. What is the rhythm and immediate intervention?
    a. Sinus bradycardia; prepare for immediate tracheal intubation.
    b. Sinus bradycardia; administer Atropine 0.5 mg IV/IO.
    c. PEA; begin chest compressions and consider the H's and T's.
    d. PEA; start bag-valve-mask ventilations giving one breath every 6 seconds.

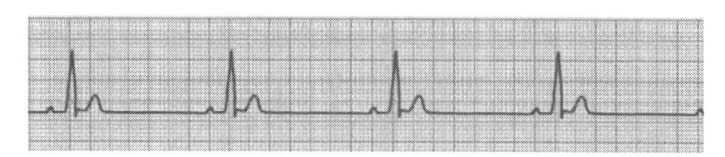

72. Four patients arrive in the emergency department. The experienced triage nurse knows the highest acuity patient is the:
    a. 15-year-old male brought in by parents who report, "he is out of control", and threatening to kill his family. He is cooperative in triage and answers questions calmly.
    b. 15-year-old female who states, "I think I'm pregnant. When I told my mom, she threw me out of the house, and I have no place to go."
    c. 8-year-old male brought in by her mother after she received a call from the school counselor that he was disruptive in class. He is cooperative and crying.
    d. 16-year-old female with a history of depression, carried in by her father. The patient is unresponsive, and the mother shows you several empty pill bottles she found next to her daughter.

73. A 50-year-old male complains of fever and retrosternal chest pain that worsens with inspiration. Assessment reveals a pericardial friction rub, so the nurse expects to see which ECG changes?
    a. Flattened T wave with U wave.
    b. Biphasic P waves.
    c. Global ST segment elevation.
    d. Peaked T wave with wide QRS.

74. Signs and symptoms of gestational (pregnancy-induced) hypertension include the following, **EXCEPT**:
    a. Proteinuria
    b. Facial edema
    c. Visual changes
    d. Increased urination

75. An unimmunized child has swollen lymph nodes and a thick gray pseudomembranous coating in the back of the throat. The most likely cause of these symptoms is which highly communicable infection?
    a. Pertussis
    b. Diphtheria
    c. Measles
    d. Mumps

76. Appropriate treatment modalities for myxedema coma include the following, **EXCEPT**:
    a. Propylthiouracil (PTU).
    b. Levothyroxine.
    c. Warming the patient.
    d. Monitor for airway obstruction due to macroglossia.

77. A patient has an open pneumothorax from a stab wound. Assessment reveals a sucking sound with inspiration and bubbling of blood around the wound on exhalation. Immediate treatment consists of placing:
    a. A nonporous, three-sided occlusive dressing.
    b. A nonocclusive, three-sided occlusive dressing.
    c. A nonocclusive dressing, taped on all four sides.
    d. An occlusive dressing, taped on all four sides.

78. A 19-year-old victim of assault kicked in the neck has anterior neck swelling and bruising. Assessment reveals subcutaneous emphysema and Hamman's crunch. The nurse suspects:
    a. Tracheobronchial injury
    b. Air leak syndrome
    c. Hemothorax
    d. Ruptured diaphragm

79. A patient with tumor lysis syndrome exhibits a tall, tented T wave on the ECG tracing. The nurse anticipates administering calcium gluconate and insulin/dextrose since he suspects which electrolyte abnormality?
    a. Hypermagnesemia
    b. Hypocalcemia
    c. Hypokalemia
    d. Hyperkalemia
80. A patient with Graves' disease presents with a temperature of 105.3 F (40.7 C), tachycardia, and agitation. Assessment reveals exopthalamus and a goiter. Laboratory results show an elevated T3 and T4. The nurse anticipates administering which of the following medications?
    a. Desmopressin acetate (DDAVP)
    b. Aqueous Pitressin IV
    c. Propranolol (Inderal)
    d. Sodium bicarbonate
81. A patient with which ocular emergency presents with severe unilateral eye pain, reduced vision, headache, vomiting, and colored halos around lights?
    a. Central retinal artery occlusion
    b. Acute angle glaucoma
    c. Retinal detachment
    d. Hyphema
82. After a camping trip, a patient presents with fever, chills, and a pink nonpruritic macular rash on the palms of the hands and the soles of the feet. The nurse suspects:
    a. Rocky Mountain spotted fever.
    b. Lyme disease
    c. Brown recluse spider bite
    d. Black widow spider bite
83. The treatment plan for hydrofluoric acid exposure includes which medication?
    a. Silvadene
    b. Polyethylene glycol
    c. Calcium gluconate
    d. Sodium bicarbonate
84. In disaster triage using the START model patients are sorted in a manner to allow the nurse to provide the most good to the greatest number of patients. The "walking wounded" are classified as:
    a. Black
    b. Red
    c. Yellow
    d. Green
85. You are discharging a patient after a temporomandibular joint (TMJ) reduction. Which diet should the patient follow for at least one week?
    a. Low residue
    b. Low fat, high fiber
    c. Clear liquid
    d. Soft diet
86. A Unit Based Council is working on building resiliency among their staff. What would **NOT** be an effective step when working towards this goal?
    a. Setting attainable department goals.
    b. Encouraging and modeling work/life balance.
    c. Indirectly addressing lateral violence.
    d. Developing and promoting self-confidence among staff.
87. Your patient is diagnosed with an incarcerated hernia. What would **NOT** be a part of the treatment plan?
    a. Applying ice to the bulging area
    b. Manual reduction
    c. Bowel regimen
    d. Surgical consult

88. You are caring for a patient who was onsite when a radiological dispersal device detonated. The nurse anticipates the patient to experience the following symptoms initially, **EXCEPT**:
    a. Diarrhea
    b. Vomiting
    c. Hearing loss
    d. GI bleeding
89. After the traumatic death of a co-worker, hospital administration decides to conduct a critical incident stress management (CISM) debriefing for the staff. Ideally the debriefing should take place within what time frame?
    a. Within hours of the traumatic event.
    b. Within 24–72 hours.
    c. Within 1 week.
    d. Within 1 month.
90. Nursing interventions suggested to prevent ventilator-associated pneumonia (VAP) include the following, **EXCEPT**:
    a. Increasing the head of the bed (HOB) 30 to 45 degrees.
    b. Providing regular oral care.
    c. Deep vein thrombosis (DVT) prophylaxis.
    d. Avoiding the use of saline lavage during suctioning.

## CEN Post Test Answers – Part 1

1. **A** – Spiral fractures are generally caused by twisting injuries, and the injury pattern above is inconsistent with the history. The other injury patterns are appropriate for the patient's age and mechanism of injury. (ENPC pg. 133)
2. **D** – 5.5 Fr. In the absence of a length-based color-coded measuring tape, uncuffed endotracheal tube (ET) sizes are calculated using (age in years/4) + 4. EX: Age 6 = 6/4 = 1.5 + 4 = 5.5 Fr. Cuffed tubes are calculated using (age in years/4) + 3.5 (0.5 size lower). Gastric tube is estimated at 2 times the ET tube size. Depth of ET tube is estimated at 3 times the ET tube size. Chest tube size is estimated at 4 times the ET tube size.
3. **B** – Flying debris and other projectiles causing impalements, fractures, and amputations secondary to the explosion. Pneumothorax, concussions, ruptured tympanic membranes, etc. occur from the primary blast. (Sheehy pg. 396)
4. **B** – Reduce the MAP by only 25% over the first 1-2 hours. The initial MAP is 167 [(120+120) + 260] = 500 divided by 3 = 167. 75% of 167 is 125 mm Hg. (Sheehy pg. 247-248)
5. **D** – Hepatitis A and E are fecal-oral route from contaminated water and poor sanitation. "Vowels from the Bowels", so the education on not sharing needle, razor, and toothbrush is for Hepatitis B prevention. Vaccines are available for Hepatitis A and B. Hepatitis D cannot occur without being infected with Hepatitis B.
6. **B** – Doppler ultrasonography shows decreased or absent blood flow in torsion. (Sheehy pg. 277)
7. **A** – Acute chest syndrome is the leading cause of death in sickle cell disease, so triage as level 2. (Sheehy pg. 315)
8. **D** – The most likely cause is urosepsis. Obtain a CBC, lactate, and blood and urine cultures immediately. Start a broad-spectrum antibiotic and isotonic crystalloid IVFs 30 ml/kg. (Sheehy pg. 127)
9. **B** – Smell or odor of bitter almonds is a sign of cyanide poisoning, as well as headache and dizziness. Treat with hydroxocobalamin, which converts into vitamin B12, causing a pink color to urine and possibly the skin. Lacrimation occurs in OP exposure. Paralysis is seen in botulism. Skin ulcer is seen in cutaneous anthrax. (Sheehy pg. 511)
10. **C** – It is preferred to have a certified translator and look directly at patient when asking questions. (Sheehy pg. 22)
11. **B** – START triage is based on RPM, respiration, perfusion, and mental status at 30-2-can do. This patient is unable to ambulate so not green, but everything else is OK so he is delayed (yellow). (TNCC pg. 366)
12. **C** – Isoproterenol (Isuprel) is first line for symptomatic bradycardia in patients who have a transplanted heart. Atropine is not effective since there is not a vagus nerve. (Sheehy pg. 234)
13. **A** – Cholinergic crisis is a side effect of Tensilon, and atropine is the treatment. Salivation, lacrimation, and bronchial secretions are symptoms of cholinergic crisis. A Tensilon test is diagnostic for Myasthenia Gravis. (Sheehy pg. 257)

14. **D** – 50% of upper GI bleeds are caused by peptic ulcer disease. Treatment of PUD includes antibiotics and proton pump inhibitors. Treatment of upper GI bleed includes starting IVFs and preparing for endoscopy. (Sheehy pg. 263)
15. **B** – S/S of inhaled anthrax include dry cough, fatigue, and mediastinal widening on chest x-ray. Report to public health officials immediately. "Ground-glass" opacities is seen in ARDS. (Sheehy pg. 174)
16. **B** – The desired outcome of nebulized albuterol is an increased peak flow reading. Pulsus paradoxus and a silent chest are ominous signs in asthma. (Sheehy pg. 220)
17. **A** – The priority intervention is to don full personal protective equipment, including gloves and goggles. The patient's clothing and vomitus must be handled with caution and disposed of carefully. Atropine and 2-PAM are administered along with 100% oxygen, and possible intubation. (Sheehy pg. 349)
18. **D** – Prepare for immediate intubation before complete obstruction occurs. (Sheehy pg. 511)
19. **B** – Glucagon relaxes smooth muscle helping move the impacted food bolus.
20. **C** – Aspirin should be avoided in thyroid storm because it can displace thyroid hormones from binding sites and worsen the patient's condition. (Sheehy pg. 306)
21. **B** – 5.4 mg is 10% of the total r-TPA dose of 54 mg for a 60 kg patient. Tissue plasminogen activator dose is 0.9 mg/kg, bolus 10%, with the remainder over 1 hour. (Sheehy pg. 256)
22. **D** – Neurogenic shock occurs in spinal cord injury that disrupts sympathetic nervous system innervation, producing bradycardia and hypotension. (TNCC pg. 172-73)
23. **B** – Lab values seen in diabetes insipidus (DI) are hypernatremia, increased serum osmolality, decreased urine specific gravity, and decreased urine osmolality due to low levels of ADH. (Sheehy pg. 304)
24. **B** – Potassium levels frequently drop precipitously with fluid replacement as potassium moves back to the intracellular space. Monitor glucose and potassium levels every 1 to 2 hours, and potassium replacement should begin after the first IV fluid bolus. (Sheehy pg. 301)
25. **C** – ECG leads I, aVL, V5, and V5 indicate lateral wall heart damage. Leads II, III, aVF look inferior. Leads V1-V4 look anterior. (Sheehy pg. 241)
26. **A** – Class I shock is up to 15%, (750 mL) blood loss. The physiologic response to hemorrhage in a 70-kg male is slight anxiousness, a pulse < 100 bpm, blood pressure normal with a narrowed or normal pulse pressure, respiratory rate of 14-20, and urinary output of > 30 mL/h. (TNCC pg. 78)
27. **B** – Blunt cardiac injury (cardiac contusion) is the most common cause of traumatic cardiogenic shock. Examples of obstructive shock are tension pneumothorax, cardiac tamponade, massive pulmonary embolus, air embolus, abdominal compartment syndrome, and supine vena cava syndrome. (TNCC pg. 208)
28. **A** – Treating pulmonary edema with noninvasive positive pressure ventilation (NIPPV), loop diuretics, and morphine is to decrease volume (preload). Digoxin is administered to increase contractility. Nitroprusside (Nipride) is used to decrease afterload by vasodilation. (Sheehy pg. 224)
29. **D** – Patients with COPD retain carbon dioxide and are in respiratory acidosis. pH will be < 7.35, and $CO_2$ will be > 45. Hypoxia becomes the drive for respiration.
30. **A** – Seventy percent of patients with myocardial contusion have sinus tachycardia with PVC's. Other common dysrhythmias observed are atrial fib/flutter, ventricular tachycardia, and right bundle branch block. (Sheehy pg. 458)
31. **C** – Adenosine may be used in stable narrow-complex tachycardia (SVT) and in monomorphic wide-complex tachycardia (VT). Polymorphic ventricular tachycardia is suggestive of Torsades de Pointes, treated with Magnesium, Sodium bicarbonate, and Lidocaine. (ACLS, 2015)
32. **A** – Rewarming frozen tissue is very painful; IV opioids should be administered for pain control. The water temperature should be maintained in the range of 37-39. NSAIDs are used to block the production of thromboxane and prostaglandins to reduce tissue damage. (Sheehy pg. 326)
33. **C** – Oral corticosteroids and antivirals are the treatment plan for Bell's Palsy.
34. **D** – Methylprednisolone is NOT indicated for Guillain Barre. Keeping the patient NPO, performing pulmonary function tests, and IV IG or plasma exchange are appropriate. (Sheehy pg. 257)
35. **B** – Serotonin syndrome is characterized by hyperthermia, agitation, hyperreflexia, but no rigidity as in malignant hyperthermia. Cool the patient immediately and do NOT administer haloperidol which will increase temperature. Medications that cause serotonin syndrome include SSRI antidepressants like Celexa, Prozac, Paxil, and Zoloft. St. John's Wort and Ginseng combined with antidepressants increase the risk. (Sheehy pg. 589)

36. **D** – Ribs 4 to 9 are the most common ribs fractured and associated with underlying pulmonary contusion and blunt cardiac injury. Fractures of ribs 1 and 2 are associated with great vessel and brachial plexus injuries. Lower rib fractures 9 to 12 are associated with liver, spleen, and renal injury. (Sheehy pg. 448)
37. **C** – Labyrinthitis is characterized by severe dizziness (vertigo), unilateral nystagmus, and decreased hearing on the affected side. Meniere's disease occurs more often in 40 to 60-year-old females and is recurrent. Treat with Meclizine (Antivert), promethazine (Phenergan), and hyoscine (scopolamine).
38. **D** – Allopurinol and colchicine are treatments for gouty arthritis. The other statements are correct.
39. **A** – Calcium channel blockers are used to decrease vasospasm which causes neurologic deterioration in subarachnoid hemorrhage from aneurysm rupture. (Sheehy pg. 255-257)
40. **C** – Administer the iodine at least one hour after the PTU, if given earlier it can increase T4 levels. Beta-blockers are administered first, then antithyroid medications such as propylthiouracil to block thyroid hormone synthesis. Aspirin is contraindicated in thyroid storm. (Sheehy pg. 305)
41. **C** – Epigastric pain radiating to the back, with elevated amylase and lipase levels are indicated of pancreatitis. (Sheehy pg. 266)
42. **A** – Erythromycin prolongs the QT interval, as well as Haloperidol, Droperidol, Amitriptyline., and many more Hypocalcemia and hypomagnesemia prolong the QTi too. (Sheehy pg. 244)
43. **A** – Flattened T wave and a prominent U wave is seen in hypokalemia. Peaked T waves is seen in hyperkalemia. Delta wave is seen in WPW. Osborn wave is seen in severe hypothermia. (Sheehy pg. 199)
44. **C** – Signs and symptoms of tuberculosis (TB) include fever, chills, night sweats, persistent cough, and hemoptysis. Place the patient in a negative pressure room since TB is carried in airborne particles and droplet nuclei. Isoniazid and rifampin are the two most powerful anti-TB drugs available. (Sheehy pg. 190)
45. **D** – Visual disturbances like "snow field" vision, drowsiness, headache, and dizziness are early S/S of methanol ingestion. Fomepizole (Antizol) is the antidote to prevent permanent vision loss. (Sheehy pg. 348)
46. **C** – Pericarditis is characterized by global ST segment elevation, and treated with oxygen, NSAIDs, and corticosteroids. (Sheehy pg. 246)
47. **C** – Early S/S of bowel obstruction include hyperactive high-pitched bowel sounds, colicky, crampy, wavelike abdominal pain, nausea and vomiting with an odor of feces. (Sheehy pg. 267)
48. **B** – Giant cell or Temporal arteritis is treated emergently with corticosteroids to avoid permanent vision loss. Definitive diagnosis is made by performing a temporal artery biopsy. (Sheehy pg. 253)
49. **D** – HHS is more insidious than with DKA so early symptoms are vague. As it progresses, neurologic symptoms such as confusion and decreased LOC may develop. Lab studies reveal a blood glucose > 600 mg/dL, serum osmolality > 320 mOsm/kg, pH > 7.30. (Sheehy pg. 302-303)
50. **A** – ST segment elevation in V1-V4 is indicative of an anterior MI, likely caused by an occlusion of the LAD. Common symptoms include shortness of breath, substernal chest pain, tachycardia, and signs of left heart failure. (Sheehy pg. 242)
51. **C** – The child struck by a car who is tachycardic and hypotensive should be seen immediately (ESI level 1). The child diving in the pool is at high risk, so triaged as ESI level 2. Hemophilia will be triaged as ESI level 2, and orthopedic injuries as ESI level 3. (ESI Triage pg. 49)
52. **A** – Nursing interventions to decrease intracranial pressure include keeping the head in a neutral position, elevating the head of the bed without flexing knees, and removing rigid cervical collars. Speak softly and limit visitors. (TNCC 8th edition pg. 114)
53. **C** – Hypocalcemia causes tetany, carpopedal spasms, facial twitching, and a prolonged QTi. Treatment includes calcium gluconate. (Sheehy pg. 200)
54. **D** – Patients with right ventricular MI are preload-dependent so administer isotonic fluid boluses to increase preload. (Sheehy pg. 242)
55. **C** – SIADH is caused by excessive amounts of ADH resulting in fluid overload and dilutional hyponatremia. Serum osmolality is typically < 280 mOsmol/kg and serum sodium < 125 mEq/L. Treat with hypertonic saline and free water restriction. (Sheehy pg. 304-305)
56. **C** – Morphine causes histamine release resulting in urticaria (hives). (Sheehy pg. 82-83)
57. **C** – After serum glucose level reaches 200 to 250 mg/dL, fluids should be converted to dextrose-containing solutions to prevent hypoglycemia. The goal of therapy is serum glucose < 200 mg/dL, serum bicarbonate > 18 mEq/L, and the venous pH is > 7.3. (Sheehy pg. 301)
58. **B** – Gastroesophageal variceal bleeding is treated with IV vasopressin or Octreotide. (Sheehy pg. 264)

59. **C** – In rhabdomyolysis, there is an increase in serum CK, potassium, BUN, creatinine, phosphate, uric acid, AST, and ALT. The patient is in metabolic acidosis, so the pH is low. (Sheehy pg. 275 and TNCC 8th ed. pg. 396)
60. **C** – Treatment of globe rupture includes securing impaled objects, shielding the affected eye, patching the unaffected eye to minimize consensual movement, keeping the patient NPO, updating tetanus immunization, and preparing the patient for surgery. Do not remove impaled objects or administer eye drops. (Sheehy pg. 370-371 and TNCC pg. 113)
61. **B** – Alkalis such as concrete, lye, and drain cleaners continue to penetrate and damage the cornea until the substance is removed. Urgent and copious irrigation is indicated. (Sheehy pg. 371 and TNCC pg. 114)
62. **B** – The symptoms are suggestive of placental abruption. The treatment priorities include high-flow oxygen, placing the patient in a lateral decubitus position or placing pillows to tilt the spinal immobilized patient 15 to 30 degrees, and starting two large-bore IV's. An ultrasound should be performed prior to pelvic examination. KB test can be done to assess for fetal blood in material blood. (Sheehy pg. 540 and TNCC pg. 295)
63. **B** – Aortic disruption should be considered in severe deceleration injury. S/S include severe chest pain, dyspnea, a loud systolic murmur, blood pressure and pulse strength discrepancies with decreased pulses in lower extremities, and mediastinal widening on a chest radiograph. Start large-bore IV's, maintain SBP between 100-120 mmHg with Esmolol, and prepare for surgical repair. (Sheehy pg. 461 and TNCC pg. 136)
64. **B** – Central cord syndrome is caused by hyperextension and results in swelling to the central spinal cord, causing a greater loss of function in the upper extremities than in the lower extremities. (Sheehy pg. 440 and TNCC pg. 175)
65. **D** – In zygoma fracture there is deformity to the infraorbital rim with flattening of the cheek (loss of malar eminence), swelling, ecchymosis, trismus, and diplopia. Patients should be instructed to avoid blowing their nose. (Sheehy 428)
66. **A** – Otitis externa or swimmer's ear causes pain, swelling, and redness of the auricle worsened by movement of the tragus or pinna. Treatment includes keeping the ear dry by using earplugs lightly coated with petroleum jelly or ear wicks and providing analgesia. (Sheehy pg. 357)
67. **B** – Reperfusion dysrhythmias such as accelerated idioventricular rhythms (AIVR) are commonly seen after fibrinolytic therapy. (Sheehy pg. 244)
68. **C** – In burn injuries > 20% TBSA begin lactated Ringer's solution at 2 mL/kg/percentage TBSA. Half of the fluid is given in the first 8 hours from the time of the burn injury. 2 x 100 x 50 = 10,000. The amount to given in the first 8 hours = 5,000. (TNCC 8th ed. Pg. 221, Box 11-2)
69. **C** – Shaken impact syndrome or abusive head injury is characterized by subdural hematoma, retinal hemorrhage, altered level of consciousness, and rib fractures. (Sheehy pg. 610)
70. **C** – The priority in ventricular fibrillation is CPR beginning with chest compressions and defibrillation. After IV or IO access is obtained administer Epinephrine 1 mg every 3-5 minutes. Antiarrhythmics such as Amiodarone or Lidocaine may be administered for refractory V Fib, and sodium bicarbonate 1 mEq/kg for cardiac arrest due to metabolic acidosis. (Sheehy pg. 229-232 and ACLS 2018)
71. **C** – In cardiac arrest from pulseless electrical activity (PEA) the priority is CPR and considering the H's and T's to find and treat the cause of the arrest. (Sheehy pg. 233 and ACLS 2016)
72. **D** – The unresponsive patient meets ESI level 1 criteria and requires immediate life-saving intervention. (ESI pg. 50)
73. **C** – Global concave ST segment elevation in ECG leads except V1 and aVR is seen in pericarditis. Treat with oxygen via nasal cannula, NSAIDs, and steroids. (Sheehy pg. 237 and 247)
74. **D** – Decreased urination may be seen in gestational hypertension, not increased urination. PIH patients are at risk for HELLP syndrome. Treat with Mag sulfate and monitor DTR's and respirations closely. (Sheehy pg. 283)
75. **B** – Thick gray coating is the hallmark symptom of Diphtheria. Pertussis is characterized by the "whooping" cough. Measles is characterized by the 3 C's and Koplik spots. Parotid and salivary gland swelling is seen in Mumps. (www.cdc.gov)
76. **A** – Hypothyroidism is caused by low levels of thyroid hormone, so the patient needs Levothyroxine (T4), rewarming, and monitoring of the ABC's. (Sheehy pg. 306)
77. **A** – Apply a nonporous (occlusive) dressing after the patient fully exhales. Tape it on three sides to allow a flap for air to escape. Monitor the patient closely for a tension pneumothorax. (Sheehy pg. 454)

78. **A** – Tracheobronchial injury occurs from blunt or penetrating injury to the neck. Subcutaneous emphysema occurs from air leaking into the chest cavity. Positive-pressure ventilation may worsen the condition. (Sheehy pg. 452)
79. **D** – Hyperkalemia is seen in tumor lysis syndrome, and is characterized by tall, tented T waves initially, then a prolonged PR interval, progressing to a Sine wave. Treatment for hyperkalemia includes calcium gluconate and a combination of insulin and dextrose. (Sheehy pg. 199)
80. **C** – Beta-blockers such as Propranolol (Inderal) are used to treat thyroid storm. (Sheehy pg. 325)
81. **B** – The increased intraocular pressure in acute angle glaucoma causes eye pain, reduced vision, headache, and vomiting. The "classic" sign is halos around lights. Treat with timolol, miotic drops, and diuretics to reduce intraocular pressure. (Sheehy pg. 375)
82. **A** – RMSF symptoms include a macular rash over the palms and the soles, as well as the wrist and ankles. The classic sign of Lyme disease is the red "bulls-eye" rash. Black widow bites produce a halo-shaped lesion. Brown recluse bites produce a red macule with a halo of pallor, then becomes necrotic. (Sheehy pg. 335)
83. **C** – Calcium gluconate is used to deactivate fluoride in hydrofluoric acid exposure (used in glass etching). Fluoride binds with calcium in the blood and can cause cardiac dysrhythmias. (TNCC pg. 228)
84. **D** – The "walking wounded" are classified as green in START triage. Red is immediate, yellow is delated, green is minor, and black is unlikely to survive. (TNCC pg. 366)
85. **D** - The patient should refrain from eating anything that requires excessive chewing or anything that would require over-expansion of the jaw. (Sheehy pg. 363)
86. **C** - Avoiding problems and hoping they disappear does not encourage resiliency in a high-stress environment. Setting goals, modeling work/life balance, promoting self-confidence, and addressing lateral violence directly promote resiliency. (TNCC pg. 339)
87. **C** - Providers may attempt to manually reduce an incarcerated hernia in the ED by applying ice to the area prior to the maneuver and following up with a surgical consult. Bowel regimen is not appropriate for an incarcerated hernia. (Sheehy pg. 570)
88. **C** - GI symptoms such as nausea, vomiting and gastric bleeding are the initial symptoms of radiation exposure, not hearing loss. Stabilize the patient, then decontaminate if needed. (Sheehy pg. 172)
89. **B** – A formal debriefing is open to voluntary participation within 24-72 hours of the critical incident. CISM is reported to mitigate the impact of traumatic events and restores adaptive functioning to those exposed to the critical incident. (TNCC pg. 339)
90. **C** – Increasing the HOB 30 to 45 degrees, regular oral care, sterile suction technique without saline lavage, and peptic ulcer disease (PUD) prophylaxis (not DVT) are suggested to prevent VAP. (TNCC pg. 401 and Sheehy pg. 120)

## PDB Nurse Education, LLC       CEN Post Test - Part 2

1. You are treating a child in cardiac arrest. CPR is initiated, and the cardiac monitor reveals ventricular fibrillation (VF). Which of the following should be performed immediately?
    a. Establish IO access and administer epinephrine.
    b. Perform synchronized cardioversion at 0.5-1.0 j/kg.
    c. Defibrillate at 2-4 j/kg.
    d. Intubate the patient.
2. Which of the following is **INCORRECT** regarding evidence collection?
    a. Avoid cutting through stains and holes when cutting clothes off.
    b. Follow the proper chain of custody.
    c. Place evidence in plastic bags.
    d. The well-being of the patient should take precedence over forensic evidence collection.
3. A patient presents to the ED complaining of shortness of breath and states that he does not have insurance at the front desk. The patient is turned away from the ED because he states that he cannot afford to pay at the time of visit. What is the department in violation of?
    a. The Joint Commission
    b. EMTALA
    c. The CDC requirements
    d. The Center for Medicare and Medicaid Services Mandate (CMS)

4. During a mass casualty incident (MCI) there are multiple pediatric patients arriving to the ED and you are applying Jump START criteria to triage the patients. You are triaging a 5-year-old patient who is unconscious, pale, and limp. She is not breathing, even after opening her airway. She has a palpable pulse. What is your next action?
    a. Categorize the as deceased/expectant and move on to the next patient.
    b. Provide 5 rescue breaths and reassess breathing.
    c. Begin chest compressions and rescue breathing.
    d. Categorize the patient as immediate and begin rescue breathing.
5. Which laboratory test detects fetal red blood cells in the maternal circulation, indicating hemorrhage of fetal blood through the placenta?
    a. Alpha-fetoprotein (AFP)
    b. Thromboelastogram (TEG)
    c. Reticulocyte count
    d. Kleihauer-Betke (KB) test
6. A 28-year-old with a history of depression dies in the emergency department from a self-inflicted gunshot wound (GSW) to the head. Who is the best person to approach the family about possible organ donation?
    a. The trauma surgeon who informed the family about the death.
    b. The trauma program manager.
    c. Organ procurement representative.
    d. The emergency nurse who is supporting the family.
7. During septic shock resuscitation, the goal of medical management is:
    a. Achieving normothermia.
    b. Restoring oxygen-carrying capacity.
    c. Maintaining glucose control.
    d. Resolving lactic acidosis.
8. If a patient enters the emergency department with hot molten tar on his hands, what is the priority of care?
    a. Contact the burn center.
    b. Cool the molten tar with cold water until it is completely cooled.
    c. Cover hands with a petroleum-based ointment and dress to promote emulsification of the tar.
    d. Physically remove the tar.
9. A patient with opioid dependence has failed at recovery several times. Which of the following medications may be beneficial for this patient?
    a. Acamprosate (Campral)
    b. Disulfiram (Antabuse)
    c. Varenicline (Chantix)
    d. Buprenorphine Hydrochloride (Subutex)
10. A patient that was previously treated for an anteriorly dislocated shoulder returns to the ED the next day with their affected arm hanging limply at their side. The nurse recognizes the patient is experiencing what complication of the dislocation?
    a. Brachial plexus injury
    b. Median nerve damage
    c. Acromioclavicular dislocation
    d. Humeral head fracture
11. Focused assessment sonography for trauma (FAST) ultrasound is a portable and inexpensive diagnostic tool that can accurately detect the following, **EXCEPT**:
    a. Hemothorax
    b. Diaphragmatic rupture
    c. Pericardial tamponade
    d. Liver injury
12. The treatment for a 3-month-old with bloody "currant jelly" stools and a palpable "sausage-shaped mass" is:
    a. Gastric tube insertion
    b. Surgical pyloromyotomy
    c. Manual reduction
    d. Barium enema

13. A sudden loss of the ETCO₂ capnography waveform is an indicator of:
    a. Return of spontaneous circulation (ROSC).
    b. Disconnected or occluded endotracheal (ET) tube.
    c. Bronchospasm.
    d. Muscle relaxants wearing off.
14. You are assisting with a precipitous delivery and the umbilical cord is protruding from the vagina. The fetal heart rate is dropping, so the immediate intervention is:
    a. Performing McRoberts maneuver.
    b. Applying suprapubic pressure to facilitate delivery.
    c. Performing Mauriceau's maneuver.
    d. Positioning the patient in knee-chest position.
15. A 15-year-old male with a history of Marfan's syndrome arrives in the ED complaining of a sudden onset of shortness of breath. He is in respiratory distress with a RR of 40, oxygen saturation of 85%, and absent breath sounds on the right side. You suspect:
    a. Dissecting aortic aneurysm
    b. Spontaneous pneumothorax
    c. Congestive heart failure
    d. Huffing of toxic chemicals
16. Which of the following treatment modalities is appropriate for the patient who overdosed on Elavil (amitriptyline)?
    a. Procainamide (Pronestyl) to treat ventricular dysrhythmias.
    b. Induced vomiting to reduce the absorption of the medication.
    c. Gastric lavage to eliminate the medication.
    d. Sodium bicarbonate to promote systemic alkalinization.
17. Urethral injuries are usually a result of high-energy impact or straddle mechanisms and should be considered with any pelvic fracture. Urinary catheter insertion should be withheld until:
    a. A prostate exam is completed.
    b. BUN and creatinine are verified normal.
    c. A retrograde urethrogram is negative.
    d. The patient voids clear urine.
18. What is the appropriate antidote for iron toxicity?
    a. Activated charcoal.
    b. EDTA (edetate disodium).
    c. Glucagon.
    d. Deferoxamine (Desferal).
19. An 8-year-old crashed his bicycle yesterday. He complains of LUQ abdominal pain radiating to the left shoulder and neck. You notice ecchymosis over the left lower chest to upper abdomen and abdominal distention. He has rebound tenderness upon palpation. You suspect an injury to the:
    a. Liver
    b. Spleen
    c. Small bowel
    d. Great vessels
20. A 70-year-old female with a history of atrial fibrillation is diagnosed with an acute subdural hematoma after a fall. She takes Eliquis (Apixaban) daily, so the nurse prepares to administer which medication while awaiting transfer to the OR?
    a. Kcentra (Prothrombin concentrate)
    b. Protamine sulfate
    c. Andexxa (Coag factor Xa)
    d. Tranexamic acid (TXA)
21. Which of the following is **NOT** a risk factor for workplace violence in the ED?
    a. Long wait times.
    b. Private patient rooms.
    c. Poor communication.
    d. Understaffing.

22. A common fear among toddlers includes:
    a. Death
    b. Darkness
    c. Bodily harm
    d. Separation from caregiver
23. Treatment for heat stroke includes which of the following?
    a. Cooling to a target temperature of 38.8 degrees C (102 F).
    b. Acetaminophen to reduce temperature.
    c. Ibuprofen to reduce temperature.
    d. Dantrolene to reduce temperature.
24. Which ECG change may you see when the child's temperature drops below 31 degrees C (88 F)?
    a. Delta wave
    b. Inverted T wave
    c. Osborn or J wave
    d. Biphasic P wave
25. Your patient was recently treated for otitis media. They present today with ear pain, fever, and difficulty hearing out of the affected ear. You recognize that they are most likely experiencing what complication of otitis media?
    a. Mastoiditis
    b. Meniere's Disease
    c. Foreign body obstruction
    d. Cerumen impaction
26. What would **NOT** be a clinical indication for an indwelling catheter placement?
    a. Turn intolerance.
    b. Spinal instability.
    c. Precise intake and output monitoring.
    d. Frequent urination.
27. You are at triage when multiple patients present simultaneously. Which patient is MOST urgent?
    a. 5-year-old with sickle cell disease, fever, and chest pain.
    b. 3-year-old Cystic Fibrosis patient with a non-displaced ulnar fracture.
    c. 10-year-old with autism spectrum disorder with vomiting for 2 hours.
    d. 7-year-old well-child with a dog bit to the leg.
28. Your patient has been diagnosed with an ovarian torsion. You know that the definitive treatment is:
    a. Pain control
    b. Antibiotic administration
    c. Methotrexate
    d. Surgery
29. Human rabies immune globulin (HRIG) is ordered for a 3-year-old child who was bitten by a bat. The emergency nurse knows the correct dose of HRIG is:
    a. 10 units/kg
    b. 20 units/kg
    c. 30 units/kg
    d. 40 units/kg
30. A 2-year-old was bitten by a racoon while on a camping trip with his family. What is the preferred site to administer the intramuscular (IM) rabies vaccine?
    a. Deltoid
    b. Ventrogluteal
    c. Anterolateral thigh
    d. Dorsogluteal
31. Issues with sexual orientation and gender identity are risk factors for which of the following?
    a. Oppositional defiant disorder
    b. Schizophrenia
    c. Suicidal ideation
    d. Body dysmorphia

32. A patient with a knee dislocation is ordered q 2-hour neurovascular checks. The emergency nurse knows they are assessing for:
    a. Sciatic nerve compression
    b. Popliteal artery damage
    c. Abnormal range of motion
    d. Tibia/fibula involvement
33. What is the most appropriate location in the emergency department for a child diagnosed with an autism spectrum disorder?
    a. A hallway stretcher for greater visibility.
    b. Near the nurse's station for ease of redirection.
    c. Away from the main hallway to decrease stimulation.
    d. In a recliner area to encourage social interaction.
34. Which of the following would **NOT** be considered a trigger for a patient with asthma?
    a. Second-hand smoke
    b. Exercising in cold weather
    c. Acetaminophen
    d. Emotional stress
35. A 5-year-old with a ventricular shunt for hydrocephalus presents to the emergency department. Which symptom is most concerning?
    a. Hyperactivity
    b. Temperature of 100.4 F (38 C)
    c. Respiratory rate of 30 per minute
    d. Unsteady gait
36. Which of the following statements is **INCORRECT** regarding wound care?
    a. Foam or alginate dressings are for chronic wounds only.
    b. Wounds with necrotic tissue require debridement prior to dressing.
    c. Infected wounds require antibacterial treatment prior to dressing.
    d. Wound vacs are used for wounds draining greater than 50 mL of fluid daily.
37. In the pediatric patient with sickle cell disease, the nurse anticipates the administration of which medication to manage the moderate to severe pain of a vaso occlusive crisis?
    a. NSAIDs such as ibuprofen.
    b. Opioids such as morphine or fentanyl.
    c. Hydroxyurea (Hydrea).
    d. Oxygen is the only medication needed.
38. Which mechanism of injury is most likely to result in a hip dislocation?
    a. A patient who suffered a seizure and fell from a standing position.
    b. An MVC victim that had their leg outstretched on the brake pedal at the time of impact.
    c. A diver that has suffered an axial loading injury.
    d. The driver of an ATV that rolled over.
39. A 6-year-old, 20-kg child presents with 10% superficial, 20% deep partial thickness, and 20% full-thickness burns from an immersion injury. What amount of fluid should be administered in the first 8 hours after injury?
    a. 1200 mL
    b. 1500 mL
    c. 2400 mL
    d. 3000 mL
40. The nurse is performing a Glasgow Coma Scale (GCS) assessment on a head trauma patient. His eyes open to cuticle pressure, his best verbal response is incomprehensible sounds, and he exhibits flexion (decorticate posturing). What is this patient's GCS?
    a. 6
    b. 7
    c. 8
    d. 9
41. The normal range for fetal heart rate is between:
    a. 60-100 beats per minute.
    b. 100-150 beats per minute.

c. 120-160 beats per minute.
d. 150-200 beats per minute.

42. The emergency nurse is performing a Full Outline of Unresponsiveness (FOUR) assessment on a head trauma patient. His eyelids are closed, but open to loud voice. The patient exhibits flexion to pain. Pupil and corneal reflexes are present. The patient is not intubated and is breathing in a Cheyne-Stokes breathing pattern. What is this patient's FOUR score?
    a. 8
    b. 9
    c. 10
    d. 11

43. Which of the following physical findings may indicate globe rupture?
    a. Flashes of light and floaters in the visual field.
    b. A teardrop-shaped pupil and vitreous humor leakage.
    c. Halos around lights and tunnel vision.
    d. Painless loss of vision and transient episodes of blindness.

44. A fluid bolus for a 15 kg child in hypotensive shock from vomiting should be:
    a. 150 ml of an isotonic crystalloid solution over 5-10 minutes.
    b. 150 ml of an isotonic crystalloid solution over 10-20 minutes.
    c. 300 ml of an isotonic crystalloid solution over 5-10 minutes.
    d. 300 ml of an isotonic crystalloid solution over 10-20 minutes.

45. A 69-year-old female discovered twelve hours after a fall where she fractured her hip has developed acute tubular necrosis (ATN). She has been normotensive since admission, so what is the most likely reason for her acute renal failure?
    a. Hemorrhagic shock
    b. Fat embolism syndrome
    c. Rhabdomyolysis
    d. Aging

46. Application of a pelvic binder is performed in unstable pelvic fractures to:
    a. Reduce muscle spasms.
    b. Prevent fat embolism.
    c. Temporarily tamponade the bleeding.
    d. Prevent compartment syndrome.

47. A toddler who recognizes his parents, but will not respond to the nurse's request is listed as which of the following when assessing mental status using the AVPU mnemonic?
    a. A for alert.
    b. V for verbal.
    c. P for painful.
    d. U for unresponsive.

48. Hypotension in tension pneumothorax is the result of:
    a. Impaired venous return to the heart.
    b. Negative intrathoracic pressure.
    c. Vasodilation from distributive shock.
    d. Hemorrhage from the internal mammary artery.

49. You are triaging for a 3-year-old who presents with stridor, drooling, and fever. He is tripoding with an SaO$_2$ of 91% on room air. What is the appropriate next step for this patient?
    a. Take the patient out of the mother's arms and lay him flat on the bed to perform a thorough examination.
    b. Have the mother hold him while an ABG is obtained to ensure that he has adequate ventilation.
    c. Use a tongue depressor to assess for enlarged, purulent tonsils.
    d. Let his mother hold him, administer blow-by oxygen, and arrange for airway assessment in the emergency department or operating room.

50. A patient with a hip dislocation is most likely to suffer from which complication:
    a. Avascular necrosis of the femoral head
    b. Popliteal artery damage
    c. Peroneal nerve injury

d. Tibial nerve and artery compromise
51. A 7-year-old patient Is brought in by his father stating that he was complaining of shortness of breath and diaphoretic. At the time of arrival, the patient is obtunded, with a heart rate of 200 on the monitor with narrow and regular QRS complex and a blood pressure of 85/43. What is the most appropriate next action?
    a. Defibrillate the patient at 2-4j/kg.
    b. Synchronized cardioversion at 0.5-1 j/kg.
    c. Administer adenosine 0.1mg/kg.
    d. Perform vagal maneuvers by having the child blow through a straw.
52. Clamping of a chest tube during transport is contraindicated since it may cause:
    a. Blood clots
    b. Tension pneumothorax
    c. ARDS development
    d. Air leak
53. A 3-week-old infant is brought to the emergency department by her parents. The patient's father states that the patient has been fussy with bilious vomiting and blood in her stool. The nurse suspects intestinal volvulus. What treatment plan does she anticipate?
    a. Antibiotics and antiemetics.
    b. Air or contrast enema and IV fluids.
    c. Gastric decompression and immediate surgical intervention.
    d. IV fluids and Protonix infusion.
54. Which of the following are signs and symptoms of epididymitis?
    a. Prolonged penile erection with severe inguinal pain.
    b. Sudden, severe onset of inguinal pain that worsens with elevation.
    c. Gradual onset of scrotal pain that is relieved with elevation, urethral discharge.
    d. Gradual onset of scrotal pain that worsens with elevation, urethral discharge.
55. A patient with a history of CHF presents to the ED with increased dyspnea. The patient is hemodynamically stable, and assessment reveals egophony and dullness on percussion over the left lung fields. The nurse prepares to assist with which procedure?
    a. Thoracentesis
    b. Needle thoracostomy
    c. Pericardiocentesis
    d. Incision and drainage
56. A 16-year-old patient presents to the ED via EMS with nausea, vomiting, and diaphoresis. Her parents reported they found an empty bottle of Tylenol (acetaminophen) in the patient's room when they tried to get her up for school. The patient states "I just wanted to sleep." What is the appropriate antidote to administer to this patient?
    a. Flumazenil (Romazicon)
    b. N-Acetylcysteine (Acetadote)
    c. Naloxone (Narcan)
    d. Fomepizole (Antizol)
57. A patient with a history of hemophilia presents to the emergency department after being involved in an MVC. The patient is complaining of arm pain with a large hematoma present, and an abrasion to the leg which is continuously bleeding despite direct pressure being applied. The following treatments are appropriate for this patient, **EXCEPT**:
    a. Aminocaproic acid to stabilize clots and inhibit fibrinolysis.
    b. Desmopressin (DDAVP) for vasoconstriction and release of factor VIII.
    c. Factor replacement and blood products.
    d. Ibuprofen for pain control.
58. A 5-month-old infant is carried to the ED by her parents. They state she has been inconsolable since yesterday. You note that the patient has a shrill cry, and your assessment reveals a bulging fontanelle, opisthotonos, and a high fever. What is the most appropriate next action for the nurse?
    a. Administer antipyretics to reduce risk of seizure.
    b. Initiate an IV and draw blood cultures.
    c. Place the patient in a private room and initiate droplet precautions.
    d. Prepare for a lumbar puncture.

59. A patient presents to the ED after being punched in the eye during a fight. The patient complains of right eye pain with vision loss and nausea. Your assessment reveals blood in the anterior chamber of the eye. What injury do you suspect?
    a. Globe rupture
    b. Orbital fracture
    c. Hyphema
    d. Retinal detachment
60. A pediatric patient who ingested a bottle of vitamins with iron was administered deferoxamine, which is a chelating agent. The patient's mother is concerned when the patient's urine appears to be pink in color a few hours later. What is the most appropriate response by the nurse?
    a. "I will let the doctor know. GI bleeding is common with iron overdose."
    b. "That is a expected effect of the deferoxamine, and it is harmless."
    c. "We will continue to monitor the patient to see if it gets worse."
    d. "I will talk to the doctor because coagulopathies are an adverse effect that can occur with deferoxamine administration."
61. Which of the following statements is **INCORRECT** in the care of the deaf patient?
    a. Wear a name tag so the patient can identify staff.
    b. Flicker the lights when entering the room instead of knocking.
    c. Allow the patient to write or text.
    d. Speak clearly and increase your volume when conversing.
62. A 13-year-old patient is diagnosed with a concussion. During discharge teaching, the parents ask when he can play football again. What is the appropriate response from the nurse?
    a. He can begin playing again once he is symptom-free for 24 hours.
    b. He should follow a graduated return-to-play protocol.
    c. He will not be able to play full contact sports for at least 6 weeks.
    d. He will not be able to play until he has a clear CT scan.
63. A 16-year-old patient presents to the ED. Her mother states she has been experiencing tremors with strange muscle contractions and repetitive movements, slurred speech, and restlessness (akathisia). The patient has a history of schizophrenia and asthma and is currently being treated for strep throat. The mother provides a list of her medications, and the nurse suspects that the symptoms may be related to which of the following:
    a. Haloperidol
    b. Albuterol
    c. Ipratropium
    d. Amoxicillin
64. Your facility is receiving several multi-trauma patients after a building collapse. Which neuromuscular blocking agent should be avoided in patients with crush injury?
    a. Rocuronium (Zemuron)
    b. Succinylcholine (Anectine)
    c. Vecuronium (Norcuron)
    d. Pancuronium (Pavulon)
65. A severely injured child is transported to the ED in cardiac arrest. To best facilitate the family's understanding of the event the nurse should:
    a. Arrange for the ED nurse manager to speak with the family members.
    b. Arrange for the parents to be at the bedside.
    c. Place the family in the family room.
    d. Call the hospital chaplain to remain with the family in the family waiting room.
66. Which of the following functions/sensations is typically preserved in a patient with an anterior cord syndrome?
    a. Motor function
    b. Pain sensation
    c. Proprioception
    d. Temperature sensation

67. A patient is demonstrating use of his crutches prior to discharge. Which action by the patient demonstrates need for further education?
    a. He is using a 3-point gait with both crutches advancing simultaneously.
    b. His elbows are flexed at a 30-degree angle.
    c. The tip of the crutches is kept 6 inches to the side of each step.
    d. The patient places most of his weight on the axillary padding.
68. A female patient arrives at the ED after escaping a house fire. There are no obvious burns, but the patient is confused and complaining of a headache and nausea. VS: HR=76, RR=18, BP=130/78, O$_2$ sat 99% on room air. An NRB is applied at 15 L/min and a carboxyhemoglobin (COHb) level is drawn. The lab calls to report a COHb level of 32. What is the priority nursing intervention for this patient?
    a. Discontinuing the O$_2$ since the oxygen saturation is 98% and the respiratory rate is within normal limits.
    b. Oxygen should be delivered at 15 L via NRB until the COHb level is less than 10.
    c. The nurse should prepare for intubation due to mechanism of injury.
    d. An IV should be obtained to give IV steroids to reduce swelling.
69. What would be an **UNEXPECTED** finding when performing an Allen's test?
    a. Non-blanching fist when opening/closing repeatedly.
    b. Pinkness returning 7 seconds after a fist is released.
    c. Blanching fist when opening/closing repeatedly.
    d. Collateral circulation from the ulnar artery.
70. Your patient has been diagnosed with a dissecting abdominal aortic aneurysm and requires emergent surgery, but they are on Coumadin (warfarin). What would be the most appropriate medication to administer?
    a. Kcentra (prothrombin complex)
    b. TXA (tranexamic acid)
    c. Protamine Sulfate
    d. Praxbind (Dabigatran)
71. You are receiving multiple patients from a warehouse accident. When triaging the patients, which is your highest priority?
    a. 35-year-old with an open tibia/fibula fracture with distal pulses intact
    b. 42-year-old with no breath sounds on the right side and tracheal deviation to the left side
    c. 28-year-old with an abdominal wound with bleeding controlled
    d. 51-year-old with confusion and an unsteady gait
72. A bladder scan reveals your patient has 300 mL urine in their bladder. Which over the counter medication is most likely responsible for the urinary retention?
    a. Acetaminophen (Tylenol)
    b. Ibuprofen (Motrin)
    c. Omeprazole (Prilosec)
    d. Diphenhydramine (Benadryl)
73. Which findings would cause you to suspect a patient was a victim of strangulation?
    a. Corneal laceration with bruising to the face.
    b. Degloving to hands and burns to the lips.
    c. Dysphonia and petechiae to eyelids.
    d. Scapular fracture and abrasions to posterior surfaces.
74. Which victim of interpersonal violence is at highest risk for stroke?
    a. 28-year-old with burns to her lips and tongue.
    b. 33-year-old with bite wounds to the face.
    c. 27-year-old with strangulation injuries.
    d. 39-year-old with Grey Turner's sign.
75. Your patient is diagnosed with urinary calculi. During your assessment, which of the following would be considered an abnormal finding?
    a. Hematuria
    b. Abdominal bruits
    c. Low grade fever
    d. Costovertebral (CVA) tenderness

76. The following are requirements of EMTALA, **EXCEPT**:
    a. Patient are stabilized to the extent possible by the referring facility prior to transfer.
    b. The provider does not need to secure an accepting physician if the patient is being transferred to a regional trauma center.
    c. Consent for transfer must be obtained from a patient or their representative after outlining risks of transport.
    d. A medical screening examination must be performed by a qualified medical provider regardless of patient's ability to pay.
77. You are discharging your patient with a new prescription for Keppra (Levetiracetam). What of the following is most important to review with your patient?
    a. "It is important to get your drug levels checked regularly."
    b. "Once you have taken the medication for one year, you can be tapered off of it."
    c. "This medication may make you dizzy and drowsy."
    d. "Make sure you take this on an empty stomach to increase absorption."
78. A patient presents to the ED complaining of pain and swelling above his right heel after hearing a "popping" sound while sprinting at track. He is unable to point his toes, so the nurse suspects an Achilles tendon tear. Which of the following medications places the patient at higher risk of tendon rupture?
    a. Fluoxetine (Prozac)
    b. Propranolol (Inderal)
    c. Alprazolam (Xanax)
    d. Levofloxacin (Levaquin)
79. After a vaginal delivery 6 days ago, a woman requests treatment for continued bleeding. What is the initial intervention for postpartum hemorrhage?
    a. Fundal massage
    b. IV oxytocin (Pitocin)
    c. Dilation and curettage
    d. Methotrexate
80. A 28-year-old female presents to the emergency department for an explosive headache that she describes as the "worst headache of my life." She has an episode of projectile vomiting while wheeling her to a room. The nurse is concerned the patient has which immediate life-threatening disorder?
    a. Brain tumor
    b. Migraine headache
    c. Hemicrania continua
    d. Subarachnoid hemorrhage
81. The nurse is triaging a 4-month-old premature infant with fever, cough, and runny nose. Assessment reveals subcoastal retractions, with crackles and wheezing audible throughout the lung fields. The nurse suspects:
    a. Asthma
    b. Bronchiolitis
    c. Epiglottitis
    d. Croup
82. A patient with blunt chest trauma exhibits severe respiratory distress, absent breath sounds on the right side, tracheal deviation to the left side, and a feeling of impending doom. The nurse prepares to assist with which emergency procedure?
    a. Pericardiocentesis
    b. Needle thoracostomy
    c. Chest tube insertion
    d. Tracheal intubation
83. You are discharging a patient diagnosed with urinary calculi. What would you include in the discharge education?
    a. "Strain all urine to send for laboratory analysis."
    b. "Take acetaminophen every 4 hours as needed for pain."
    c. "Limit oral intake until the stone passes."
    d. "Follow up with urology in 3 days if you have increased pain, uncontrolled vomiting, or fever and chills."

84. You are discharging a patient diagnosed with diverticulitis. Which statement by the patient indicates an understanding of their diet regimen once inflammation has resolved?
    a. "I should reduce the number of calories I consume."
    b. "I should eat a higher fiber diet."
    c. "I am on a 1,500mL fluid restriction."
    d. "I need to consume a consistent amount of Vitamin K. "
85. Which infectious disease is characterized by conjunctivitis, coryza, cough, and Koplik spots?
    a. Varicella
    b. Mumps
    c. Measles (Rubeola)
    d. Pertussis

**CEN Post Test Answers – Part 2**

1. **C** - CPR and defibrillation are the priorities in VF, along with finding the cause of the arrest and epinephrine. (PALS pgs. 89-92)
2. **C** – Evidence should be placed in paper, not plastic bags. The other options are correct. (Sheehy pgs. 596-98)
3. **B** – EMTALA is a component of COBRA which states that a qualified provider must perform a medical screening exam and treatment to stabilize emergency medical conditions on all patients who present requesting emergency care (Sheehy pgs. 9-11)
4. **B** – The difference between START and JumpSTART triage criteria is that 5 rescue breaths are to be provided to a pediatric patient who is not breathing but has a palpable pulse, and breathing is to be reassessed prior to categorizing the patient as dead/dying. If this patient begins breathing on her own after 5 rescue breaths, she would be categorized as immediate. (ENPC pg. 349)
5. **D** – The KB serum test detects fetal red cells in the maternal circulation, used to predict abruptio placentae. It is important in determining the need to administer Rh immune globulin when the mother is Rh negative, and the fetus is Rh positive. (TNCC pg. 299)
6. **C** – The person who approaches the family about donation must be a trained requester or local organ procurement representative. Early notification gives the OPO representative adequate time to prepare the family for the request to donate a loved one's organs or tissue. (Sheehy pg. 142, 146 and TNCC pg. 334)
7. **B** - Therapeutic interventions should be guided with a goal of increasing the body's normal oxygen-carrying capacity to limit any further organ damage. (Sheehy pg. 228)
8. **B** – Stop the burning process by cooling in water until the tar or asphalt is cool to the touch. Physical removal is not an emergency. After cooling, adherent tar should be covered with a petroleum-based ointment. (TNCC pg. 227)
9. **D** - Buprenorphine is another option for patients that have had multiple failed attempts at recovery using methadone and other drugs. Campral and Antabuse are used for alcohol addiction. Chantix is used for nicotine dependence. (Sheehy pg. 637)
10. **A** - Shoulder and elbow dislocations can often lead to brachial plexus damage which can present up to 48 hours after the injury. (Sheehy pg. 494)
11. **B** – Providers are trained to assess the hepatorenal fossa, the splenorenal fossa, the pericardial sac, and the pelvis. FAST cannot diagnose hollow visceral and retroperitoneal injuries, and it is user dependent. (TNCC pg. 129 & 157, Sheehy pg. 470)
12. **D** – The initial treatment of intussusception is a barium enema. Surgical intervention may be necessary if the enema does not reduce the obstruction. Pyloric stenosis is treated with a gastric tube and pyloromyotomy. Testicular torsion may be treated with manual reduction. (Sheehy pg. 570)
13. **B** - A sudden loss of waveform is an indication of a disconnected circuit or an occluded ETT. ROSC suddenly increases ETCO$_2$ during CPR. Bronchospasm results in a "shark-fin" appearance. Muscle relaxants wearing off results in a cleft in the waveform. (TNCC pgs. 68-70 and 399)
14. **D** – Therapeutic intervention in prolapsed cord is aimed at relieving pressure on the cord and minimizing fetal anoxia. Either elevate the mother's hips or place the mother in the knee-chest position. McRoberts maneuver (legs hyper flexed) and suprapubic pressure are indicated in shoulder dystocia. Mauriceau's maneuver is used in breech delivery. (Sheehy pgs. 286-87)

15. **B** - Spontaneous pneumothorax. Marfan's is a genetic defect of the connective tissue which is characterized by elongated faces, limbs, fingers, and toes. The risk of spontaneous pneumothorax and aortic aneurysm is higher. These symptoms are suggestive of pneumothorax. (ENPC pg. 86)
16. **D** – Systemic alkalinization (urine alkalinization) can narrow the QRS, improve blood pressure, and control ventricular dysrhythmias seen in in tricyclic antidepressants overdoses. Induced vomiting and gastric lavage are contraindicated because CNS depression can develop rapidly. Do not treat ventricular dysrhythmias with type 1A antidysrhythmic agents. (Sheehy pg. 347)
17. **C** – Retrograde urethrograms should be completed prior to insertion of a urinary catheter when urethral injury is suspected. Evaluate for blood at the urethral meatus and gross hematuria. Most injuries require a suprapubic cystostomy. (TNCC pg. 157 and Sheehy pg. 474)
18. **D** – Deferoxamine (Desferal) is the antidote (chelating agent) for iron (Fe+) ingestion, seen most common in children who ingest prenatal vitamins. Activated charcoal does not bind with heavy metals. EDTA is used for lead toxicity. Glucagon is used in beta-blocker toxicity. (Sheehy pg. 350)
19. **B** – Splenic injury. LUQ pain radiating to the shoulder (Kehr's Sign) is consistent with a spleen injury. (Sheehy pg. 471)
20. **C** - Andexxa is the reversal for Eliquis (Apixaban) and Xarelto (Rivaroxaban). Kcentra is the reversal for warfarin. Protamine sulfate is the reversal agent for heparin. (Sheehy pg. 409)
21. **B** - Long wait times, poor communication, and understaffing all contribute to the potential for violence in the ED, not private rooms. (Sheehy pg. 48)
22. **D** - Fear of death, darkness, and bodily harm are all common fears for preschoolers. A toddler is most afraid of being separated from their caregiver (Sheehy pg. 557)
23. **A** – Heat stroke can quickly lead to multiple organ failure so cool quickly to a target temperature of 38.8 degrees Celsius. Use evaporation, ice packs, cold-water immersion, and administer benzodiazepines to prevent shivering while cooling. (Sheehy pg. 322)
24. **C** – Osborn or J wave may be seen in cardiac irritability from hypothermia. A delta wave is seen in WPW. (Sheehy pg. 323)
25. **A** - Mastoiditis is infection of the mastoid bone which is most often a result of otitis media. (Sheehy pg. 359)
26. **D** - There are many external collection devices that can be used for patients that require frequent toileting. Placing an indwelling urinary catheter should be avoided unless necessary to prevent CAUTI. (www.CDC.gov and www.AHRQ.gov)
27. **A** - This patient would be an ESI level 2 as they are at high-risk for acute chest syndrome. (Sheehy pg. 568)
28. **D** - Ovarian torsion should be treated much like testicular torsion and emergent surgery is required to avoid infertility, infection, and necrosis. (Sheehy pg. 290)
29. **B** – All postexposure prophylaxis should begin with a thorough cleansing with soap and water. For those not previously vaccinated, HRIG dosing is 20 units/kilogram. If feasible, the full dose should be infiltrated around and into the wound. Any remaining volume should be administered IM. HRIG should not be administered in the same syringe as vaccine. (Sheehy pg. 108)
30. **C** – The outer aspect of the thigh is appropriate in younger children. The vaccine should never be administered in the gluteal area due to decreased absorption and risk of sciatic nerve injury. The deltoid area is the only acceptable site of vaccination for adults and older children. The vaccine is given on days 0, 3, 7, and 14. (Sheehy pg. 108)
31. **C** – When screening for suicidal ideation, use direct simple questions and without the caregiver's present. Risk factors include issues with sexual orientation and gender identity, chronic or terminal illness, psychiatric diagnosis, previous attempts, and history or abuse or bullying. (ENPC pg. 247)
32. B - Patients with a dislocated knee require frequent neurovascular checks to assess for potential compromise of the popliteal artery and peroneal nerve. (TNCC pg. 199)
33. **C** – Patients with autism are more sensitive to sound and light, so place the patient in a room away from main hallways. Move slowly and avoid touching the child any more than necessary. Maintain consistent team members. (ENPC pg. 249)
34. **C** – Acetaminophen is not a trigger for asthma, but NSAIDs, aspirin, and beta-blockers may trigger an acute, as well as smoke, cold weather, dust, and emotional stress. (Sheehy pg. 218)
35. **D** – Older children with hydrocephalus exhibit headache, diplopia, and unsteady gait. Infants present with vomiting, sleepiness, irritability, "sun-setting" eyes, and seizures. (ENPC pg. 155-156)

36. **A** – Foam dressings work well for abrasions, lacerations, and incisions. Alginates and wounds vacs work well for surgical wounds producing excess fluids. Infected wounds require antibacterial treatment. (Sheehy pg. 105-106).
37. **B** - Patients in a vaso-occlusive crisis typically require opioid administration to manage their moderate to severe pain. Hydroxyurea daily reduces the frequency of painful crises. Oxygen and NSAIDs are used for minor pain. (Sheehy pg. 568)
38. **B** – There is a high probability of hip dislocation when there is a high-impact collision, and the leg is extended (outstretched). (Sheehy pg. 495)
39. **A** – The Parkland formula for children is 3 ml lactated ringers solution multiplied by weight in kgs multiplied by percentage TBSA of deep partial and full thickness (not superficial) burns. Half of the fluid is given in the first 8 hours from the time of the burn injury. # x 20 x 40 = 2400. 1200 ml will be given in the first 8 hours from the burn injury. Adequacy of fluid resuscitation is measured by minimum urine output of 1-2 mL/kg/hour. (TNCC pg. 246)
40. **B** – The GCS score ranges from 3 to 15 and provides a measure of the patient's level of consciousness as well as a predictor of morbidity and mortality after brain injury. This patient receives a 2 for best eye opening (to pressure), a 2 for best verbal response (incomprehensible words), and a 3 for best motor response (flexion), totaling 7 out of 15. GCS is limited due to sedation, fractures, or spinal cord injury. (TNCC pg. 101)
41. **C** – The normal fetal heart rate is 120-160 beats per minute and may be heard using a Doppler ultrasound by 10 weeks gestation. (TNCC pg. 297)
42. **D** – FOUR score evaluates four parameters - eye response, motor response, brainstem reflexes, and respiration. Each parameter is scored from 0-4, with 16 as best score. This patient scores 2 for eye response, 2 for motor response, 4 for brain stem reflexes, and 3 for respiration, totaling 11 out of 16. FOUR score is more reliable than GCS in intubated patients. (TNCC pg. 101)
43. **B** - A teardrop-shaped pupil and vitreous humor leakage is indicative of globe rupture. (TNCC pg. 113)
44. **C** - 20 ml/kg over 5 to 10 minutes for severe shock using the "pull-push method" with 20 ml syringes. You may infuse over 20 minutes if not severe shock. Use smaller fluid boluses of 5-10 ml/kg over 10-20 minutes if you suspect cardiogenic shock. Monitor closely for signs of pulmonary edema. (PALS pg. 201)
45. **C** – Rhabdomyolysis is muscle damage, releasing myoglobin. Myoglobin obstructs renal perfusion and glomerular filtration. Acute kidney injury/renal failure occurs in 24% of patients with rhabdomyolysis. (TNCC pg. 396)
46. **C** – Pelvic binder application will help attain stabilization and control hemorrhage by exerting external pressure. (TNCC pg. 156)
47. **A** – Toddlers may be cautious of strangers, and may not respond to healthcare provider commands, which is a normal response. (TNCC pg. 235)
48. **A** – Air enters the pleural space but cannot escape on expiration, increasing intrathoracic pressure. As pressure rises, venous return is impaired, cardiac output decreases, and hypotension occurs. (TNCC pg. 134)
49. **D** – The S/S may indicate epiglottitis. Allow the patient to assume a position of comfort. Avoid activities that will cause the patient to cry. Airway assessment and intubation should be performed in the emergency department or operating room with a surgical airway prepared as backup. (ENPC pg. 190)
50. **A** - A dislocated hip can result in necrosis of the femoral head without timely reduction. (TNCC pg. 199)
51. **B** – This patient is experiencing unstable SVT and requires immediate cardioversion. Adenosine administration and vagal maneuvers would be appropriate for a patient with stable SVT. Defibrillate a patient with pulseless VT or VF. (PALS pgs. 262-263)
52. **B** - Clamping a chest tube for transport or any other extended periods of time is contraindicated due to the increased intrathoracic pressure that can lead to tension pneumothorax development. (TNCC pg. 138)
53. **C** – Intestinal volvulus (malrotation) is when loops of bowel twists around each other. Malrotation is a congenital condition in which the intestines have an abnormal rotation which often leads to volvulus and compression of the mesenteric artery, which compromises blood supply to the intestines. Treatment is immediate surgical intervention. Gastric decompression may be performed while waiting for surgery. (ENPC pgs. 201-202)
54. **C** – Epididymitis is an acute bacterial infection often caused by Chlamydia or Gonorrhea. It is characterized by scrotal pain with a gradual onset that is relieved with elevation (Prehn's sign), urinary frequency, and urethral discharge. Evaluate for STI's, treat with antibiotics and NSAIDS. (Sheehy pg. 277)

55. **A** – Egophony and dullness are symptoms of pleural effusion. Pleural effusion occurs in heart failure, pneumonia, lung and breast cancer, pancreatitis, and pulmonary embolus. A thoracentesis is performed to remove fluid. Purulent fluid is an empyema. Thick white fluid is a chylous. (ENA Core Curriculum pg. 465)
56. **B** – N-Acetylcysteine (Acetadote) is the antidote for acetaminophen overdose. It should be administered within 8 hours of ingestion. Activated charcoal can be administered within 1 hours of ingestion if the patient is alert. Acetaminophen overdose can lead to severe hepatotoxicity. (Sheehy pgs. 341-42)
57. **D** – Medications such as ibuprofen and aspirin should be avoided in patients with hemophilia. The other treatments are appropriate. Acetaminophen, rest, ice, and compression may be used for pain. (Sheehy pgs. 316-317)
58. **C** – This patient is exhibiting S/S of meningitis and should immediately be placed on droplet precautions. The nurse would anticipate initiating an IV and performing a septic workup including bloodwork, IVFs, and antibiotic administration. Diagnosis and determination of viral vs bacterial is made by performing a lumbar puncture. (Sheehy pg. 572)
59. **C** – A hyphema is a collection of blood in the anterior chamber of the eye. Treatment includes bed rest with the head of the bed elevated to 30-45 degrees. Rebleeding may occur, and usually occurs within 3 to 5 days after initial injury. Instruct patient to return to the ED if signs of rebleeding occur. (Sheehy pgs. 369-70)
60. **B** – Deferoxamine is a chelating agent that is the reversal agent for iron. It often turns urine pink as it is excreted. (ENPC pg. 280)
61. **D** – Do NOT increase your volume but do speak clearly and distinctly. Use dry erase boards to communicate with the patient. When using a sign language interpreter, look at and speak directly to the patient. (www.ADA.gov)
62. **B** – It is recommended that patients follow the graduated return-to-play protocol after suffering from a concussion. Activity is gradually increased as the patient can reach each step without symptoms. (Sheehy pg. 350)
63. **A** – The symptoms described are extrapyramidal symptoms (EPS) which are often caused by antipsychotic medications. Dystonia (muscle spasms) can be treated with diphenhydramine. Akathisia symptoms may be treated with beta blockers and benzodiazepines. (Sheehy pg. 592)
64. **B** - Succinylcholine (Anectine) is contraindicated in Guillain Barre, patients with a history of malignant hyperthermia, crush injury, burns > 24 hours, and hyperkalemia. (TNCC pg. 66)
65. **B** - Arrange for the parents to be at the bedside. Current research shows most family members want to be present during the resuscitation of a loved one. Family presence during resuscitation assists in the grieving process, provides closure for survivors, and reduces questioning if personnel were adequately attempting resuscitation. (Sheehy pgs. 112-13)
66. **C** - Anterior cord syndrome is characterized by immediate onset of complete motor paralysis and loss of pain and temperature sensation. The posterior column is preserved, sparing vibration sense, position sense (proprioception), deep pressure, and light touch. Anterior cord syndrome mimics complete cord syndrome and has the worst prognosis of the incomplete injuries, with only 10-20% recovery of motor function. (TNCC pgs. 174-75)
67. **D** - The axillary padding should be 2 to 3 finger widths below the axilla, with no weight placed on the axilla. (Sheehy pg. 500)
68. **B** - Deliver oxygen via 15 L NRB until COHb normalizes (<10%). The oxyhemoglobin dissociation curve shifts to the left in CO toxicity, so hemoglobin holds onto oxygen, yielding pulse oximetry unreliable. All patients exposed to CO should receive high-flow oxygen to expedite the separation of CO from the Hgb molecule. Pregnant patients are more likely to need hyperbaric oxygenation to support fetal circulation. (Sheehy pg. 509)
69. **A** – An Allen's test is traditionally performed before radial artery cannulation to assess collateral blood flow to the hand by the ulnar artery. Have the patient repeatedly open and close their hand while you simultaneously apply pressure to radial and ulnar arteries. The hand will blanch from occluded flow. Release pressure on the ulnar artery and the hand should turn pink in 7 seconds. (Sheehy pg. 121)
70. **A** - Kcentra rapidly decreases INR which allows the patient to get to the OR faster than traditional treatment with fresh frozen plasma. (Sheehy pg. 256)
71. **B** - Absent or decreased breath sounds and tracheal deviation to the unaffected side are indicators of a tension pneumothorax, which would be the highest priority following the ABC's. Additional S/S include shortness of breath, chest pain, and a sense of impending doom. (Sheehy pg. 454)

72. **D** - Over the counter (OTC) decongestants containing anticholinergic ingredients like diphenhydramine can cause urinary retention. (Sheehy pg. 272)
73. **C** - Dysphonia and petechiae to the eyelids are indications of strangulation due to injuries in the neck and periorbital region of the face. Additional S/S include dysphagia, odynophagia, ligature marks, and subconjunctival hemorrhage. (Sheehy pg. 598 and TNCC pg. 312)
74. **C** - Strangulation patients are at high risk for stroke due to the impediment of blood flow and vascular injury that can occur. (TNCC pg. 312)
75. **B** - Abdominal bruits can be indicative of an aortic or iliac aneurysm and are not associated with renal calculi. Symptoms of urinary calculi also include lower abdominal pain radiating to the groin and urge to void. (Sheehy pg. 276-77)
76. **B** - The sending provider must speak to the receiving provider and the patient must be accepted by the receiving facility prior to initiating transport. (Sheehy pgs 9-11)
77. **C** - Common side effects of the anticonvulsant Keppra include drowsiness, dizziness, headache, and fatigue; especially in the first few weeks. Patients may have thoughts of suicide, so ask the patient about depression and suicidal thoughts. (www.drugs.com)
78. **D** – Fluoroquinolones such as levofloxacin (Levaquin), ciprofloxacin (Cipro), and moxifloxacin (Avelox) are associated with tendon rupture. Classic S/S of Achilles tendon rupture are hearing a "popping" or "snapping" sound, followed by pain, and swelling above the heel. (WebMD)
79. **A** – Fundal massage to promote uterine atony is the initial management of postpartum hemorrhage. In addition, apply oxygen, initiate IV access, and administer oxytocin (Pitocin). (Sheehy pgs. 287-88)
80. **D** – The "worst headache of my life" is the hallmark sign of subarachnoid hemorrhage (SAH). The headache is maximal at its onset, followed by vomiting, and a deterioration of LOC. SAH is caused by a cerebral aneurysm or AV malformation rupture. (Sheehy pg. 255)
81. **B** – Bronchiolitis is common in infants under 2 years of age and characterized by copious thick mucus and nasal drainage. RSV is the most common source, so it is highly contagious. Educate caregivers hygiene and nasal suctioning with a bulb syringe. (Sheehy pg. 562)
82. **B** – Needle thoracostomy or decompression is the emergency treatment for tension pneumothorax. Relieve intrapleural pressure with a 14 to 16-gauge needle (7 cm long) at the 4 to 5$^{th}$ ICS, anterior axillary line for best management. Definitive treatment is chest tube insertion. (Sheehy pg. 454)
83. **A** - Straining the urine for calculi allows for testing to determine the type of stone and may predict the likelihood of future occurrences. Pain control includes narcotics and NSAID's. Dietary restrictions include coffee, cola, and tea. Patients are encouraged to drink large amounts of water to facilitate passage of the stone. Return to the ED for excessive pain, vomiting, or fever. (Sheehy pg. 277)
84. **B** - Diverticulitis is inflamed diverticula associated with a low fiber diet. Patients should increase their fiber intake by eating more fruits and vegetables. (Sheehy pg. 267)
85. **C** – Measles (Rubeola) is characterized by the 3 C's (cough, coryza, and conjunctivitis) and Koplik spots on buccal mucosa. (ENPC pg. 290)

** As a thank you, order the CEN Supplement at **http://www.pdbnurseeducationllc.com/** and use code "**AMAZONCEN1991**" to download the PDF for FREE. Please give a review.

Made in the USA
Monee, IL
19 May 2022